Understanding Personal Security and Risk

A Guide for Business Travelers

T0293150

Understanding Personal Security and Risk
A Guide for Business Travelers

Charles E. Goslin

CRC Press
Taylor & Francis Group
Boca Raton London New York

CRC Press is an imprint of the
Taylor & Francis Group, an **informa** business

CRC Press
Taylor & Francis Group
6000 Broken Sound Parkway NW, Suite 300
Boca Raton, FL 33487-2742

© 2017 by Taylor & Francis Group, LLC
CRC Press is an imprint of Taylor & Francis Group, an Informa business

No claim to original U.S. Government works

Printed on acid-free paper
Version Date: 20161011

International Standard Book Number-13: 978-1-4987-6578-7 (Paperback)

Library of Congress Cataloging-in-Publication Data

Names: Goslin, Charles E., author.
Title: Understanding personal security and risk : a guide for business travelers / by Charles E. Goslin, CPP, CISSP.
Description: Boca Raton : CRC Press, [2017]
Identifiers: LCCN 2016040414 | ISBN 9781498765787 (pbk.) | ISBN 1498765785 (pbk.) | ISBN 9781498765794 (web pdf) | ISBN 1498765793 (web pdf)
Subjects: LCSH: Business travel--Safety measures. | Businesspeople--Crimes against--Prevention.
Classification: LCC G156.5.B86 G67 2017 | DDC 613.6--dc23
LC record available at https://lccn.loc.gov/2016040414

Visit the Taylor & Francis Web site at
http://www.taylorandfrancis.com

and the CRC Press Web site at
http://www.crcpress.com

Printed and bound in Great Britain by
TJ International Ltd, Padstow, Cornwall

For my son, Sgt. Cabot Goslin, USMC, Iraq, 1979–2015

Contents

Contents

Contents

Acknowledgments

I have a debt of gratitude to several individuals in the Central Intelligence Agency and the US State Department, which over the course of my lifetime taught me through their own experience how to survive for extended periods in dangerous places in the world. We lived and worked in the shadow world of intelligence work abroad, watching each other's back as we served our country. For reasons of confidentiality, they must remain anonymous but will never be forgotten.

The nuts and bolts of our work required the development of skills to assess risk on a very personal level and live with it day in and day out for years on end. Not enough time is spent, in my candid opinion, in the development of quality personal security programs. The easy work is to design and develop security within the gates of the castle, so to speak. When one gets outside those gates, it is hard and sometimes defies disciplined engineering—it is a world that does not sit still for drawings and blueprints. It requires the development of good instincts, judgment, habits, and preparation. This latter point is one I cannot emphasize enough—preparation is the key to survival, the long pole in the tent of a well-rounded personal security program.

I must first credit the impetus and the encouragement for writing this book to Thomas Norman, who provided me the initial introductions to my publisher and exhorted me to put my bent for writing to work on a book-length exposition on personal security. Without the strong support, the positive environment of professional security consulting, and the interest shown by Benjamin Butchko, this book would not have gotten off the ground. Ben's razor sharp judgment and rare good humor has been a tonic throughout the endeavor, and I am fortunate to call him a friend, a colleague, and a mentor in the field of security. Megan Bradley's outstanding editing skills and observations on the work were of incalculable value, and her irrepressible good humor and professionalism when the book was being scrubbed could not have been more welcome. The security industry is indeed fortunate to have individuals like these on its rolls.

One does not put prose to paper for a book-length topic without having had someone from the beginning who unfailingly encouraged the project. My wife Cinthya Trueba's tremendous patience and unfailing support is of incalculable value. My mother and my father's active encouragement to follow my muse and write got me started on the habit at an early age, and coupled with their spirit of exploration and adventure, I got the itch to live and work abroad. Not seen, but very present between the lines of my exhortations on what one should do to survive and stay secure, are my children. A routine 9-to-5 job in our cities here in the United States was not to be my lot in life. My kids were a tether on my heart that always got me home, no matter the destination. Alexandra Goslin Boren and Sebastian Goslin are in the heart and the soul of this book.

Finally, my late son Cabot Goslin, my guiding spirit throughout the long weekend nights writing this book. He would have wanted me to write this book.

Author

 **Charles E. Goslin** is a retired Central Intelligence Agency operations officer who served throughout the world in a wide range of capacities that bridged covert technical and human intelligence operations. He continues actively consulting in retirement on international intelligence, security, and risk issues faced by multinational corporations operating in some of the world's most hostile regions. Goslin's experience offers unique value for the business traveler that must, out of necessity, venture into "Indian country." His perspective is one drawn from years of working in the trenches of the third world, rather than the relative comfort of a Washington office. Goslin has authored and published numerous white papers on security threats and business risk issues, and he lectures regularly on terrorist radicalization and the threat of jihadist groups to Europe and the United States. He has worked abroad in India, Africa, Central and South America, Europe, and the Middle East with personal experience in crisis management and evacuation of facilities and personnel on numerous occasions. His expertise has been solicited by national media, both broadcast and print.

Author

Introduction

I am a retired Central Intelligence Agency operations officer. Much of my working life both during and after my company days was spent in dangerous, third-world urban environments: India, Tanzania, Uganda, Kenya, Central and South America, Europe, Syria, Yemen, Saudi Arabia, and the Arab Gulf States, to name a few. Unlike many expatriate professionals, my work required that I spend a great deal of time on the streets and the alleyways of urban slums of the developing world, in the dangerous and unpredictable world of human intelligence operations. In the course of my long career, I learned through training and trial and error the street skills necessary to survive and thrive.

In this book, I endeavor to tease out those engrained instincts for security and survival in the third world that are in my bones and articulate them into words. I believe that my own practical experience offers very useful lessons in personal security, and I want to pass along what I have learned. This book is for those professionals who find themselves in the trenches of some third-world garden spot or a picturesque European city that is suddenly transformed into a hostile environment because of shifting security threats and events, who need to keep themselves and those for whom they are responsible alive and well. It is also for expatriate contractors, midlevel office employees and managers, consultants, nongovernmental organization workers, or journalists who quite frequently find themselves in one of the three predicaments. They accept jobs in high-risk locations at short notice, where they must live and work in an environment that is unfamiliar, dangerous, and unforgiving of mistakes. The second predicament can be even worse. With little notice, a trip is scheduled into an unknown environment, where there is no contact on the receiving end and little or no information about circumstances on the ground. Ironically, when I began writing this book, my focus was on the developing world and hostile places. Sadly, crises in Paris, San Bernardino, Brussels, and quite a few places in between happened, so I must add a third predicament: when your benign environment is turned upside down by terrorism and the fallout from an attack.

Most large corporations have adequate journey management programs that are supposed to address travel security issues, to include briefings for employees traveling into dangerous areas of the globe. This book will be a very useful supplement to required security orientation and familiarization training for existing corporate programs. However, my focus is those individuals who do not often receive the familiarization and the training afforded employees and executives in larger corporations or governments. In today's threat environment, lack of familiarity and training in personal security can leave one acutely exposed to terrorist attack, terrorist hostage takers, kidnap for ransom, express kidnap, and violent street crime. Corporate security programs typically focus their perennially limited resources on physically securing facilities and (perhaps) executive protection of senior executives traveling to a high-risk region. If there is a corporate journey management program, it can be limited to travel security awareness briefings and/ or tracking the employee's travel. Should an incident occur—assuming that the employee's contact and tracking information is up to date—remediation measures are reactive, rather than proactive. I hear a lot about emergency response programs. That is fine. However, I am all about giving you the tools and the instincts to avoid having to be plucked from the jaws of kidnappers or terrorists in the first place. I put a great deal of emphasis on the front end of the security cycle—the detection and deterrence element. It is proactive and less reactive.

Workers, midlevel employees, and managers need a way to develop that intuitive sixth sense required to make fast, smart judgments on what to do and how to behave when they travel to or live and work in high-risk environments or low-risk environments in the throes of social transition. Also, this book is intended as a blueprint for corporations that need to develop in-house intelligence reporting about their global operations.

CHAPTER 1

Important Personal Security Concepts

INTRODUCTION

Security is a broad discipline that embraces a wide spectrum of activities and concepts. The sphere of personal security is no exception. Personal security applies to you and, taken in a business context, the safety and the well-being of your team, colleagues, or employees. It is the portable set of wisdom that is most critical when you or your colleagues step outside of the relatively safe confines of the workplace, the familiarity of hearth and home. When you get on a plane or a train and travel outside of the developed world into the developing world, whether by design or by accident, the principles of personal security are what will distinguish those who survive and thrive from those who become victims. Like its cousins in the physical or cyber realms, personal security shares similar concepts in protection, such as layering defense against threat. Likewise, the concepts of threat, risk, and asset value are similar. There are key theoretical distinctions that must be made, however, to separate personal security from related disciplines. Examining these distinctions helps throw into sharp contrast the aspects of personal security that are unique to this category.

CONCEPT OF EFFECTIVENESS

The first concept of personal security is that of effectiveness. For example, a good physical security plan would be utterly ineffective if the layers of defense were procured and laid out but not implemented. A perimeter fence that is not erected offers no deterrence. A closed-circuit television camera (CCTV) that has not been connected offers no detection of threats. Or a duress alarm that cannot be assessed is of minimal use. While all of these measures might, on the designer's drawings, seem to be present for the purpose of security, they are just that—security on paper, not in reality. This absurd example is used to illustrate a point regarding personal security: if the measure cannot be remembered and acted on when it is most needed, it is useless. Just as the effectiveness of physical security is measured in how well the various layers of defense are implemented, the effectiveness of personal security is measured in how well the various layers of defense are available for immediate recall from memory. Personal security is, unlike other security disciplines, much more intimate because it is principally focused on one key asset: you.

CONCEPTS OF THREAT, VULNERABILITY, AND RISK

The second set of concepts within personal security that are different are those of threat, vulnerability, and risk. These discrete elements of risk take on new meaning when considered in the personal security sphere. The terms *threat* and *risk* are often used interchangeably. In fact, these terms are not the same. It is important to have a clear understanding of what each term really means and how it applies to your personal security.

A threat, defined in the context of personal security, is an event with an undesired impact on your health and well-being. It is a supplemental ingredient to risk and should never be substituted for it. The components of a threat include the threat agent, or the actor, and the undesirable event. Threat events can be classified by type and category into intentional events that are planned and carried out or unintentional events such as accidents and natural disasters.

Vulnerabilities are weaknesses intrinsic and inherent to you that can be exploited by a threat actor or are susceptible to hazard events. In terms of personal security, these can include bad practices, such as never varying your routine or schedule, and bad habits, such as being easily distracted or inattentive, drinking too much, or being indiscreet about your location or business. Another example of bad practice is checking into a hotel, on the 40th floor beyond the reach of fire-fighting rescue ladders.

Risk is a more complex term. It is a calculus that, technically speaking, takes into measured consideration the loss potential to an asset that will likely occur if a threat is able to exploit a vulnerability. Another way of stating this is that it is the potential harm to you if a threat actor such as a kidnapper or a terrorist is able to take advantage of a weakness in your personal profile. Notice that conditional words such as *potential* and *likelihood* are included in the description of risk—these are important conditional terms that can be scaled up or down depending on the weight and the relevance of threat, vulnerability, and impact to you.

There are much more sophisticated definitions and implementations of risk evaluation—security is a broad discipline that embraces a wide spectrum of activity. However, for the purpose of developing a solid personal security program, it is sufficient to understand risk in these most basic terms.

Threats and vulnerabilities in personal security are very dynamic and multidimensional: dynamic, in the sense that there is movement through an ever-shifting risk environment, and multidimensional, in the sense that threats and vulnerabilities can be both external and internal. An integral part of a personal security plan is having an informed, internalized course of action that is capable of anticipation as well as reaction. Being able to identify a risk context as it is unfolding and identify indicators of change in the risk environment mitigates apprehension and reduces fear within the individual. Being able to correctly identify these changes does not eliminate fear, nor should it. However, a good plan of action directly addresses the vulnerability that we all have to *paralyzing* fear in the face of danger, identifying and reducing the paralysis itself without entirely removing the fear. Fear, if properly harnessed, can motivate the right reactions at the right time. As will be pointed out in later chapters, having a good sense of timing and acting on it can make the difference, for instance, between being a kidnap victim or not. Good personal security planning provides this benefit.

CONCEPT OF TIME

Time is a valuable commodity in personal security. The time that it takes to identify, react, and mitigate a potential or validated threat event as it blossoms against or around you or those for whom you are directly responsible is much shorter—generally speaking—than in other fields of security. For this reason, this book puts special emphasis on threat pattern and indicator recognition and detection of (i.e., gang signs, symbols, tattoos, graffiti) potentially threatening profiles or behavioral traits. This has consistently been useful to me over the course of my career and lifetime. Taken together, sensitivity to detail on the street provides you the anticipatory skill needed to react in a timely fashion to a potential threat event as it is developing and not after it occurs. The importance of good timing cannot be overestimated. Like physical security or cybersecurity, a good personal security program is subject to a methodical assessment and design process. However, to be resilient, effective, and of maximum use, the repository of that program cannot be sitting in a tabbed binder on the corporate security officer's shelf at headquarters. Since there is really only one principal asset—you—a significant part of the design process is having a knowledge transfer method that embeds critical reactive elements—*good timing instincts*—into your memory.

COMMITTING A SECURITY PLAN TO MEMORY

I have never been a proponent of security plan by checklist, and this is why: checklists, although well intended, are impossible to remember unless you have a photographic memory. When you need them the most, you are likely on an airplane buckled firmly in a middle-row seat on final approach to an airport and a city that is completely unfamiliar or in the back of a darkened taxi or motor rickshaw in a monsoon rainstorm. The checklist will likely be out of reach.

Principled security planning, constructed around a simple framework, is a way of contextualizing and then internalizing in your memory your security design around layers of defense. Doing this makes it much easier to remember what needs to be done next, rather than randomly choosing from a smorgasbord of security must-do options. A principled security plan is crucial to getting street smart. This simply means that you are able to think clearly, rationally, and quickly on your feet without having to resort to a map or a global positioning system application of your smartphone or some other crutch.

There are two reasons this is an important way to develop a personal security plan. First, a structured approach to layering personal security measures via key principles is easier for training purposes—it lends itself to instructing large groups of nonsecurity professionals.

Second is the individual. The most important place for a plan of action is in one's head, not a piece of paper or a smartphone. A layered approach built around a few key concepts provides essential memory pegs on which one can hang several concepts. Knowing that you can remember what to do when it comes to all aspects of one's personal security builds confidence, a sense of clear thought, and a more deliberative way to approach the environment out there in the real world. These qualities are very important. When a crisis event happens, how you react and what you choose to do in the moment are crucial to your survival. With regard to personal security—unlike other elements of the security discipline—I pay particular attention to the importance of feelings (listening to your gut) and emotions. How you manage your emotions in any given situation is crucial. Crisis events always have their own dynamic; to the extent that you can mitigate (not eliminate) feelings of panic, fear, or confusion, you will be capable of thinking through your emotions and ultimately survive the event. You turn panic into a sense of urgency and focus, fear into action, and confusion into ordered deliberation.

THREAT AGENTS AND THREAT ACTORS

There are also important distinctions between what is considered a threat actor and a threat agent. A threat actor is an individual or a group that has the resources, the capability, and the motivation to execute an undesirable threat event. A threat agent is the causative element of what becomes a hazard event, which is a specific condition, or a set of conditions, such as a hurricane, a tornado, or an earthquake. Threat agents and consequent hazard events have follow-on catalytic properties that can evolve into cascade threat events or, simply put, unanticipated consequences.

Understanding threat agents and hazard events is relevant to the development of a personal security program, because of these threat cascade effects. An earthquake, a hurricane, or a tornado may be the initial undesirable event—but, in each instance, secondary or tertiary cascade events unfold into the rise of threat actors such as looters or thieves who take advantage of a chaotic situation to loot and assault innocent victims who get in their way.

It is important to understand threats and threat actors, because each one exhibits specific tactics, history, and characteristics as an adversary, understand who they are and where they operate, but more importantly, understand their motives and how they execute against their targets. Another way to look at it is this: on the street, it does not matter that the hooded gunman coming for you is a terrorist with political motives, a kidnapper with pecuniary motives, or a common mugger who wants your shiny new watch. What matters, at that instant, is what you do to survive the attack itself. At the end of selected chapters in this book, there will be a brief monologue focusing in on specific threat actors. This chapter is intended to put some flesh and blood behind the normally anodyne descriptions of who threat actors are. Much of this narrative is anecdotal, from my own experience and that of others in my acquaintance. In addition, later in the book, I go into some detail about the signs, the tattoos, the graffiti, and the behavior of the major international criminal gangs both in the United States and around the world. Recognition of telltale indicators of individuals who are potential gang members in an urban setting or an urban setting that clearly hosts gang activity can provide you the small but important clues needed to make quick, informed decisions about your own security.

Understanding the risk environment is important for you in terms of the tools that you select to mitigate the risk. If you are living in an earthquake zone, for instance, it is prudent to ensure that your home is built to standards that can withstand the threat of an earthquake. Similarly, if you live along the Florida coastline, your home is built to standards that can weather high winds and storm surge tides. If you are smart, you have a generator, extra food, water, and backup communications options. You have an evacuation plan, should the storm threat rise to a very dangerous level. In fact, whether you are in a hurricane zone or an earthquake zone, many of the countermeasures that you select to mitigate your risk are very similar. These all reflect an understanding of your risk environment and the measures that you need to take to mitigate or address those risks.

As applied to international risk environments, if you travel to Tampico, Mexico, or Tripoli, Libya, for instance, it is prudent that you take measures to mitigate specific risks in those countries. In Tampico, the risk of kidnap for ransom by criminals is high. In Tripoli, Libya, the risk of hostage taking by a terrorist group is likewise high. While the threat actors may have different motives, their tactics can be roughly similar. The countermeasures that you must learn to mitigate these threats are likewise similar. Learning and developing that certain set of skills will set you apart from the average traveler and keep you and those for whom you are responsible safe and alive.

CHAPTER 2

Personal Security Principles

INTRODUCTION

There are five key elements to building an effective personal security plan. These principles are preparation, detection, deterrence, delay, and defense. Do they sound familiar? They should. The world of physical security planning and design conceptualizes layering key elements of security when developing protection measures for facilities or infrastructure. Personal security can employ the same conceptual principles, with some key differences. First, *you* are the principal asset. Yes, others for whom you might be responsible also require attention—but within the sphere of personal security, if you abdicate responsibility for your own security plan in favor of concentrating solely on others, you fail. Note that I did not say that you focus on your security to the exclusion of others. If you are required to protect the lives of others, your ability to think ahead, plan, and execute a well-thought-through plan professionally that keeps you alive, as well as your principal, means that you must accept that you are an asset as well as your principal. A well-designed personal security plan, in fact, can be a good extension to a personnel or an executive security plan. Its focus is on your survival and security. To the extent that you can extend a well-thought-through plan as an umbrella of protection to others such as family members and colleagues, it succeeds. This book will provide a set of skills, both mental and physical, that can be employed to address the potential for various threat scenarios. The good news is that despite the many different threat actors active around the world, the skills needed to counter their tactics are in fact applicable across many different scenarios.

PRINCIPLE OF PREPARATION

Abraham Lincoln wisely summarized the importance of preparation when he remarked, "If I had eight hours to chop down a tree, I'd spend six hours sharpening my axe." Planning and preparation are terms that should not be confused. Planning provides you awareness. Preparation is action oriented and leads to readiness. Developing a solid, successful personal security plan is like baking a cake—there are specific ingredients that are important to ensuring that the cake comes out right. One of the first ingredients in your personal security plan is doing your homework by preparing your travel security in advance. As a first principle, preparation is crucial because it mitigates an internal vulnerability that we all have—fear of the unknown. The absence of knowledge breeds unfamiliarity, apprehension, and fear. Traveling to an unfamiliar location, particularly if it is high risk, can understandably raise one's sense of apprehension and fear—not preparing to address these feelings in advance of travel is a recipe for failure.

There is a right way and a wrong way to research and internalize knowledge as part of preparation planning. Reading or researching sites on the Internet is informational and necessary but not functional for what you need it for. Research for action is different from research for information. Your need is not casual or curious but crucial to your survival in the environment to which you are traveling. For this reason, the research element of your advance planning must be methodical and goal driven.

Preparing for Contingencies

Expect the unexpected in your travel. Preparing for contingencies means putting some thought toward provisions for future events or circumstances that cannot be predicted but can potentially occur. Your preparation phase should address the following topics: area familiarization and threat orientation, geographical memorization, physical and mental health (I include both technical and procedural communication preparations as part of engineering mental health), your appearance and clothing, documentation, packing for mobility, and preparing defense tools.

Developing a Threat Profile: Preparation for Incidents

You should develop a threat profile of the location to which you are traveling. There is a specific way that you should approach this part of your homework. First, look for the threat actors—that is, the criminal gangs, the petty criminals, the kidnappers, the terrorist groups, the corrupt police, and the rival militia groups—and list them. Second, look for the most recent, frequent, and recurring threat incidents that are happening in the city or the region to which you are traveling: petty crime, pickpocketing or muggings, express kidnaps, carjacking, or worse. Third, take into consideration noncriminal- or terrorist-related threat agents and hazard events such as violent seasonal storms (cyclones, typhoons) or regional geophysical hazards such as earthquakes, sandstorms, and flooding. Finally, develop a list of relevant scenarios involving potential threat actors and incidents based on your research. More often than not, in areas of persistent crime or terrorism, these scenarios play out repeatedly and can be found in recent news reports or threat advisories for the locale.

To research for threat information, do not restrict yourself to the usual suspects (embassy websites, Overseas Security Advisory Council [OSAC], etc.). Make no mistake about it; these are good sources for initial, baseline threat information. However, they are not updated as frequently as they could be. Get granular. Besides perusing guidebooks about a city or a country's charms and tourist attractions (for some hot spots, the guidebooks will be very dated and useless…like guidebooks for, say, Yemen), take the time and the effort to dig out information about the location's underbelly—street crime, dangerous neighbor- hoods, history of terrorist incidents, civil unrest, or kidnap—and the things that the Ministry for Tourism does not really want you to know about. To the extent possible, try to determine what threats are relevant and consider what undesirable actions could occur. Websites that are useful for collecting information include the following:

- US State Department (http://www.travel.state.gov/alertsandwarn ings)
  - Travel warnings: The US State Department issues travel warnings when they want you to very carefully consider whether you should go to a country at all. Examples of reasons for issuing a travel warning might include unstable government, civil war, ongoing intense crime or violence, or frequent terrorist attacks. The State Department wants you to know the risks of traveling to these places and strongly consider not going to them at all. Travel warnings usually remain in place until the situation changes; some have been in effect for years.
  - Travel alerts: The State Department issues travel alerts for short-term events that they think you should know about when planning to travel to a country. Examples of reasons for issuing a travel alert might include an election season that is bound to have many strikes, demonstrations, or dis- turbances; a health alert such as an outbreak of H1N1; or evidence of an elevated risk of terrorist attacks. When these short-term events are over, the travel alert is cancelled.
- US Department of State OSAC (http://www.osac.gov)
  - The OSAC was created by the secretary of state to pro- mote an open dialogue between the US government and

the American private sector on security issues abroad. The OSAC is directed by a council of 34 representatives from companies and government agencies concerned with overseas security. The director of the Diplomatic Security (DS) Service is one of the cochairs of OSAC, and a DS special agent serves as OSAC's executive director. OSAC has a constituency of 4600 US companies and other organizations with overseas interests. Its website offers visitors the latest in safety and security-related information, public announcements, warden messages, travel advisories, significant anniversary dates, terrorist group profiles, country crime and safety reports, special topic reports, foreign press reports, and much more. One feature of the OSAC that is very useful is its staff of international security research specialists that are dedicated solely to serving the US private sector. Additionally, the OSAC uses a network of country councils around the world that bring together US embassies and consulates with the local US community to share security information.

- UK Foreign and Commonwealth Office (http://www.gov.uk/for eign-travel-advice)
  - This website is one of my favorites, partly because it is so easy to use and also because of the maps available for download of specific countries and regions as well as other very useful in-country travel advice. There are more British citizens outside the country, on any given day, than there are inside Britain. For this reason, the UK government has a very robust in-country informational network that provides the Foreign Commonwealth Office the latest travel advice by country; rights at the airport and getting help; and foreign travel advise for 225 countries and territories that includes terrorism, crime, safety and security, natural disasters, health hazards, and the like.
- Lonely Planet travel forums (http://www.lonelyplanet.com/thorn tree/categories/country-forums)
  - Lonely Planet's travel forums are powered by its community of independent travelers covering every place on earth (from Afghanistan to Zimbabwe). Take the time to read the frequently asked question threads. There is a lot of useful information in them that will help you develop a refined threat profile of the country or the city to which you are traveling. With that said, the backpacker/youth hostel crowd can be endearingly naive, so take what is posted with a grain of salt.

- Virtual Tourist (http://www.virtualtourist.com)
  - Like Lonely Planet, Virtual Tourist is a web-based community where travelers and locals can share advice and experiences. Combing through the site can yield some good insider threat information about specific cities and areas around the world.
- Wikitravel (http://www.wikitravel.org)
  - Wikitravel is a project to create a free, complete, up-to-date, and reliable worldwide travel guide. Its site provides relatively up-to-date travel alerts and warnings for specific areas around the globe.

It is not enough to just be aware of a potential threat. Use this information to then pair various potential threat actors with undesirable events that could occur and develop possible scenarios (see Chapter 9). This emergency conditioning helps you become mentally prepared should something like or similar to the scenario occur. You will be able to handle the situation much better because it will not feel new. Despite the fear or the shock of the incident, you will be better able to think through the event and understand how to handle it.

Guidebooks as a Resource

There are guidebooks, and then there are *guidebooks*. If you want guidebooks that hold your hand, tell you what you should see, and where you should eat and stay, then invest in a Michelin guide, an Arthur Frommers guide, a Fodors, or a Zagat. Lonely Planet guidebooks are useful because they provide a bit more detail about areas of a city or a country that are more dangerous than others, criminal offenses that might otherwise be unfamiliar, and social or religious taboos and underbelly stuff. Information to look for includes very basic items such as local currency requirements, transportation/costs to or from the airport and other terminals of entry, availability of automated teller machines (ATMs) in the airport (dictates whether you should carry extra cash with you in advance), pharmacies, emergency clinics, embassies and consulates, major hotels, and police stations. These are all locations that should be marked on your map and, if possible, committed to memory. In particular, study the precincts in an urban area or a province that are considered unsafe. Pay attention to your ingress or egress routes into and out of those areas and assess whether you will be exposed to them during your trip.

Geographical Memorization: Preparation for Movement

It is important to invest time and effort into planning both the regional and specific (local) aspects of where you are going. Study the route your flight, train, or vehicle will take. If traveling into the country overland, memorize intermediate stops along the way. If coming in by air, think about what airports might be used as a diversion should weather or an incident be encountered during the flight requiring an emergency landing.

Geographical memorization requires interactive study of the terrain. Obtain and memorize a map of the location to which you are traveling. If it is a city, get a basic street map and study it. A reliable technique that I use to memorize and internalize this information is a bit old school, but it works for those of us who do not have photographic memories. I draw by hand a rough map of the city or the route while I am studying it, identifying points of the compass—basic locations of ports, main roads, and neighborhoods. I then use this hand-drawn map as I research various areas of the city to identify and characterize sectors of the city, the locations of interest, the good and bad places to go, and the metro and bus routes. As the information is drawn in, my narrative research is put into an already familiar context and is, at the same time, mentally internalized right where I need it. You do not need a perfect memory to accomplish this; the purpose of this technique is to focus your research. It is important to do this research before you leave on your trip, not en route to your destination. Once you are on the ground, in a taxi, a bus, or a train, it could be at night or when you are exhausted from an overnight flight or both. The surroundings will be unfamiliar at best, but if you have done your homework, you will have a *basic set* of expectations about where you are and where you are going. This baseline of knowledge mitigates fear of the unknown to manageable levels, which is precisely where you want it. If the taxi takes an unfamiliar turn, you have enough knowledge to immediately ask the driver why he/she turned and where he is going. It may be that he/she is avoiding a traffic jam or a new set of police or military roadblocks or an area of civil unrest. Or it could be different (in some third-world countries, drivers run up the meter by taking the long way to your hotel). Either way, if your own internal radar is attuned enough to the terrain, you can react and get answers to any changes to your route. You have researched for action and not just for information.

Physical and Mental Health

An important part of physical security planning is ensuring that your physical and mental well-being, otherwise called *peace of mind*, is closely addressed in the preparation stage. Not preparing for illness or even a minor injury leaves you vulnerable to unanticipated ailments that can leave you feeling debilitated, distracted, and unfocused—all conditions that weaken personal security defenses. Your mental health is equally crucial. Handling unexpected developments to your personal

CIVIL UNREST IN THE MOST UNEXPECTED PLACE

Having a good mental picture of your surroundings, particularly in urban settings, can save your life. In situations where there is civil unrest, your options for escape and evasion can become very limited, very quickly, simply because of the chaotic actions of the mob. In 2001, I was providing an on-the-ground threat assessment during massive protests at the European Union Summit in Gothenburg, Sweden. A State Department colleague and I had spent nearly a week memorizing the city and its layout, prior to the arrival of dignitaries that included President George W. Bush. While the protests began peacefully at first, they quickly deteriorated into violent street riots. There were pitched battles with the police, with protesters and police charging and retreating through a warren of cobblestone streets. Innocent bystanders were caught up in the riots and, not knowing where to go, were trampled or severely injured. We had a solid, mental picture of where streets and alleyways led and where there were potential points of refuge. Without this clear mental map of the urban landscape, we would have been hopelessly confused and potential victims of the violence.

situation when your environment suddenly changes or breaks down requires composed, sensible thinking. When there are doubts, unfinished business, or disruption in communications back home, this can directly impact your mental well-being. A healthy state of mind translates to hope and the will to live, in a critical situation where your very life and survival are at stake.

Physical Heath: Medical Necessities

A basic travel health kit is important no matter where you travel. First aid supplies and medications may not always be readily available in other countries, a fact that is chronically underestimated by travelers. A good travel health kit contains enough supplies to prevent illness, handle minor injuries and illnesses, and manage preexisting medical conditions for *longer than the duration of your trip*. It is very inconvenient to be traveling abroad and not have basic relief medicine. I might add that having extra supplies of these items can be very useful if you have the responsibility for other team members or associates. More often than not, they forget these items, particularly if it is their first foray into third-world travel. When they become ill, they can become a burden on movement and travel, so if you can provide some basic medicine to lower a fever, reduce a cough, or relieve diarrhea until they can be seen by a doctor, that will be a huge benefit. The following are the basic items that you should include in your travel medical kit and why:

- Antidiarrheal medication (for example, bismuth subsalicylate, loperamide): Getting a case of so-called Delhi belly or Montezuma's revenge is no joke. Almost 90% of travelers' diarrhea (TD) cases are caused by bacteria. TD may also be caused by viruses, such as norovirus or parasitic TD such as *Giardia intestinalis* (Kozarsky, 2010). Speaking from personal experience, I have seen this common ailment completely sideline an entire project team (in India). Dehydration sets in, and if you are in an area where water is not clean or available, your situation can become quite serious. In Africa, I once had to rehydrate by drinking fresh coconut milk while in a provincial hospital after a severe bout of diarrhea.
- Antihistamine: Its principal use is for nasal congestion, hay fever, itching, or insect bites. However, in a pinch, it is also good to counter motion sickness and nausea. Having been caught in thick sandstorms in the Middle East, I found it very useful to have to counter the congestion that arises during these events.
- Decongestant, alone or in combination with antihistamine: Over-the-counter nasal spray or Sudafed is sufficient.
- Anti–motion sickness medication: There are two ways to treat motion sickness. One is by taking scopolamine (an anticholinergic drug), which should be taken at least eight hours before traveling. The second is by taking an antihistamine, such as diphenhydramine (Benadryl), dimenhydrinate (Dramamine), cyclizine (Marezine), and promethazine (Phenergan). Seasickness, the most common malady, can be crippling. Having a way to mitigate the risk of this illness in advance is very prudent, since you may need to be flexible and travel by sea at short notice. Also, if you are leading a team, chances are there will be someone on that team who is prone to motion sickness, and Murphy's law indicates that they will not be prepared for it!
- Medicine for pain or fever (such as acetaminophen, aspirin, and ibuprofen): I pack more of this medicine than any other. Food poisoning or flu can be absolutely debilitating—I once spent three days in a Madrid hotel room burning up with fever that mild pain relievers could not make a dent in. Airlines will typically not let you fly if you are ill. So you need something strong enough to get a handle on the ailment, sufficient to allow you to travel—even if it is across town to a doctor's clinic or the US

Embassy (embassies always have local doctors to whom they can refer you). My recommendation is to bring the strongest dosage of pain/fever medicine that you can obtain without a prescription.

- Mild laxative: While you do not want diarrhea keeping you in the bathroom your whole trip, constipation is no less unpleasant. Being unable to have a bowel movement can cause abdominal pain, discomfort, gas, and bloating. To the extent possible, veteran travelers stick to their usual schedule and diet while traveling and avoid the use of sleeping pills. Schedule changes, diet, and sleeping medications can all trigger constipation. Dulcolax is an oral laxative that can be packed into your kit.
- Clove oil: Clove oil is a natural analgesic and antiseptic—its primary use is for toothache. Third-world dentists can be a hit-or-miss proposition. I once had a tooth extracted in up-country Kenya by a local dentist, without anesthetic. I highly recommend keeping this in your medical kit for just this sort of contingency.
- Cough suppressant/expectorant: Pack an oral cough suppressant, such as Mucinex D, Delsym, and Benadryl tablets.
- Cough drops: Sore throat, coughing, sneezing, and runny nose interfere with concentration, making it difficult to focus. Colds interrupt sleep and drain energy for even the simplest tasks. Zinc cough drops are effective in reducing the effects of a cold, used in conjunction with antihistamines or cough suppressants/expectorants.
- Antacid: Antacids are available over the counter and are taken by mouth to quickly relieve occasional heartburn, the major symptom of acid reflux. Examples are Alka Seltzer or Pepto-Bismol (in tablet form), Tums, or proton pump inhibitors such as Nexium and Zantac.
- Antifungal and antibacterial ointments or creams: Antifungal and antibacterial ointments or creams are applied to wounds to prevent infection.
- Hydrocortisone cream (1%): This preparation relieves both itching and swelling/redness. It actually has anti-inflammatory effects, not just symptomatic relief like the topical anesthetics. However, it does take longer for full effect than topical anesthetics.

Specialty medicines and items:

- Antimalarials: These are medications that are designed to prevent or cure malaria. The considerations when choosing a drug for malaria prophylaxis are the following:

- If headed to remote areas where mosquito-borne diseases such as malaria, dengue fever, and the Zika virus are prevalent, carry mosquito netting to sleep beneath. How do you know whether to pack this? Check the destination-specific current health reports from the Centers for Disease Control and Prevention (CDC) for information (Davis, 2016).
- Recommendations for drugs to prevent malaria differ by country of travel and can be found in the country-specific tables of the *Yellow Book* (CDC Health Information for International Travel).[1] Recommended drugs for each country are listed in alphabetical order and have comparable efficacy in that country.
- No antimalarial drug is 100% protective and must be combined with the use of personal protective measures (i.e., insect repellent, long sleeves, long pants, sleeping in a mosquito-free setting, or using an insecticide-treated bed net).
- For all medicines, also consider the possibility of drug–drug interactions with other medicines that the person might be taking as well as other medical contraindications, such as drug allergies (CDC, 2012).

- Prescription antibiotic for self-treatment of moderate to severe diarrhea: TD is the most predictable travel-related illness. Attack rates range from 30% to 70% of travelers, depending on the destination and the season of travel. Traditionally, it was thought that TD could be prevented by following simple recommendations such as boil it, cook it, peel it, or forget it, but studies have found that people who follow these rules may still become ill. Poor hygiene practice in local restaurants is likely the largest contributor to the risk for TD. Antibiotic prophylaxis is not recommended by the CDC even for high-risk travelers because it can lead to drug-resistant organisms and may give travelers a false sense of security. Although antibiotic prophylaxis does not prevent viral or parasitic infection, some health care professionals believe that it may be an option for travelers who are at high risk of developing TD and related complications (e.g., immunocompromised persons). *Prophylaxis with fluoroquinolones is up to 90% effective.* Rifaximin (Xifaxan) may prove to be the preferred antibiotic because it is not absorbed and is well tolerated, although data on its effectiveness for prophylaxis have not yet been published (Rendi-Wagner et al., 2002a). The use of prophylactic antibiotics should be weighed against the result of using prompt, early self-treatment with antibiotics when TD occurs, which can limit the duration of illness to 6–24 hours in most cases. Prophylactic antibiotics may be considered for short-term travelers who are high-risk hosts (such as those who are immunosuppressed) or who are taking critical trips (such as engaging in a sporting event) during which even a short bout of diarrhea could affect the trip (Rendi-Wagner, 2002b).

Supplies to prevent illness or injury:

- Insect repellent containing N,N-diethyl-meta-toluamide (DEET) (30–50%) or picaridin (up to 15%): This is for protection against ticks and mosquitoes. A repellant with at least 20% DEET will last up to several hours, so stronger is better. Products containing DEET (diethyltoluamide—the most common ingredient in insect repellants) include Off!, Cutter, Sawyer, and Ultrathon. Products containing picaridin (also known as KBR 3023, Bayrepel, and icaridin) include Cutter Advanced, Skin So Soft Bug Guard Plus, and Autan (outside the United States)).
- Sunscreen (preferably SPF 15 or greater) that has both ultraviolet A and ultraviolet B protections: If you are also using sunscreen with insect repellant, apply sunscreen first and insect repellent second.
- Antibacterial hand wipes or alcohol-based hand sanitizer containing at least 60% alcohol

First aid supplies:

- Lubricating eye drops: Lubricating drops or artificial tears relieve dry eyes when it is windy or dry. If you wear contact lenses, these are a must—I wear them, and these are important enough to be in my carry-on backpack. Keep an extra small bottle filled with emergency saline solution, which also acts as a general-purpose eye lubricant. Also, have your glasses handy in case that your eyes swell up and you cannot wear your contact lenses.
- First aid quick reference card: If you have not received first aid training, or combat aid training in the military, then I highly recommend a small, portable first aid reference card. Even if you have had the training, it is a good reference in an emergency.
- Basic first aid items (bandages, gauze, ace bandage, antiseptic, tweezers, scissors, cotton-tipped applicators)
- Moleskin for blisters: Pack cut-your-own sheets or precut templates of various sizes, depending on your preference.
- Aloe gel for sunburns
- Digital thermometer

- Oral rehydration solution packets
- Health insurance card (either your regular plan or supplemental travel health insurance plan) and copies of claim forms

In addition to the basic medicines outlined previously, you should include enough of your own prescription medicine to last the entire trip, and a week's extra supply in the event that your trip is delayed. Ensure that you pack prescription medications in your carry-on luggage in their original containers and pack a copy of all of your prescriptions including the generic names of the medications. This information can be obtained from your local pharmacy.

If you have medication that is a controlled substance, or injectable, make sure that you have a note on letterhead stationery prescribing the medicine to you from your physician. If you have doubt about whether you can bring in a certain medicine to the country to which you are traveling, check with the US Embassy or Consulate to make sure that the medicine is allowed. You do not, under any circumstances, want to get held up at a border because you neglected to prepare an explanation for certain medicines. Finally, you should leave a copy of your prescriptions at home with a friend or a relative.

Physical Health: Health Insurance

Ensuring that you are insured is an important part of your travel preparations. Insurance options for travel overseas can be complicated. The first thing you should do is to look at the insurance policies that you already have to see what they cover. Some health insurance policies will cover medical emergencies overseas, while others do not. Many homeowners' policies also cover baggage loss. Credit card companies (particularly gold cards) offer their members baggage loss, international medical assistance, and accidental death and dismemberment insurance. The caveat, of course, is that airline tickets and reservations must be charged on the card.

Severe illness or injury abroad can impose an immediate and severe financial burden on travelers. Although planning for every possible contingency is impossible, travelers can reduce the cost of a medical emergency by considering the purchase of three types of insurance for their trip: travel insurance, travel health insurance, and medical evacuation insurance. These insurance policies can be purchased before a trip to provide coverage in the event of an illness or an injury and may be of particular importance to travelers with chronic medical conditions. Basic accident or travel insurance may even be required for travelers to certain destinations.

Examine your coverage and planned itinerary to determine which medical services, if any, will be covered abroad and the level of supplemental insurance that you believe will be needed. The following is a list of characteristics that you should consider (Stoney, 2016):

- Exclusions for treating exacerbations of preexisting medical conditions
- The company's policy for out-of-network services
- Coverage for complications of pregnancy (or for a neonate, especially if the newborn requires intensive care)
- Exclusions for high-risk activities such as skydiving, scuba diving, and mountain climbing
- Exclusions regarding psychiatric emergencies or injuries related to terrorist attacks or acts of war
- Whether preauthorization is needed for treatment, hospital admission, or other services
- Whether a second opinion is required before obtaining emergency treatment
- Whether there is a 24-hour physician-backed support center
- Travel insurance: Travel insurance protects the financial investment in a trip, including lost baggage and trip cancellation. Travelers may be more likely to avoid travel when sick if they know that their financial investment in the trip is protected. Depending on the policy, this type of insurance may or may not cover medical expenses abroad, so travelers need to carefully research the coverage offered to determine if additional travel health and medical evacuation insurance is needed.
- Paying for health services abroad: Medical care abroad usually requires cash or credit card payment at the point of service, regardless of whether the traveler has insurance coverage in their home country. This could result in a large out-of-pocket expenditure of perhaps thousands of dollars. Additionally, the existence of nationalized healthcare services in a given destination does not ensure that nonresidents will be given full coverage. When paying out of pocket for care, travelers should obtain copies of all bills and receipts and, if necessary, contact a US consular officer, who can assist US citizens with transferring funds from the United States. A discussion of insurance options is an important part of any pretravel consultation. In addition to covering costs of treatment or medical evacuation, the travel health insurer can also assist in organizing and coordinating care and keeping relatives informed. This is especially important when the traveler is severely ill or injured and requires medical evacuation. Although all travelers should consider insurance, it is particularly important for travelers who plan extended travel outside the United States, have underlying health conditions, or plan to participate in high-risk activities on their trip, especially if the destination is remote or lacks high-quality medical facilities.

- Supplemental travel health and medical evacuation insurance: Travel health insurance and medical evacuation insurance are both short-term supplemental policies that cover healthcare costs on a trip and are relatively inexpensive. Many commercial companies offer travel health insurance, which may be purchased separately or in conjunction with medical evacuation insurance. Frequent travelers may consider purchasing annual policies or even policies that will provide coverage for repatriation to one's home country.

Although travel health insurance will cover some healthcare costs abroad, the quality of care may be inadequate, and medical evacuation from a resource-poor area to a hospital where definitive care can be obtained may be necessary. The cost of evacuation can exceed US$100,000. In such cases, medical evacuation insurance would cover the cost of transportation to a facility where adequate care can be provided. Medical evacuation companies in some parts of the world may have better resources and experience than others; travelers may want to ask about a company's resources in a given area, especially if planning a trip to remote destinations. The traveler should scrutinize all policies before purchase, looking for those that provide the following:

  - Arrangements with hospitals to guarantee payments directly
  - Assistance via a 24-hour physician-backed support center (critical for medical evacuation insurance)
  - Emergency medical transport to facilities that are equivalent to those in the home country or to the home country itself (repatriation)
  - Any specific medical services that may apply to their circumstances, such as coverage of high-risk activities
  - Even if an insurance provider is selected carefully, travelers should be aware that unexpected delays in care may still arise, especially in remote destinations. In special circumstances, travelers may be advised to postpone or cancel international trips if the health risks are too high.

- Finding an insurance provider: The following resources, although not all inclusive, provide information about purchasing travel health and medical evacuation insurance:
  - Department of State (http://www.travel.state.gov)
  - International Association for Medical Assistance to Travelers (http://www.iamat.org)
  - American Association of Retired Persons (http://www.aarp .org) (For information about Medicare supplement plans, see the following below.)

Mental Health: Engineering Peace of Mind:
Technical Communication Preparation

Communication is how you stay connected with those who are most important to you. In terms of security planning, it is an important component of your mental health—if you do not have peace of mind because no one knows where you are, where you are going, or what is happening to you, it impedes your ability to clearly think about other aspects of your security. Being worried is a significant distraction and ultimately leaves you vulnerable.

There are three aspects of communications to which you should pay particular attention. They are electronic communications, point-of-contact (POC) arrangements, and duress planning.

Electronic Communications: Mobile Phones Global wireless networks and agreements are complex, confusing, and—if you are unprepared—expensive. Your primary requirement is having communications that work on arrival. Secondarily, however, is the importance of keeping a low profile—and that includes not having a flashy mobile phone that is a tempting target for criminals. I have found, both from a practical standpoint and from a security perspective, that it is useful to put my US mobile phone and associated plan into a backup communication role and utilize a local phone and a subscriber identity module (SIM) card subscription as my primary communications. The following are important points to consider when preparing for travel:

- Confirm that your mobile phone will work in the region or the country to which you are traveling. Assess if your carrier has an international calling plan that covers the country or the region to which you are traveling. Most major US phone companies give you the option of choosing a plan that allows you to make international calls. These plans may be offered on an ongoing basis or as a temporary service that you can set up for a single month when you know you will be leaving the country. Each company offers different plans for various prices that work for a number of phone models and in designated countries. Major cell phone providers have coverage maps that show in which countries your network works. Be sure to check that your plan covers the destination in which you plan to travel. Per-minute calling rates vary for different countries. This is the most convenient option if you do not want to use another mobile phone. However, in terms of personal security, it is not recommended.
- With the caveat that your primary home country phone is a smartphone, ensure before departing that you have preloaded

messaging apps such as WhatsApp, Viber, and Skype onto the phone. This gives you the option of using the phone to communicate with colleagues or family through a Wi-Fi connection.

- Try to confirm if you can purchase a local phone in the country to which you are traveling (if you are not certain, you can usually purchase an inexpensive unlocked mobile phone in the airport if you are connecting internationally). Local calling plans are often similar to the one you have on your current cell phone; domestic rates are cheap, and the most basic cell phone models are quite affordable. Research cell phone companies in the country that you will visit or look for a local cell phone store or a kiosk once you arrive. Once this local phone is activated, it becomes your primary number in that country. Make sure that this local phone is unlocked and can work with SIM cards from other countries in the region. Your primary mobile phone reverts to a backup role, as an emergency phone (it should be tested to ensure it works), or for use—in emergencies—in Wi-Fi hot spots with WhatsApp or Skype (this is also a risk, as outlined in this book in Chapter 7 covering cyberthreats and risks to personal security). Frequent travelers who spend a lot of time in one international location will be best served by purchasing a phone in their destination. Students studying abroad and travelers with international vacation homes or family in another country should also consider purchasing an international cell phone.
- Before departing, confirm if your mobile phone is unlocked. In an emergency, this gives you the option of purchasing and using a local SIM card in your phone. In most countries, you must register your name and passport number in order to purchase a SIM card or a mobile phone. While you can still secure unregistered SIM cards through sources such as taxi drivers and shop keepers (I have preferred this in the past as I can enjoy a relative degree of anonymity on my mobile phone), doing so increasingly exposes you to the risk of fines or worse if caught.
- Your mobile phone, whether it is the local phone or your home country phone, should have key contacts programmed in, both in the country to which you are traveling and outside of the country. This should be part of your security preparation protocol with your communications devices.

Electronic Communications: Public Switched Telephone Network and Calling Cards Before you travel, work out the long-distance dialing protocol from the country (and surrounding countries) to which you are traveling. This applies both to mobile phones and to hard-line public switched telephone network (PSTN) telephones. These phones will typically work during a crisis, particularly when the mobile phone network gets over-loaded and will not work or is taken out by some other incident. You can purchase prepaid calling cards for long-distance (domestic or interna-tional) calling. Each card has an 800 number or a local access number. It also has a personal identification number (PIN) or an account number. Just dial the 800 number or the local access number, enter your PIN number, and then you will be prompted to enter the phone number that you are calling. Calling cards are most useful when making international phone calls, particularly while traveling abroad. They can be purchased in the airport terminal or at convenience stores. Vendors typically only accept cash for the prepaid cards. Most calling cards provide detailed usage instructions on the card itself or inside the packaging. Whether calling domestically or internationally, begin by dialing the toll-free number listed on the instructions. When prompted, enter the PIN. You will be provided with account information, such as the remaining dollar amount on the card, and then typically asked to enter the phone number that you wish to call, including the country code. Before using the card, research the country codes of nations that you may call as well as the steps for calling outside your country. Due to different rules and regu-lations, some nations restrict the use of calling cards, so research your destination's guidelines before you buy a card with a high dollar value that ends up going to waste.

Electronic Communications: Voice over Internet Protocol   Voice over Internet protocol (VoIP) is a technology by which telephone calls are placed over the Internet rather over the standard PSTN, also known as the land-line network. Making an international call from a VoIP telephone line requires the same dialing format as a landline phone: international dial-ing prefix + country code + area code + local number. Skype and Vonage are two examples of VoIP applications that can be used. It is important to anticipate that your VoIP connection could be blocked in some coun-tries. Before you leave, it is worthwhile to download a tunneling proxy server service or "a virtual private network" (VPN). When you connect to a VPN, your computer acts as if it is on the same local network as the VPN server. When you browse the web through a VPN, your browsing traffic is forwarded through the VPN server. In other words, if you are in the UK and you connect to a VPN in the United States, websites will see you as browsing from the United States. The VPN server acts as a sort of intermediary.

Electronic Communications: Satellite Phones   In remote locations, without cell phone coverage, a satellite phone may be your only option. A satel-lite phone is not generally a replacement for a mobile phone, as you have to be outdoors with a clear line of sight to the satellite to make a phone call. The service is frequently used by ships, including pleasure craft, as well as expeditions that have remote data and voice needs. I have also used them in war zones where there is absolutely no phone service at all. Your local telephone service provider should be able to give more information about connecting to this service. Rates are generally much higher than using ordinary mobile phones, even if the other party is in the same country as you are.

The Thuraya network, using a Thuraya handset, allows roaming from global system for mobile communications to satellite depending on network availability. Check to see if they have an agreement with your home network. Some networks (for example, Vodafone UK) charge a very high rate for incoming calls (GBP6.00/min). If you plan to make a lot of calls, buy a SIM card from a satellite phone provider. Calls on the Thuraya system cost from US$0.50–US$1.30/min. The Thuraya network uses geo-stationary satellites over Europe, Africa, Asia, and the Middle East, so check for coverage in the area that you are traveling to. You may have to orient the antenna of the device toward the satellite for best reception.

For truly global walk-and-talk roaming, you are going to need an Iridium handset. Iridium uses a constellation of low-earth orbit satellites, so unlike Thuraya, you can use Iridium everywhere as long as you have line of sight with the sky. Iridium works on all landmasses and oceans including both poles. Expect to pay about US$1.50/min for outgoing calls, although this can be as low as US$0.99/min to call another Iridium phone. Iridium does not sell directly and only sells phones through dealers who may rent units as well. Another consumer satellite telephony network is Globalstar.

Satellite phones may not be available for purchase or are illegal to use in Saudi Arabia, China, India, Myanmar (formerly Burma), Cuba, Iran, Libya, North Korea, and Syria. Technically, they will still function in these areas. Some countries require a special permit for using satellite phones within their territory (Wikitravel, 2016).

Mental Health: Procedural Communication Preparations It is important to take some time to choose the right Point of Contact (POC) before you travel. For personal travel, your POC can be a friend or a family member that you trust can verify your identity and move quickly and efficiently should your travel plans go sideways. For business travel as an executive representing your corporation, make certain that your POC is someone who can do the following:

- Be available and fully engaged on short notice
- Be capable of quickly rallying the team to engage in your support
- Has the authority to make decisions on your behalf

- Has backup that can step in, if he or she is unavailable, to respond to your requirements
- Negotiate basic business contracts or negotiations on your behalf

Leave a copy of your itinerary with your POC, as well as copies of your prescriptions and copies of important documents. In addition, make certain that you have the full name, the address, and the contact details of your POC with you.

Other important considerations include paying your bills before you leave for a trip and advising your bank and/or credit card companies of your travel and where you expect to be. This is especially important because credit card security often flags foreign charges, freezes your account, and will not approve any further use of the card until you are able to contact them personally. That can be difficult, depending on where you are located.

Mental Health: Duress Plan   A duress plan is also an important element of your advance planning. It is a simple word, or phrase, that you and your POC alone understand that signifies that you are under duress and need help. This signal is a way for you to discreetly convey certain circumstances of your situation should you be taken hostage or kidnapped.

Clothing and Appearance Preparation

A key principle of security is deterrence, which we will discuss in more detail later in this chapter. Your advance planning preparations should keep this principle in mind, because it is an important component of your overall security plan. Having the capacity to blend in means dressing appropriately for the region and the location to which you are going and having the option of changing your look if needed. Consider where you are going and what your functions will be and could be should a sudden shift in plans occur. An easy rule of thumb to follow is this: dress for your travel, with an eye on your destination. For instance, dressing up for a business meeting in Riyadh on Monday morning makes you a rather conspicuous target when jammed into an airport waiting room with 150 Asian workers at midnight because your flight was delayed and the airline rescheduled you. Conversely, high heels and a dress are quite impractical if you need to run the length of an airport because your flight was suddenly changed.

Documentation

Ensure that you have color photocopies of your passport and visa, a second means of photo identification card (driver's license, for instance), photocopy of details of credit cards and emergency phone numbers, and doctor's prescriptions. While traveling, you should keep the original documents on your person, in your backpack, or in a briefcase. Upon arrival in a hotel or wherever you are staying, secure the original documents in the hotel or in a room safe, and while on the street, carry the photocopies of the original with you.

Packing for Mobility and Portability

An important, but sometimes overlooked, measure that should be taken before travel to any destination abroad—and most particularly high-risk locations—is packing. Over the years, I have learned to pack light, for

---

DURESS CODE: COVERT CALL FOR HELP

A duress code is used to communicate that the caller is under threat such as a kidnapping or hostage situation. Also, it can be used to wave off someone from coming to a certain place, such as a safe house that is compromised. A simple but effective duress code used over the telephone by Special Operations Executive (SOE) agents in occupied Europe during World War II was to give a coded answer when someone checked whether it was convenient to visit a safe house. If it was genuinely safe to visit, the answer would be "No, I'm too busy." However, if the safehouse had been compromised (i.e., the Nazis had captured it, forcing the occupants to answer the phone at gunpoint in order to lure in other members of the SOE network), the captured agent would say "Yes, come on over." Having been warned that the safehouse had been compromised, the other agent would hang up the phone and immediately inform his team members so that they could take appropriate action.

   There are three ways to create a simple duress code. First, the duress phrase can be as simple as "Don't forget to clean the pool." This would be immediately understood by my wife as a signal for duress, since we do not have a pool. However, we would have agreed in advance on the phrase and she would understand exactly the meaning of the phrase and act according to our predetermined plan. Second, a duress code can be a series of two or three words, spoken in a prespecified sequence. Using the previous example, I might say to my wife "Call the pool cleaner and have them put in some chlorine." "Pool" and "chlorine" would be the words, in that sequence. Finally, a call and response can be a duress code. I might say "Take my shirts to the cleaners." My wife's reply, "to the cleaners on Dallas Street?" My reply (if under duress) "No, the one in Galveston." This sequence of conversation would signal I was under duress.

efficiency of movement through airports, streets, and hotels. Being flexible enough to move fast gives you an edge over the average traveler moving through the world's crowded airports. Also, a tight, efficient pack is much easier to manage.

Limiting the Luggage Load

Restrict your luggage load to two cases—preferably an over-the-shoulder backpack and a small roller board case or a close variation to this profile. The roller board should be able to fit into the overhead luggage rack on an airplane, a train, or a bus. The ideal size should be no larger than 22″ × 14″ × 9″ (56 cm × 36 cm × 23 cm). An over-the-shoulder rucksack is good because you do not have to put it down whenever you need both hands for a transaction. The reason for this is simple: the less luggage you have, the easier it is to manage rapidly changing situations while traveling. Whether it is disengaging from the masses when changing flights or getting to the passport counter more quickly upon arrival, having a lean, low-drag luggage profile ensures that your movement through public areas is more effective and therefore less obvious. A large, cumbersome luggage profile makes you distracted, frustrated, late and a target.

Spreading Your Risk

Be smart about where you carry your most valuable items. Keep critical documents such as passport, tickets, money, and credit cards closest to you—that is, *on your person*. It is worth investing in a small fanny pack with a zipped compartment; otherwise, have a shirt with large button-down pockets in which you can keep your passport and other critical items. Do not put these items in the side pocket of a blazer or jacket, since the risk of being pickpocketed or losing the jacket (and its contents) is greater. Also remember that if you need to get off the X fast—whether it is out of an airplane emergency exit, out of a taxi, or otherwise, with your passport, money, and credit cards—you can buy what you need to replace what you left behind.

Before you leave, consider what combination of cash, credit or debit cards, and/or checks you plan to carry on your person. US dollars or Euros are very good bartering tools to have in most third-world countries. Before you get on a plane to depart for a high-risk destination, make sure that you have cash in the local currency in small denominations. This cash should be kept in a separate pocket and not your wallet. It is there for quick, easy access—it prevents you from fumbling with your wallet and showing the public your stack of credit cards and US dollars upon arrival at your destination. To the extent possible, you want to make your transactions in the local currency fast as you attract less attention to yourself.

You should double the amount of local currency kept on your person typically required to get from the airport to the hotel, because taxi drivers are a prime source of current threat/risk information. A nice tip for that information not only is appreciated but also often ensures that you have an ongoing source of information and (potentially) a trusted method of discreet transportation.

Preparing Delay Measure Tools: Throw-Down Wallet

Delay is an important principle of personal security, which we will discuss in more detail later in this chapter. One delay measure of a personal security plan that will require prior preparation in the advance planning phase is the throw-down wallet. It is a tool that is exactly as the term implies, a wallet that appears filled with cash that can be thrown down in the event you encounter a mugger or an assailant. It accomplishes two things. First, it is a diversion for the threat actor, and second, it gives you the chance to make a tactical withdrawal. The wallet should be filled with some low-denomination currency such as $10–$20 bills and some singles sandwiched in between to give it the appearance of a "wad" of cash. Second, fill it with some pocket litter—just make certain that none of the cards inside has your name or address on it. An alternative to the wallet is a money clip that can be kept in your front pocket and is there for the express purpose of use as a throw down should you need it. You can trim your name off of expired credit cards and plant them inside the wallet's pockets to add the appearance of value. The importance of this tool is not just in having it but in practicing how to use it—to plant the bait and withdraw when and if necessary. This should also be practiced several times in the planning phase.

A supplement to the throw-down wallet is to have a throw-down phone and watch. Often, assailants will ask for more than just your money. Rather than say no—if you can peel off other supposed "valuables" as you simultaneously back away—you create a distance, and you increase your chances of withdrawal and survival of the situation. In the absence of an offensive weapon such as a gun, a knife, and a club, having the capability to simultaneously respond and move away can be very effective.

PRINCIPLE OF DETECTION

In the world of physical security, detection is the layer of physical protection that determines that an unauthorized action has occurred or is occurring. A good detection measure must be capable of sensing the action or the potential threat event, communicating the alarm to a control center, and providing an immediate and effective way to assess the alarm event. Detection is not considered complete without assessment of the intrusion attempt—or threat.

In the world of personal security, while the general ideas of anomaly detection and assessment remain the same, the crucial difference is that you must be the sensor that detects potential threats. What this requires is the development of observational skills. Observation of one's environment is not just seeing, but sensing and knowing.

Most humans conduct their daily lives simply by seeing the environment around them. In fact, their internal dialogue about their own personal lives and external distractions such as music on their car radio or their iPod virtually blind them to what is actually happening in their environment. In high-risk environments, this will ultimately make you a victim. How many times have we heard the refrain, "...they seemed to come out of nowhere." I have heard this lament, whether it is a tourist who has had their bag ripped from their shoulder or someone driving to their office whose car is suddenly blocked front and back and hooded men jump out and are on them before they knew what had happened. People are seeing, not observing.

Observation is a skill that requires focused effort of looking at the world around you and assessing as you move through it.

As noted earlier, doing your homework in advance helps create a baseline of knowledge that is crucial to building a foundation of familiarity, mentally, for a key element of detection. It is the first step in positively engaging with what could potentially be a high-risk environment, rather than remaining passive to the risk and the potential dangers around you.

Observing, detecting, and assessing are a learned skill. You get a sharper edge to your observation skills if you have a baseline of your environment from which to work. It is not absolutely necessary, but it is very helpful. There are two components to use while on the street. First, switch up your internal dialogue to one focused outwardly on your surroundings. Mentally say to yourself what you see, as you move along.

"Coffee shop on the left."
"Mailbox on the corner."
"Alleyway on the opposite side of the street."

This exercise mentally draws your attention span into the here *and* now. The dialogue should then be refined to noting those things that are relevant to your movement, your safety, and ultimately your security. You are basically attaching observed caveats to your mental dialogue as you move along.

"Pavement narrows ahead because of a sidewalk vendor."
"Someone loitering near the ATM but not using it."
"Alleyway ahead, with no overhead light."

THE AFRICAN GAME SCOUT

Years ago, I hunted Cape buffalo near a vast stretch of East Africa known as the Selous Game Reserve. I was with a wizened old Tanzanian game scout. As we drove our Land Rover deep into the bush, the landscape of Savannah—interspersed with thickets of thorn trees—all looked the same to me. I would try to peer deeply at the forests, the grassy plains, for some sign of the animals that we had come to hunt. I saw nothing.

Suddenly, the game scout barked out "buffalo!" I looked but saw nothing. After letting me flounder for a minute or so, he pointed to a small stand of trees, and suddenly, I saw what he had seen much earlier than I: indeed, two buffalo, about 300 m distant. I would never have seen them without his assistance because they were shaded and blended in with the landscape. Only the scout's trained eye could pick them out at such a distance. He, unlike I, had a baseline of knowledge, familiarity, and experience in the African outback. He was observing, not just seeing—as I was. Later, the scout pointed out to me the subtle signs that we were near our quarry; the fresh tracks of the buffalo across the path that we were on; the broken Savannah grass through which they had plodded, foraging along the way, to the tree stand; and the fact that the trees shaded a wet, muddy area where the buffalo could wallow and rid themselves of the ever-present Tsetse flies biting them. All of them were subtle clues that were right there in front of me.

I learned an important lesson from that game scout about observation, as opposed to just seeing what is around me. First, he had a crucial baseline of mental familiarity with what was normal in his environment. Because of this, as we ploughed along across the Selous, he was looking and assessing, not just seeing. When the scout detected something that was out of the ordinary in the environment, he could make a mental deduction about what he saw and come to a conclusion—was it relevant to the hunt or not? The buffalo tracks were fresh and deep. Conclusion: They were made very recently, within the past hour. Following the direction of the tracks, there was the telltale disturbance of the grass through the sea of Savannah grass, which led to the trees, and eventually the two Cape buffalo, switching their tails and chewing their cuds.

When you see these things, ask yourself, "So what?" This forces your mind to draw a conclusion—a spot assessment—of the potential threat.

The second key component is developing triggers for what is wrong. This is done by looking for the absence of familiar and the presence of strangeness. A part of this technique, which is particularly relevant to security, is the déjà vu effect. This technique is useful whether you are on a street or in a vehicle, either as a passenger or as a driver (Figure 2.1).

We often sense it before we actually realize it—it is our intuition telling us something is not right. This skill is not hard to develop—it requires practice until the technique and what you see and conclude become muscle memory. Having a sense of where you are and where you are going in space, time, and direction is crucial. The temptation to rely on a global positioning system (GPS) to find your way through unfamiliar terrain should be fiercely resisted. First, the GPS is a crutch that will give you the excuse not to do your homework, as outlined previously in the section "Principle of Preparation." Second, reliance on the GPS

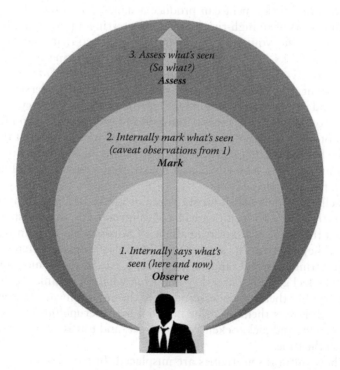

FIGURE 2.1 As you move through your environment, focus your observations and mental dialogue externally. It will naturally give you the focus required to detect anomalies. (Courtesy of Openclipart, http://www.openclipart.org.)

means you will not learn your environment once you are immersed in it. Being told where to go means you will never know where you are or where you are going.

PRINCIPLE OF DETERRENCE

In physical security, deterrence is the layer of physical protection that is employed to discourage an adversary from attempting an assault, by making a successful assault appear very difficult or impossible. The keyword is *appear*—deterrence, whether applied to physical security or personal security, has an element of deception to it.

As with the previous principle, applying deterrence to one's personal security plan means thinking through how to deceive a potential adversary that you are not a viable target.

The human herd, in today's urban environment, is more distracted than ever before. Compounding distraction with a disregard for how you fit into your environment can produce a dangerous combination when you find yourself in high-risk locations. Deterring a potential adversary means caring for your appearance and demeanor so that, together, your adversary thinks "these aren't the droids we're looking for," to paraphrase Obi Wan Kenobi's famous line from the movie *Star Wars*. To a great extent, this requires knowledge and some basic understanding of what kind of adversaries you might encounter and what they look for. It may not be what you expect. Tourists and their naivety can illustrate what not to do—a good rule of thumb is simply not to do what they do, and the likelihood that you will be targeted diminishes. I have observed this consistently in Abu Dhabi and Dubai, in the United Arab Emirates (UAE), for example.

Well-meaning female tourists from Europe or the United States often assume that since both cities are in a Muslim country, they must apply to all what they have heard or read about *all* Muslim countries (in general), and so, they arrive at the airport with headscarf in place, often wearing a loose-fitting robe and sandals, no makeup, etc. So that is nice, and perhaps they feel good because they are being what they think is culturally sensitive—but their misunderstanding of the environment to where they are traveling sets them up to be targeted by unscrupulous taxi drivers, petty thieves and pickpockets on the street, and tourist vendors. It happens all the time.

Their cultural sensitivities are misplaced. In fact, both cities in the moderate UAE are quite cosmopolitan. Over 86% of the populations are expatriates from other countries, including a substantial number from the West. In Dubai, a well-heeled woman tastefully made up and well coiffed with fashionable clothes and accessories that blend in is less of a target. Why? In this environment, it is assumed that she is a resident of the country, knows her way around, may be well connected, may have a wealthy husband, etc.; in short, there would be unacceptable consequences should she be assaulted or cheated.

Strive to blend in, be discreet, be boring! It is one of the keys to surviving on the street. Do not drive a shiny black GMC Yukon with blacked out windows through Tampico, Mexico (or any other northern Mexican town, for that matter), and not expect to get separated from your fancy sport-utility vehicle (SUV)—it will go into some cartel kingpin's fleet of vehicles and you will go hooded into some grimy safe house with a price on your release. Drive a dented, dusty, mud-splattered pickup truck through the same areas, and you increase your chances of being overlooked. You would not be that interesting, which is exactly the profile that you want.

How you look is an important deterrent, as well as how you behave, where you are, and what you do.

In downtown London's Piccadilly Circus, if you are wandering aimlessly along the sidewalk with your head tilted up, gaping at the sights and sounds, iPhone headsets plugged into your ears, and wearing a T-shirt and shorts and bright red rubber clogs, there is a good chance that you are a clueless bumpkin of a tourist, and the chances your wallet will be missing by the time you go from Piccadilly Square to Regent Street are very, very good. Some of the best pickpockets in the world operate in this area and salivate at targets such as this. In the same vicinity, how

HOW TO STAY SAFE IN YEMEN

While working in a Yemen just a few years ago, I chose to move around the city using unmarked cars with a trusted local driver or taxis. Using this mode of transportation accomplished two things. First, I could vary my time and route to and from business meetings in the city. Second, a boring old sedan or dirty, dented local taxi and a driver are a much lower profile than an armored SUV with armed bodyguards. In fact, there were attacks on just these sorts of high-profile, allegedly "high-security" convoys by Al Qaida in the Arabian Peninsula operatives. I further made myself more "boring" as a target by replying that I was a "Swedish" or a "Canadian" when asked where I was from. Having a small cover story to back your identity claim helps validate it in small talk. Having a thick wad of rial or dirham (UAE) currency was also important, to pay for everything in regional or local currency as opposed to using western cash and drawing attention.

you behave—combined with how you look and what you do—makes a real difference. If you are smartly dressed, are alert (no iPhone glued to your ear), are purposeful in your stride, and seem to know exactly where you are going, your chances of being a target diminish significantly. Pickpockets look for someone who is distracted or can be easily distracted (the bump-and-pick method). If your movement down the sidewalk includes conscious efforts to create a space between you and other people or chokepoints (such as at crosswalk intersections where the crowd bunches up waiting for the light), the risk of being a target drops even further—you are making yourself a hard target through deterrent measures.

PRINCIPLE OF DELAY

In physical security, delay is the element of a physical security system designed to impede adversary penetration into or exit from the protected area.

When applied to personal security, delay measures are implemented as a distraction to allow the *creation of distance* and ultimately escape from the confrontation. This principle and those that follow are significantly different from the previous ones, because the application of these measures assumes that an adversary has actively targeted you and is engaging. One or more individuals wish to do you harm. The measures used to delay an adversary's attack overlap with measures to deny and ultimately to defeat the attack. These collectively represent close-in self-defense measures that are distinctly different from the previous more passive measures described. The use of these rings of defense requires a rapid, crisp execution. For this reason, the concept of scenario building is useful when committing self-defense responses to memory.

In an encounter with someone who wants to harm you, the old saw that distance is your friend is very true. Whether the assailant wants to assault you physically or with a knife or a gun, your survival rate increases as your distance from the assailant and the speed at which you can achieve that distance increases. Techniques to achieve distance include the use of a throw-down wallet or purse, pepper spray, and whistle.

A throw-down wallet, as described earlier, is a wallet purposely made to look attractive and worth an assailant diverting attention to it and not you. Giving the assailant the wallet, or the purse, is a presentation technique that should be done in conjunction with simultaneously moving away and out of the area—hence the term throw-down wallet. It should be fat with cash that visually looks like a lot—the wad can be a relatively small amount, such as US$50–US$100, but made to look like a lot by converting $60 of the amount to $1s and $5s and bracketing this wad with two $20s. Hence, when the adversary thumbs through it, at a glance, it looks like a lot. Salting in some foreign currency notes only makes it look more enticing—especially if they appear to be large denomination bills. Plastic cards for expired memberships, offers or other pocket litter should be included with the wallet to further enhance its attractiveness. The top two-thirds of old expired credit cards can be stuffed in, to add to its attractiveness (make sure to clip off identifying information).

This delay measure is one that can be pulled together and included in your packing list for overseas destinations. It is part of your street kit when you go out, from the time you leave the airport or the train terminal (Figure 2.2).

I also include a cheap cell phone that is kept charged and minimally functional and a cheap watch that I can unclip and toss away without hesitation. The trick is to pass off these items while simultaneously moving away, so that you can run. If it is possible, another delay measure that you can include is pepper spray. This measure is a second line of defense, should your assailant not take the bait with the throw-down wallet/watch or if they are taken and they keep on coming. If you have

FIGURE 2.2 Example of some of the author's own street toolkit items. Counterclockwise from right is a wad of low-value currency collected from around the world; a very basic, reliable mobile phone loaded with pay-as-you-go minutes for local communications; a cheap but reliable watch that can be quickly tossed away; and a throw-down wallet filled with expired credit cards and what appears to be a thick wad of cash. The phone, watch, and wallet are simply delay measure tools to hand off to an assailant and simultaneously move away to obtain distance, before running.

pepper spray, it is important to test it before carrying it—you will not have the time to do so in an actual encounter—if you fumble with it, there is the chance that it will just further antagonize your assailant. Testing it in a safe location helps you understand the spray's range and its pattern. When using it, aim for the eyes—even if you do not hit the eyes directly; the old principle of aim small, shoot small ensures that you get within the vicinity of your target. Inhaling a healthy dose of pepper spray will considerably slow an assailant down.

The third delay measure is the whistle, and this should be used at the same time as the pepper spray. Have it around your neck, where you can get to it quickly. The throw-down wallet creates distraction through attraction, the pepper spray creates delay through sensory discomfort, and the whistle creates an alarm that forces the assailant to decide whether to continue to assault. Most assailants, whether they are thieves, muggers, or sexual predators, are looking for an easy, soft target to exploit. Each of these measures, taken together and escalated one after the other, very quickly makes you a much harder target than they bargained for.

PRINCIPLE OF DEFENSE

If the threat to you has not been deterred or delayed enough that they withdraw and/or you escape from the situation, you must defend yourself. The best form of self-defense is avoidance of situations where confrontation escalates into violence. If you studiously follow the principles previously outlined in this book, there is a very good chance you will minimize the risk of a situation where you must resort to violent measures to defend yourself. *Self-defense is always the last resort.* The objective should you be required to defend yourself is—as with the previous principle of delay—to use sufficient force to remove the threat and then withdraw quickly and, basically, to hit and run.

It is not within the scope of this book to provide you a comprehensive set of skills and training for active self-defense. However, based on our own experience and accounts from colleagues over the course of our years living in high-risk environments, we can provide some useful tips and practical guidelines for what you need to expect in a violent encounter and what you need to look for in self-defense training to complete your personal security program.

Reality of Confrontation

At the heart of your personal security program, ultimately, is you—not the adversary, the mugger, the rapist, the kidnapper, nor the terrorist.

It is all about you, your mental attitude, and what you are prepared to do to survive. When it gets to the point where you must defend yourself on the street, you must be willing and confident that you will defeat your adversary, no matter what. If you do not have this mental attitude, you could end up raped, beaten, and dead in a body dump; hooded in the back of a kidnapper or a terrorist's SUV, headed for a nameless safe house; stabbed or shot; and bleeding out in some third-world alleyway. That is a cold, hard fact. It is okay to be afraid. It is not okay to let your fear rule you. Make it work for you.

There are tools that you should have for self-defense, and for the purposes of this book, we will only provide you some familiarization with them. The three basic areas are as follows:

- Delivering effective violence (fighting)
- Protecting yourself from blows
- Getting out of holds

Delivering Effective Violence (Fighting)

The rules: The first rule of fighting, if you are cornered, is that there are no rules. If you do not have anything at hand, then you will have to use your natural weapons, which are hands, elbows, feet/shins, knees, teeth, and head. Consider the following when fighting back barehanded:

- Instinctively, one strikes with a punch or with the open palm of their hand (slap). If that is what you are going to do, make that strike count. Choose an area that is relatively unprotected and easy to strike quickly, such as the throat or the nose.
- If you are being held closely, or cannot strike with your hands, use your fingers—or nails if you have them. Scratch the face, the groin—and wherever you can get purchase.
- Again, if you are being held closely or are very close, knee your adversary's groin (if it is a man) as sharply and quickly as possible. It is very effective.
- Do not be afraid to bite, especially if you are being held. A hard bite to the face or the ear is tremendously painful (just ask Evander Holyfield!).
- Avoid flamboyant, high kicks—it can put you off balance and on your back very quickly. If you are being held from behind (your arms trapped), a quick downward stamp of your heel to the foot or your adversary's shin can be very effective.

Something at hand: If you can find something to hit with, grab it and use it: your purse, an umbrella, a piece of scrap metal, a broken bottle, a rock, and car keys bunched in your fist. If you have a club or other similar item, do not swing it like a baseball bat or stab downward with it—it can be blocked more easily. Jab upward in a stabbing motion—aim for the face (eyes), the throat, or the chest area.

If you are on a beach or around dirt, grab a handful and throw it in your assailant's eyes. If you have hot coffee in a mug, throw it in their face. *Taking action gives you a fighting spirit*, which you will need when and if that adversary keeps coming at you. If any of these tactics work, take advantage of the respite and withdraw and run. Your objective is to survive the encounter, not to conquer your adversary. That is only a last resort (see the following).

Make noise: When you hit, slap, punch, or kick your assailant, yell and scream. This has three practical uses. First, it keeps you breathing and gets your blood oxygenated and pumping through your circulatory system. You need oxygenated blood for stamina, so you can fight. Second, it alerts anyone within earshot that you need help. Third, when your adversary punches you, yelling gets air out of your lungs and you are less apt to have the wind (and your fight) knocked out of you.

Know your opponent's vulnerabilities: Knowing how and where to kick your assailant is important. There are three general areas to aim for:

- Face and head—Aim for the eyes, the tip of the nose, and the throat. Ears are also vulnerable to pulling/ripping, as is hair. Keep your fingers clear of the mouth area (you do not want to get bitten).
- Torso—The solar plexus is very vulnerable but can be easy to miss if you do not know what you are doing. The testicles/groin of male and the female genital areas are excellent locations to attack, as they are sensitive.
- Legs and feet—A hard strike to the thigh can actually render someone unable to walk. The shins are vulnerable to hard kicks, and a hard stomp with the heel of your shoe on the feet can be very effective.

Guns, Knives, or Other Weapons   The premise of this personal security book is that you will not be carrying a knife or a gun. Not having a gun, or a knife, in a certain sense should make you smarter about your personal security. If you understand that you do not have lethal weapons on which you can rely and you have studiously paid attention to the other elements of this security program, you will make smarter risk-based decisions that will keep you from getting into difficult situations to begin with. You will become street smart and wisely cautious. As previously said, if you are not familiar with the use of firearms and knives, it is well worth the time, the investment, and the effort to become proficient in their use. The reason for this is that should the occasion arise where you have these weapons available to you, not knowing how to employ them against your adversary can become a severe liability to your survival (see "Hesitation Kills").

Weapon familiarization: Part of a weapon familiarization course is learning what kinds of rifles, shotguns, and handguns are used around the world. You do not need to know how to strip it down, clean it, and maintain it—you just need to understand where and how the safety mechanism works, how to load and chamber a round, and how to cock it, aim it, and pull the trigger. You will likely not have a choice as to what gun you are able to secure, so you must know how to use the one you do get. Also, it is important to understand how to hold the weapon if/when you are able to get your hands on one. For instance, if you have a handgun, keep it pulled in close to your body. If you hold it out away from you, it is easy for an adversary to grab and twist the muzzle away before you have a chance to pull the trigger—the gun is rendered useless

HESITATION KILLS: LESSON OF THE OPEC SIEGE, 1975

On December 21, 1975, six militants led by infamous terrorist Ilich Ramirez Sanchez, aka "Carlos the Jackal," stormed the Vienna, Austria–based headquarters of the Organization of Petroleum Exporting Countries (OPEC) and took 60 hostages. Three hostages were killed in the attack; an Austrian policeman, an Iraqi OPEC bodyguard, and Yousef Al-Azmarly, a young Libyan statistician assigned to OPEC. The story of how Al-Azmarly died is a particularly good example of why weapon familiarization is critical. Carlos and the terrorists had already killed twice and were moving rapidly through the corridors of OPEC's offices. Al-Azmarly unexpectedly confronted and surprised Carlos and was able to wrest his Beretta M12 machine pistol away from him. The young Libyan suddenly had a loaded automatic weapon in his possession and had the drop on the world's most dangerous terrorist. Unfortunately, he did not know what to do next. As he clumsily fumbled with the weapon, it was clear that he had no idea how to operate it. Carlos calmly drew another automatic pistol from underneath his leather jacket and deliberately shot Al-Azmarly in the hand (disarming him), in the leg, then in the stomach, and finally the coup de grace, in the back of the neck. Hesitation, and unfamiliarity with the weapon, robbed the young OPEC employee of his momentary advantage and ultimately his life.

and can easily be wrested away from you. You should be fully prepared to use it, if you have it. There should be no hesitation in this. Hesitation will kill you, as surely as if the adversary themselves had it.

If you have a knife, know how to defend yourself with it. Using a knife as a weapon is an acutely intimate experience—it is not for the fainthearted. You really need to steel yourself mentally and prepare for close-in violence in the encounter—you will be looking your adversary in the eye. A knife should not be drawn except as a last resort. If your assailant has a knife, be prepared to defend yourself against the assault. There are some practical measures that you can and should take when knives are involved. First, if you have the option, the type of knife that you should have ought to be double edged, not single edged—a double-edged knife in a fight gives you 100% more advantage than a single-edged blade, and you can be less predictable about your slashes—it cuts both ways (see Figure 2.3 for example). Ensuring that the first inch and a half of the blade, from the point down toward the hilt, are razor sharp is critical. The knife should have a hilt guard and a long handle, prefer-ably rubberized. It should be kept in a cheap sheath that can be thrown aside and not missed. If you are wearing short sleeves or are otherwise bare armed, pull off your shirt or use your jacket wrapped around your forearms as protection. Sometimes, the act of doing this in a deliber-ate way—wrapping your forearm, tossing away the sheath, and palming the knife alone—signals to your adversary that you know what you are doing and they will back off.

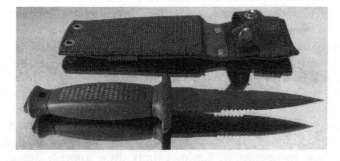

FIGURE 2.3 If you have the option to choose to have a knife, pictured is the ideal type of weapon you should select. The sheath can be tossed away, the rubber grip is counterweighted for balance, the tang provides your hand a protection, and it is double edged, giving you the ability to slash both ways and increase your advantage. The serrated edge to the tip should be kept razor-sharp.

Protecting Yourself from Blows

The simplest ways to block an adversary's blows are the best, because you will not forget them if you need to remember them. They are as follows:

> Blocking a punch—if someone tries to punch you, you naturally move your head in the opposite direction of the punch. Support this natural movement by instinctively throwing your forearm at the adversary's punching arm. Use the bony part of your arm that runs from the point of your elbow to the outside edge of your wrist. Practice daily to see how this feels—it helps to rotate your arm as you push it at the punch. Using this part of your forearm is important for the following reasons:
> - Because it is bony, it will hurt the adversary more.
> - It is least likely to be badly damaged—if you are attacked with a knife, it can sustain a deep slash and not disable the use of your hands (see tips for fighting with a knife and/or an adversary with a knife).
> - By using this part of your arm, your physical balance will be maintained. In the instance that the power of your adversary's punch is deflected away from you, for a fraction of a second, they are off balance. With practice, this can be used to your advantage.
>
> Blocking a kick—If someone tries to kick you, avoid the temptation of blocking with your legs. This can leave you off balance (on one leg) and vulnerable. Instead of kicking out, lift your knee and absorb the kick on the shin and not your thigh.
>
> The essential element of blocking is not so much the technicalities—unless you are a trained fighter—you will not have the time or the instincts to respond perfectly. The main point is to get something between your vulnerable areas and the strike or kick being thrown and push the energy of the attack away from your body. You would not be able to block forever. The goal is to effectively block when the attack starts, get the adversary off balance, and strike early and hard.

Getting Out of Holds

It is important to understand that if your adversary is trying to hold/restrain you, it is because the attack is in a transition phase—they are moving to the objective of their attack, which could be a sexual assault or a kidnap attempt where they are moving you to a van or a car. The three key elements to break a hold are (a) ensure that you can breathe, (b) loosen the hold, and (c) inflict injury.

Headlock: A headlock can be used to strangle. If you are being held from behind in a head lock, move your fingers to the crook of your adversary's elbow and turn your head—this gives you space to breathe. Once you can breath, strike back.

Neck grab: Release yourself from a neck grab by forcing your arms rapidly up or down between your adversary's arms. Strike hard and then withdraw as quickly as possible (run).

Grab from behind: If you are held from behind, attack the genital area with your hand, kick the shin with your heel, or hit at the face with the back of your head (rear head butt—very painful!). Strike hard and then be prepared to run.

Keep It Simple

If you find yourself in a situation where you have *no choice* but to fight to defend yourself, keep your strategy simple and keep thinking. As noted earlier, it is quite alright to be afraid—you would not be human if you were unfearful. But do not let your fear paralyze you. One construct for not letting your fear take over is to repress your emotions and think of what you have in front of you as a series of tasks you need to accomplish for your safety—nothing more, nothing less. Mentally, keep it simple and matter of fact. You do not need to fight someone to a standstill. You just need to use enough force to give you a chance to run.

SELECTED THREAT ACTOR PROFILE: STREET GANGSTERS

Street criminals are commonly dismissed with labels such as *thugs* and *scumbags*. Of all of the threats that one might encounter, this class of criminal is the most prolific and the one you are most likely to meet. Personally, I do not put labels on criminals such as this because, as a professional, I believe that I have an obligation to understand their nature, motives, character, and modus operandi. Labels are dangerous because they unconsciously shut down further inquiry by putting a mask on the actor and a focus on bad things...not bad people. It abstracts the actor. I always try to truly understand my adversary. I do not have to like them or empathize with them, but I do believe that nothing is lost by trying to learn more about them since they are a category of threat actor that is common and widespread. I start with putting the colorful labels aside.

Street gangsters and criminals are usually brought up in abject poverty and have nothing to lose by taking incredible risk—in this sense, they are risk takers. Violent behavior is commonplace with them, and most, if not all of them, have survived severe beatings, stabbings, or being shot before the age of 14 (see Chapter 5, which catalogs in detail the kinds of gangs that you might encounter abroad). If their trust is won, it is transitory and must be consistently fed. They live by quid pro quo, and this transactional principle is seared into their DNA. If they survive into their 20s, it makes them hardened, shrewd, and ruthless in the business of crime. They lead by example, because their reputation is sometimes all they have. This kind of criminal is easier to deal with one on one; within a group, they must maintain face, and no matter how well you think you may know them or trust them, all bets are off if they are within the gang when encountered or dealt with. They expect you to understand and accept that and can be dismissive if you do not. They are incredibly resourceful and have a constant ear to the street. Finally, their network of contacts—for those that survive—is impressive. They know with whom and where to fence stolen items, and they know where to get weapons, drugs, information, and dirt on corrupt officials or businesses. As an adversary, they are to be respected in terms of capability (not character)—these are typically the foot soldiers for more organized prison gangs, cartels, or organized criminal groups. If they sense at all that you are sympathetic to them, they will take complete advantage of you and whatever you have to offer—if you are victimized by them, pleading, begging, or crying will only harden their resolve to escalate abuse. Likewise, they do not trust anyone outside of their circle who apes their language or the way that they talk to each other or others. Next time that a security professional indulges in a labeling exercise for these kinds of adversaries, ask him/her who—specifically—he/she is describing. There is a good chance that you will not receive an answer that tells you anything of value about who the threat actor(s) are, their range, capability, scope of influence, or history.

REFERENCES

Center for Disease Control (CDC), "Choosing a drug to prevent malaria," http://www.cdc.gov/malaria/travelers/drugs.html (2012, November 9, 2012).

Davis, C. E., "What's in your travel medical kit?" http://www.travelinsurance review.net/tips-and-advice/travel-safety-tips/packing-a-travel-medical -kit/ (February 2016).

Kozarsky, P., "Travelers diarrhea: What you need to know," http://www .webmd.com/digestive-disorders (2010).

Rendi-Wagner, P. et al., Abstract for "Drug prophylaxis for travelers' diarrhea," *Clinical Infectious Diseases* 34, http://www.ncbi.nlm.nih.gov/pubmed/11803509 (2002a), pp. 628–633.

Rendi-Wagner, P. et al., Abstract for "Choosing a drug to prevent malaria," *Clinical Infectious Diseases* 34, http://www.ncbi.nlm.nih.gov/pubmed/11803509 (2002b), pp. 628–633.

Rhett J. Stoney, "Travel insurance, travel health insurance, and medical evacuation insurance," *CDC Yellow Book*, 2, http://wwwnc.cdc.gov/travel/yellowbook/2016/the-pre-travel-consultation/travel-insurance-travel-health-insurance-medical-evacuation-insurance (2016).

Wikitravel, "Telephone service for travel," accessed April 16, 2016, http://wikitravel.org/en/Telephone_service_for_travel (February 17, 2016).

ENDNOTE

1. *CDC Health Information for International Travel* (commonly called the *Yellow Book*) is published every two years as a reference for those who advise international travelers about health risks. The *Yellow Book* is written primarily for health professionals but is a useful resource for anyone interested in healthy international travel.

CHAPTER 3

When Travel Plans Go Sideways

INTRODUCTION

When considering this chapter, I made the decision to combine two classic scenarios that together pose what I believe can be one of the more terrifying experiences that business travelers face: the unexpected arrival in uncharted territory, without any backup on the ground, and the unavoidable necessity of navigating by road into the capital city or some regional backwater late at night. This has happened to me several times in the course of my lifetime living and working abroad, and I still get uneasy when it happens. The principles of personal security outlined in the previous chapter can make all the difference in how you manage this situation.

We have heard the ideal advice from security experts regarding ground travel in hazardous areas of the world. Typically, it goes like this:

- Do not travel after dark.
- Travel in armored vehicles, preferably with an armed escort.
- Avoid any travel to (insert city or country of concern).

All very nice. Unfortunately, these maxims sometimes do not square with reality. In international business, the dictates of profit margins and competition make the world a messy place. Not all corporations have the global resources to field top-tier security teams, equipment, and coordination in dangerous regions of the globe. Sooner or later, you might find yourself alone, late at night in a crowded, grimy airport in the third world, about to break the very nonspecific, general cautionary rules that the so-called security experts laid out so glibly at the last conference that you attended. You will have to travel after dark, and your only available mode of transportation is not a shiny black armored Cadillac Escalade, but more likely a beat-up taxi driven by a local who does not speak your language.

Welcome to the real world. This uncharted territory is quite frequently the kind of security challenge that overseas travelers face. If you are one of the fortunate few who has a dedicated company expeditor who can whisk you through customs at four o'clock in the afternoon into an armored vehicle, with private security kitted out in cargo pants, bulletproof vests, wrap-around dark sunglasses, headphones, tattooed biceps bulging, and automatic weapons, that is great. You get to brag about having been to a real danger zone, without actually having had to deal with or experience the real danger for yourself. See it through smoked out, bullet-resistant windows as you are driven at high speed to your five-star luxury hotel—someone else will take care of it for you.

If you are not apt to be one of the fortunate few, but one of the unwashed majority who is compelled by business or operations to travel into the third world on a moment's notice, then read on—the following guidelines are just for you.

ARRIVAL AT THE AIRPORT

Consider this scenario: You have arrived alone, late at night, in a deserted regional airport in a conflict zone, no local expeditor, no driver, no armored car, and no bearded bodyguard contingent. To make it more interesting, your mobile phone does not work, and it is 20 miles into the main city from the airport. This is where you need good, solid security advice on what to do and what not to do.

At Arrivals

The customs official glared at you, thumbed through your passport several times, glared at you again, and then—to your surprise—hammered the entry stamp on a blank page and let you into the country. Congratulations—he actually stamped your entry visa. Make sure to check that this was done—just accepting your passport from the official without confirming that it is actually stamped can lead to problems when you leave the hellhole in which you have just found yourself.

From that point on, the first principle—that of preparation—is focused on one thing only: getting you, and—if you are so lucky—your team of nervous, greenhorn teammates squabbling with each other, safely and securely out of the airport and into relatively secure transport to wherever your accommodations will be. This principle is not just for the comfort of your office or home before leaving your home country. It is also one that should be implemented to get you ready for show time, which is your entry into the arrival hall. If you do not have anyone expecting you, the less known about who you are, what you do, and where you need to go, the better.

Before you proceed to the arrival hall, step off to the side and make the following preparations:

First, there is the issue of bags or tools that you may have checked before departing. Once you have retrieved them, check to make certain that you do not have any obviously identifying information on them such as company logos and business cards used as identity tags. If you have your team of greenhorns, make certain that they do the same thing. The object of this is to lower your profile and that of your team, building in a measure of deterrence. The absence of obvious information about you gives you a small measure of control about how much or how little information you decide to provide to a potential source of transportation once you get into the arrival hall. Every little bit counts.

Second, make sure you have secured your passport, some small denominations of cash, and only the most important credit cards on your person. Also, have a printed copy of your itinerary and the address of your hotel—in the language of the country where you have arrived—on your person where it is easily retrievable. The remaining cash and credit cards, copies of passports, and anything else (such as your shiny new watch) should go into your backpack. The cash will be for transportation and tips, as you move through the public space of the airport, to transportation, to the hotel. If you are traveling with a team, advise them to do as you do. Having printed copies of your itinerary and the address of your hotel in the local language will minimize confusion later.

Third, if possible, check to see if your mobile phone works or—if you have secured one in advance that will work in the region—activate it.

Arrival Hall: Public Space

With this preliminary preparation done, you push through the entry hall into arrivals and are greeted by a throng of people. Besides family members and friends, there are individuals collectively known as *expeditors* who have either been hired by or work for companies or individuals. They have signs, with the name of the arriving businesspersons or clients, who they are to meet and transport into the city.

Unless your company was able to arrange someone in advance of your arrival, none of these individuals is waiting for you. It is at this point where you must have a clear strategy on how to expedite yourself through the airport, to trusted transportation.

1. Technically speaking, *there is* someone waiting for you in the arrival hall. You have not met him, but he knows you. He is Jamal, or Carlos, or whoever . . . hustling for business, for his cousin Ibrahim, or Juan, waiting outside in an unmarked car. He is looking for you—the tired business traveler with a shell-shocked glaze in your eyes, mouth agape, aimlessly shuffling out of the arrival hall looking for something or someone that is not there, looking for familiar in a strange place. Word of advice: the first element of your airport exit strategy should be *not* to be that person I just described. Further, if you are traveling with a greenhorn, a junior employee or a colleague, or your boss—*take charge*. The last thing you want is for your team, whether it is the two of you or more, to exhibit the aforementioned characteristics of the clueless traveler. Herd them, keep them together, and firmly communicate what the plan will be. First impressions are important in places like this. Even if you do not feel like it, you need to appear confident, knowledgeable, and alert.

2. Be aware of anyone who has a placard bearing your name on it. If you were not expecting someone, then this is an individual who got your information from someone on the airport staff handling the immigration cards, as you came through customs. This individual phoned in the information about you to his accomplice, who quickly prints your name on the placard. It is a scam. He will introduce himself as a driver for a named, reputable hotel in town. If you are not prepared for this, it can be easy to fall for—after all, he knows your name and hotel. What happens next can be a very expensive ride to the hotel or an express kidnap scenario where you are robbed and then dumped somewhere in town. If you are not expecting someone to meet you at the airport, check their credentials. Do not let them lead you out of the crowd, into their vehicle. Go to the airport information desk and ask to contact the hotel for confirmation of the driver and his bona fides.

3. Do not go immediately to the exit. Consciously ignore the hustlers soliciting your business. Do not engage in conversation with them, and do not query them. For now, they are not your priority (they could be later, but you want to solicit on your terms—not theirs). Your priority is to maintain control of your selection of transport for yourself and—if you are accompanied—your team.

4. Logistical needs: If local cash and communications are available, approach the requirement as follows:
   a. Money: Look for a recognized brand name exchange bureau, if you need to exchange cash into the local currency. Unscrupulous money changers in some countries will set themselves up as a currency exchange bureau and then proceed to charge whatever rate they like, as well as commissions that are exorbitant. They are taking advantage of your unfamiliarity and often your language difficulties.
   b. Communications: You may be in a situation where your mobile phone is not working or cannot roam with the local cellular provider. Be very wary about using phones in the airport that take credit cards, particularly if there are no call rates posted on the phone. Even if the rates are posted, there are more often than not hidden charges that end up being quite a lot. Also, be careful about cell phone rentals. What is often not revealed is the exorbitant rates that you will pay while using the cell phone, plus the security deposit and other changes. Instead, try to find airport booths that sell SIM cards for a fixed price that work in your own phone (you should have an unlocked phone when you travel). Alternatively, purchase a cheap unlocked phone that will take a locally purchased prepaid SIM card. Activate that phone before departing, and try calling ahead to the hotel or the accommodation where you will be staying.

5. Transportation:
   a. Look for kiosks that are often part of the arrival hall in third-world airports. These kiosks are service desks for large hotels, driver for hire or trusted taxi services, or rental car services. If you are fortunate enough to spot one of these—go to one that is manned and ask if the hotel at which you are staying has airport transportation to the hotel. With luck, you might be directed to the hotel's transportation service, and your most immediate problem—trusted transportation—will be resolved.
   b. If there are no service desks, your next option is an airline representative. If one is on duty, go directly to them and ask about transportation and what should be trusted.
   c. If there are no service desks, taxi services, hotel transportation, or airport information desk, then the time has come to head for the exits. Once outside, look specifically for a taxi stand—with marked taxis queuing up for travelers. This keeps control of your transportation in your hands and further reduces the risk of being accosted by an unscrupulous

operation by keeping the taxi selection random—which is in your favor.

d. The taxi operations outside airports in third-world countries are often haphazard and confusing at best. If this is the situation on the curb, your next option is to engage with Ahmed or Carlos, the hustler-for-hire operation. But do *not* engage with the first one that you encountered—in fact, on arrival, you should have made a note of who first sought you out. If there is one, there will be many operators like this. Select the second or the third individual looking for your business. This keeps you in control of transportation selection and keeps the element of randomness in the equation. With regard to personal security, the *element of randomness* is important because it allows you to inject a measure of unpredictability into any given situation, which in turn reduces the risk that you become a target for exploitation. This concept is especially important in counterkidnap or counterterrorist tactics and is one of the most important tools in your personal security toolkit.

e. For tip for service and tip for information, do not be a grinch. Both are valuable commodities in a strange place, and showing your gratitude can win influence that could come in handy later.

Phase 1 is completed; you have kept your risks to a minimum in identifying and securing trusted transportation, under the circumstances. Now, the second phase of your arrival in "Indian country" begins.

ON THE ROAD: CHECKPOINTS AND ROADBLOCKS

One of the inevitable difficulties of living and working abroad in high-risk regions is understanding and negotiating your way through various kinds of checkpoints or roadblocks. There are fundamental rules that need to be considered when encountering roadblocks, and not understanding these unique rules of the road in dangerous environments can get you incarcerated or killed. In keeping with the theme of principled personal security, knowing how to identify, approach, and get beyond roadblocks ultimately lies with you. Whether you are in a taxi, with a company driver, or driving by yourself, it is important to understand the first rule of roadblocks: get that roadblock safely in your rearview mirror. Period.

For this book, we will discuss general guidelines that apply to most third-world roadblocks. We will also characterize five different variants of checkpoints. They are checkpoints or roadblocks established by police, by regular military forces, by paramilitary or militia forces, by operational or flying checkpoints, and by criminal roadblocks.

General Guidelines for Roadblocks

There are some very important basic guidelines that should form the basis of your roadblock strategy. These apply to just about any situation involving a checkpoint manned by armed individuals, whether they are police, military, or civilian.

Preparation

Have your passport or photo identification (ID) in a place where you have it at hand, ready to show if asked. *Know exactly where it is, and be deliberate and calm about how you retrieve it and hand it over.* You do not want to be in the position of leaning over, digging for your documents in a bag, at a dimly lit police or military checkpoint. The quicker you respond, the more you increase your chances of getting past the checkpoint. They are following a checklist, and you are accommodating that list quickly and efficiently. It is usually as simple as that—so keep it simple and do not complicate matters, or let someone in your party do that.

Communications

If you are with a taxi or a company driver, let that individual initially do the talking. Be prepared to respond, if or when asked for ID. Keep the tone of your answers polite, short, and to the point. If you speak the language fluently but are in a taxi or with a driver, do not let on that you do. Stick to English—whipping out your best Spanish, or Farsi, or Arabic might make you feel good and impress your girlfriend or other companions, but more often than not, in third-world countries with ongoing security issues, it raises suspicion. Listen carefully to the local dialogue between the driver and the police or military guard at the checkpoint, but keep your own knowledge of what is being said to yourself. You might gain some valuable information in the process, because what the driver and the police say to each other is unguarded. Once you are through the checkpoint, you can surprise your driver by asking in his own language what the police or military meant if there was a conversation. It will be unexpected and give you an element of control with the driver.

Managing Your Team

Ensure that others in the vehicle understand the protocol—let the driver do the talking, only speak when spoken to, and if anyone else needs to do the talking, you do it, in English. Stupid or random why questions, or questions about directions, can quickly confuse the situation and upset the police or the military. The less said, the better. (If you have someone on your team that just cannot understand or comply with your rules, take a mental note and keep them at a distance later on. People like this can cause serious security issues during a visit, and they rarely get it.)[1]

Approach and Interaction

If you are driving a vehicle, here are some basic principles that should be followed when approaching police or military checkpoints:

- Slow down and dim your lights. Driving up on roadblocks with your lights blaring and windows up will just upset the guards stationed at the checkpoint. With your lights dimmed, they can see you, and it is an initial acknowledgment by you that you respect them.
- Roll down your window and keep your hands at 10–2 on the steering wheel, where the police can see them. You have not said a word yet, but unconsciously, the security see you respect them (dimmed lights, slowed down), and feel more secure.
- Have your photo ID, passport, driver's license, registration, and insurance ready on the dash. Keep it together and in a place where the police or the military can consistently see your hands. Do not secure these documents, until the last minute, in the glove box or closed console next to your elbow.
- Be pleasant and polite. Keep your salutations short and to the point—but use them. Your nonverbals to this point have indicated respect, so let your first verbal encounter confirm it. Then, let the police ask their questions. Typically, they will ask for your ID, where you have come from, where you are going, and the nature of your business. Have quick, confident replies ready for them. They might ask the nationality of you and others in your vehicle. Keep the answers brief and truthful. In Mexico, they might ask if you have drugs or weapons in the vehicle. The answer to both questions is no—unless you wish to spend your time in Mexico in a fetid jail cell. Do not be cute, and do not be chatty. Be polite, brief, and direct to the point. Your objective is to be moved on, as there is nothing about you or your companions of interest.

Police Checkpoints

In the third world, the uniformed police—although corruptible—are at least relatively predictable. Bribes are common, so be prepared to pay a token amount. If handled appropriately, the police will wave you through without incident and—if you are nice—actually provide some advice on what lies ahead on the road. Even the worst police still have some innate sense of duty to order, even if it is heavily weighted on the side of enforcement. This is a subtle difference that is worth remembering because it generally holds true with all third-world police.

Police in Conflict Zones

Police forces operating in areas where there is an ongoing insurgent or terrorist activity have a thankless job. Quite often, they are poorly armed with obsolete weapons, sporadically paid, and reliant on informal local relationships with criminal gangs or militias for compensation in return for cooperation. For example, in Uganda, during the civil war of the mid-1980s, the police were poorly armed with a mix of World War II era Lee–Enfield rifles, ancient Webley Revolvers, and old .45-caliber M3 submachine guns—otherwise known as the *Grease Gun*. In South America, the regular police had .38-caliber revolvers and shotguns (more elite counternarcotics forces received automatic rifles and submachine guns). In Algeria, regular police were expected to fend off periodic terrorist forays into the countryside with worn-out Belgian Fabrique National—Carabine Automatique Legere (FN CAL) rifles, and in Yemen, police manned roadblocks with worn-out Kalishnikovs. Police in these locations have the thankless task of trying to maintain civil order in a capital city or a province that has long since deteriorated into armed camps of different insurgent factions. Along with crime, they must deal with ongoing military operations and drunken firefights between rival groups or even within groups that are little more than gangs.

Police at established roadblocks periodically check the occupants of vehicles that seem out of place, and usually, they simply wave taxis and locals through. Most of the time, they are exhausted, doing a thankless job in a gritty, dangerous environment. The worst thing that you could do with this lot is to question them, question their authority, or argue with them. There is a fine line between bored cursory checks and a hair-trigger temper that, when aroused, can result in one getting hauled out of the vehicle at gunpoint, slapped around, and hauled away for questioning. It is best not to poke the bear at all; the smart play is to always have an ID at the ready, a pleasant demeanor, and, if necessary, some currency to grease passage through the checkpoint.

Police in Criminal-Controlled Regions

In Mexico and Central/South America, checkpoints may be manned by local police who are working with the cartels or the regional criminal gangs operating in the region. Local police departments in Mexican towns and cities, for example, are notorious for being corrupt. Part of it is understandable—the police officers themselves are paid a pittance, not well trained, poorly supported, and led by local politicians themselves who are corrupt. As a result, they collect *mordida* ("bribes"; when translated, it means "bite"). It is almost customary. Their job is usually to direct traffic and deal with traffic accidents or other incident-driven problems in the town or the city. They usually do not have an investigative function; this is done by the state or the federal police—the municipal police simply secure the scene. In these instances, the police will not just be interested in where you came from or where you are going. They will want a bribe. Police may also pull you over, for the same reason. These kinds of shakedowns typically follow a script, which can progress as follows.

The police will pull you over or stop you at a makeshift roadblock and ask if you have some obscure safety item in your trunk such as a safety triangle, a fire extinguisher, or other item. They might say that you were monitored passing someone in a no passing zone. The "violation" is obscure and is likely a complete fabrication. Just understand that this is how the game is played.

Once the violation is explained, the consequences are then laid out—they usually involve a large fine, confiscation of your license, etc. Getting your documents back is also described as a drawn-out affair and made as inconvenient as possible by saying that it must be done at a police station 20 or 30 km away. The officer will then give you a way out, by offering to accept an amount of cash on the spot, which can typically be negotiated. Once this is paid, you are on your way.

There are some ground rules to handling these kinds of situations:

- First, never hand over original documents such as your license, or passport, to the officer. This is why you carry copies with you.
- Second, even if you are fluent in the language, resort to your best broken version of the language. This gives you an advantage of understanding the officer better than he understands you. The officer may become frustrated that you are taking so much time, and this will throw him off his game. He might let you go or reduce the amount of the bribe if you mildly stand your ground and push back on the amount that they want. Ultimately, complicating their script works in your favor, as long as you do not get too aggressive or unpleasant.

Military or Paramilitary Checkpoints in Conflict Zone

If you have landed in a country that is engulfed in a civil war, there is the chance that the airport at which you have landed is under contested military control. As this is being written, this is the case in Sana'a, Yemen, where the Houthis from the north of Yemen have captured the capital; accepted the current president's resignation; and have taken control of the airport, the capital, and all related infrastructures. You must keep in mind that these kinds of checkpoints, unlike semipermanent police or regular military checkpoints on main roads, are usually hastily assembled blockades manned by combat troops, as opposed to professional police or garrison-conditioned military units. The reason for the blockade may be to prevent or divert traffic away from ongoing combat operations further down the road. It could also be simply to check for weapons or combatants moving in and out of recently captured territory or key objectives—such as the airport.

Standard Military Checkpoint

A good rule of thumb to use in distinguishing what type of military roadblock that you are approaching is how the checkpoint is deployed and what physical security measures have been used to block the road and the channel traffic. If there are security lights in use (spotlights that are directed toward oncoming traffic), concrete jersey-type barriers, a boom gate, a shelter of some kind for the guards, and heavy weaponry such as a truck or armored personnel carrier (APC)-mounted 12.7 mm DShk Dashka[2] heavy machine gun off to the side with sweeping coverage of the road, you are likely going through a standard, semipermanent roadblock. These kinds of checkpoints are typically manned by garrison-conditioned troops who have become somewhat familiar with civilian traffic and behavior. Their uniforms will probably be cleaner, they may have boots and helmets, and they will have relatively good weaponry. There will be at least one officer in charge of the roadblock detachment, in the event that some intervention and decision are required. You will likely receive a cursory once-over and be on your way.

Paramilitary, Militia, or Flying Checkpoints

Using the same physical security assessment rule of thumb, if the roadblock that you are approaching is relatively darkened, guards are disheveled, are using flashlights, are armed, and behave as operational infantry, then there is a good chance that they are. This is a different kind of roadblock. Look for light infantry weapons such as Kalishnikov (AK-47s) with magazines taped together (yes, it is a bad idea but very common among third-world fighters), hand grenades clipped to their belts, and rocket-propelled grenades (RPGs). They may be using a hastily arrayed coil of concertina or razor ribbon or just two mud-spattered Toyota Hilux pickups pulled across the road nose to nose. Their behavior will be that of a third-world combat grunt, not a garrison-conditioned trooper. This means that you will likely be looking down the business end of an AK-47 leveled directly at your head, and the soldier behind it with bloodshot eyes could be in his early teens. If these are insurgents or local militia, they will be undisciplined and have very rudimentary training, if any.

It is important to understand that the individuals stationed at these kinds of roadblocks are not used to dealing with the public or civilians. Many are fresh from combat; hence, they are tense and wary, and the slightest wrong move can set them off. If you are with a driver, he is likely to know if this roadblock is not a usual checkpoint. Defer to his instructions, have your ID at hand, and coach everyone in the vehicle to stay calm and not engage in idle questions, chat, or otherwise. Stay calm and collected; keep your tone deferential and polite, and you will get through without difficulty. In other words, stay boring!

If you are driving the vehicle, follow the same basic principles previously outlined for military checkpoints, with some exceptions:

- *Flying checkpoints:* The roadblock may be to prevent you from entering an active area of combat operations. These kinds of roadblocks are set up by active combatants to divert civilian traffic or to catch enemy combatants who are trying either to outflank them or to escape the battlefield. If this is the case, pay very close attention to any hand signals or otherwise from the individuals stationed at the checkpoint. Do not sit observing them, with your lights on and engine running. This is suspicious behavior and will very soon earn some automatic rifle fire across the top of your hood or directly into your windshield. If they are waving you off, stop, dim your lights, and put your vehicle in reverse and back slowly away from the blockade. Once at a safe distance, turn and go back in the opposite direction.
- *Nighttime:* If the roadblock is at night—particularly late at night—this is a very dangerous situation. In many third-world countries, particularly in Africa, the troops or the insurgents stationed at the blockade are very young and untrained, hopped up on drugs or alcohol, or both. Be prepared to give them what they want—usually it is money or alcohol. Once you have parted with some cash, cigarettes, or that bottle of Scotch from Duty Free (yes, you should get a couple for just these sorts of situations), carefully make your way forward and get as much distance as possible between yourself and the roadblock.

Criminal Roadblocks

There are parts of the world where insecurity within the country is due more to ongoing, low-intensity insurgencies or transcriminal organization influence, such as drug cartel activities in Mexico or Colombia.

In provincial areas where there is an ongoing conflict between rival drug cartels, random roadblocks on rural roads at night are one form of criminal roadblock. There are two general types of criminal roadblocks, and it is important to understand the distinction because this dictates how you respond to the roadblock.

The first kind is thrown up by criminal gangs blocking a police or a military response to a drug shipment or ongoing armed confrontation between rival gangs. It is essentially preventative in nature. These hastily assembled blockades of vehicles or buses (they often set them on fire) are meant to disrupt traffic flow and confuse the response of local law enforcement. These are called *narcobloqueos* in Mexico, and your vehicle may or may not be hijacked in this kind of narcobloqueo, but in this instance, it will be used as part of the blockade or as a getaway vehicle. If you are lucky, they will take the vehicle and leave you on the side of the street.

The second kind of criminal roadblock is exploitative in nature. Criminals will utilize these quickly assembled roadblocks to stop you, rob you of cash or other items, take your vehicle if it fits with what they need or want (most popular are extended cab pickup trucks, SUVs, or luxury cars), and—if it looks like you come from a relatively wealthy family or are affiliated with a large multinational company—kidnap you for ransom.

This kind of roadblock and activity is particularly common in Mexico and can be found on rural back roads in areas that are controlled by cartels. These back roads often lead to ranches owned by wealthy businesspersons in the state (this is currently the case in northern Veracruz). The criminals have good information networks, which are used to develop information about individuals and companies with money. They know that on holidays or weekends, these ranches are used to host large social events, between other wealthy individuals coming in from outside of the province, surrounding towns, or nearby companies. For this reason, these thoroughfares are targets. If your company's plant, headquarters, or area of operations happens to be along the same road, you will be targeted as well. Here are some guidelines for dealing with fake roadblocks:

- Before venturing out on the road, talk to locals who live in the area. They will know where the fake roadblocks are most prevalent, so you can avoid them in the first place.
- If you are on the road and come across a checkpoint, there are some telltale signs that indicate that it is fake. As mentioned earlier, use your observation skills, and look for the absence of normal and the presence of the abnormal:
    - Some fake checkpoints can be more elaborate than others. On the lowest end of the scale, the gunmen at the checkpoint

would not even try to disguise their intentions or appearance. On the other hand, the police or military vehicles might appear real, and the uniforms could be equally convincing. Look at their weapons. They can be different from the standard issue (AK-47s, for example, are not standard-issue weaponry for the police).

- Fake roadblocks do not last long and spring up where they are not expected. The purpose of these is to ensnare and exploit unsuspecting targets. For this reason, they will be set up on a bend in the road or at a bridge.

- They may wave through the old farmer, with a rusty, wheezing 1985 Ford filled with manure or a battered Toyota or Hyundai sedan. If you have local tags, you will be more likely to blend in. But if you are driving a late-model truck or SUV or even a sedan in good shape with out-of-province tags, you are likely to get targeted. Expect it.

- If you have the option to discreetly withdraw (i.e., other vehicles are in front of you and currently going through the shakedown), you can do so and return to a city or town. Try to get to a police station, a military checkpoint, or some area where you can be protected. More often than not, you will be unable to back away from the blockade, so there is no choice but to go through it. There are several things that can be done to raise your chances of survival. Again, having some idea of how these blockades work is important, because you do not want to panic. Keep your cool.

- You should have with you a throw-down wallet stuffed with low-denomination cash and other pocket litter (see previous chapter). This is a very useful option to have, so that you can part with it easily and quickly—and hopefully buy time to move on away from the blockade. Your jewelry in areas such as this, if you wear any, should be cheap and expendable. The same goes for watches and cameras. All these items are expendable, and there should be no hesitation about giving them up. If you have taken photographs that you consider valuable, then plan in advance to have two secure digital high-capacity (SDHC) digital cards—one for the photos you have taken and one for security purposes in case that the camera is stolen. Switch out the cards, before going in transit mode between locations in country. You can always reinsert an SDHC card with valuable photos into another camera.

- They will want your ID, and they want it fast! Have it ready; ultimately, they do not care about it. If the guards are not immediately confrontational, then it is a negotiation.

- In Mexico, if you are driving an extended cab or a late-model pickup truck, expect to have your keys and the truck taken from you. Just expect it: you are asking for trouble, being out after dark in these kinds of areas, with this kind of transportation. The same goes for late-model SUVs. You have a better chance to survive if your mode of transportation is an older sedan, that is, a bit dirty and has a few rust patches on it. A couple of dents help as well. It lowers your profile significantly and makes you less of a target.

SELECTED THREAT ACTOR PROFILES: ROADBLOCKS AND MILITARY, INSURGENTS, AND POLICE

Military Roadblocks

There are military roadblocks, and then, there are "military" roadblocks and police roadblocks. In Uganda, in the 1980s, during the civil war and afterward, it became routine to encounter the many different variations of these kinds of checkpoints over a course of years. Roadblocks can get tiresome when living for a protracted period in a combat zone. This attitude itself can be dangerous, because sooner or later, they become a routine part of life, and it becomes tempting to let your guard down. The type and the quality of guards at these checkpoints vary depending on whether they are police manning long-established checkpoints, garrison military, operational government, or insurgent forces under pressure to block entry or exit into fluid areas of conflict during battle or a mix of both. In all respects, dealing with these kinds of potential threat actors requires caution—particularly after dark.

In a third-world country that is in conflict, military roadblocks can be tricky to navigate. It is important to be able to recognize the type of roadblock, the demeanor, and the appearance of the soldiers stationed at the roadblock and respond accordingly. As with any conflict, there are long periods or lulls in fighting. During this time, military units are stationed at established, semipermanent roadblocks that are usually put up at chokepoints in and out of the major cities; around the airport; or other transportation hubs, the parliament, and houses of the government/regime. These can be interchangeably or sometimes even jointly operated with the police. During high traffic periods (daytime), checks are cursory, if at all. Nighttime checks are a little more intrusive, but as long as your documents are ready, there is a very little chance of a problem. In fact, if you are a long-time resident, it is wise to go out of your way to be affable and polite to the soldiers/police staffing this checkpoint—they will recognize you, remember it, and appreciate it. As an example, while in Uganda, during the civil war, there were at least two semipermanent roadblocks manned by government troops on a route that I frequently traveled. For the first few times that I passed through the roadblock, they approached me with customary suspicion, rifles leveled at the car (and me). I decided to purchase an extra carton of Marlboro cigarettes from the commissary at work. I later passed along the cigarettes to the soldiers stationed at the roadblock, and they quickly warmed up to me. I never had a problem after that and, in fact, always received smiles as their Kalishnikovs were shouldered as they approached to greet me and solicit more cigarettes. In times of heightened tension, you increase the likelihood that they will remember you and wave you through so that they can concentrate on individuals and vehicles with whom they are unfamiliar. An important point to remember is that if you have other individuals in your vehicle, advise them in advance to keep quiet and speak only when questioned. If it is a quiet night, they really prefer to go back to their post and smoke a cigarette and drink their beer. Keep it uncomplicated. Asking for directions, particularly if it comes from a stranger in your car, can be a trigger. You had better know where you are and where you are going if you are out driving in this kind of environment. Otherwise, take a taxi.

Insurgent Roadblocks

Roadblocks manned by insurgent fighters can be dangerous and unpredictable—they are usually related to ongoing operations. They can also be in areas of the city recently overrun. In this case, they will take over the established roadblocks. Do not expect a police presence. Most of the time, the troops are "green," recently arrived from battle in the field and on a hair trigger for anything out of the ordinary. In Kampala, these soldiers were often boys as young as 11 or 12 (called *Kadogos*). Some had old Kalishnikovs or Soviet-era Mohsin–Nagant rifles that were bigger than they were. Their approach to each vehicle was with the weapon extended out in front of them, their fingers on the trigger. It can be unnerving. As noted before, this is *not* the time for inane questions, picture taking, or chatter from any passengers in your car. Documents had better be ready. The guards can be aggressive, and tension can escalate like chain lightning at roadblocks such as this if they sense something out of the ordinary. It is worth knowing that at these kinds of roadblocks, there is typically a machine gun emplacement set back from the checkpoint itself or—as is very popular in Africa—a soldier with an RPG at the ready.

ENDNOTES

1. This is an important point. If you are a team leader, group care is critical. I have sent people out of the country in situations like this, for this very reason.
2. The 12.7 mm Dashka is a Russian-made heavy machine gun that is extremely common in third-world countries. It is a durable, effective weapon that more often than not is mounted on a tripod in the bed of a Toyota Hilux pickup truck (these trucks are known as the *war chariot* of third-world armies). The author has had the misfortune of being on the receiving end of directed Dashka fire over an extended period. When in use, the weapon has an ear-splitting, very distinctive report and is highly effective.

CHAPTER 4

Kidnapping

INTRODUCTION

One of the worst fears for anyone working and traveling abroad is being kidnapped. On the face of it, being abducted represents the worst-case outcome. It is not—it can get much worse. Kidnapping for ransom is a violent crime. Violent crimes are negative events that usually happen suddenly, generating fear and helplessness, threatening people's physical or psychological well-being, and leaving victims in an emotional state which they are unable to deal with using their normal psychological resources. Any kind of trauma—and a violent crime is a type of trauma for the victim—involves a collapse of the person's feelings of security, also indirectly affecting their immediate family circle (Koleoso and Akhigbe, 2013). For kidnapping victims, freedom almost always brings a sense of elation and relief. However, adjusting back to the real world after being held hostage can be just as difficult as abruptly leaving it. Upon release, many hostage survivors are faced with transitioning from conditions of isolation and helplessness to sensory overload and freedom. This transition often results in significant adjustment difficulties. Released hostages need time to recover from the physical, mental, and emotional difficulties they faced. However, it is important to keep in mind that human beings are highly resilient and can persevere despite tragedy. Research shows that positive growth and resilience can occur following trauma. Hostage survivors may feel lost or have difficulty managing intense reactions and may need help adjusting to their old life following release (Hanbury and Romano, 2013). Kidnapping statistics are difficult to obtain—primarily because incident classifications vary from country to country and many kidnappings are not reported for fear of retaliation by the kidnappers or fear of police corruption and ineptitude (red24.com, 2012).

Understanding the dynamics and the realities involved with various types of abduction is important to developing a reliable personal security plan. Also, when kidnap or hostage situations are involved, understanding what needs to be done to create mental resilience is crucial.

The difference between the mind-set of a victim and the mind-set of a fighter can spell the difference between life and death. As with all elements of good personal security, preparing in advance with the potential eventuality of abduction in mind is often the best remedy to being vulnerable to kidnapping in the first place. Distinctions are very important when it comes to kidnap/abduction operations. I have heard that "it does not matter whether the bad guy is a terrorist or a criminal, an abduction is an abduction." Broad, very simplistic assumptions like this might be acceptable for statisticians, but for security practitioners, it is unwise to generalize about events while excluding specifics about the threat actors and their motives. This is true for several reasons. First, when you are developing a security plan for yourself or others (executives, employees, or contractors), it is important to know the kinds of actors who conduct kidnap/abduction operations in the area to which you or those for whom you are responsible are traveling. While your value as a commodity with a price on your head is the common denominator among kidnappers, your commodity status is where the similarities begin and end. This is true whether the threat actors are state-sponsored terrorists such as Hezbollah; transnational Islamic insurgents such as al Qaeda, Al Shabab, or the Islamic State in Iraq and Syria (ISIS); a transnational criminal organization such as the Zeta Drug Cartel in Mexico; or a common criminal gang in Venezuela. Ultimately, the kidnap operation is a business transaction. The transaction may require ready cash, potential ransom cash (from a company or family), information, prisoner exchange, or—in the case of some Islamic extremist groups—quite literally your head and the propaganda value of posting the video of you losing it on the Internet. If you know who the specific actors are and what motives drive their kidnap operations, you will be able to make tactical adjustments to your own personal security profile that make you less of a target. Second, if you are abducted, knowing more about who took you hostage and what motivates them can go a long way toward informing your mental expectations about what comes next. Fear of the unknown and being confused about how to mentally brace yourself for what your captors may have in mind can be incapacitating and lead to panic. This is a state of mind you do not want to be in, when in this situation. An important part of incorporating the eventuality of kidnapping into your security plan is the development of credible scenarios and outcomes. In order to do this, you need to research the motives, the tactics, and the geographic operating areas of threat actors with a history of kidnapping, operating in the area where you are planning travel. This is a key part of travel preparation. As noted earlier, it is a mistake to assume that every abduction, once it is set in motion, unfolds in the same way. They are not. Every kidnapper's scenario has variations that are dependent on timing, resources, police response, and victim cooperation, among other variables. Threat actors—be they criminal or political—possess different motives. While the tactics used in the actual abduction operation have broad similarities the world over, there are distinctions in how you are treated as a hostage, what to expect, and what negotiating strategies and communications are used in the transaction.

CLASSIFYING TYPES OF KIDNAP/ ABDUCTION OPERATIONS

Part of effective preparation is good analysis. When researching the threat of kidnap/abduction, using the motivation of kidnapping provides a useful way of classifying and analyzing kidnapping. Mark Turner, in his paper "Kidnapping and Politics," published in 1998 by the *International Journal of the Sociology of Law*, developed a typology of four types of kidnapping based on the motive for abduction (Turner, 1998). Turner's kidnapping classification uses two contrasting dimensions of political and material characteristics. For the political dimension, there are nonpolitical motives on one end and highly political motives on the other end of the spectrum. For the material dimension, there is nonmaterial gain on one end and maximum material gain on the other end of the spectrum. From this, four types emerge.

Type 1: Money but No Politics

Type 1 kidnapping is the classic kidnap for ransom (KFR) type of abduction. Kidnappers seek to extract the maximum economic return for the sale or the release of their victims. The kidnappers have no political agenda to pursue. KFR operations in Mexico have steadily risen in direct proportion to the steady growth and proliferation of drug trafficking cartels and associated criminal street gangs. Kidnap operations in Mexico are on the rise and are increasingly targeting middle- and working-class Mexicans. Variants of KFR in Mexico are express kidnap, where a gang temporarily abducts a hapless businessperson or tourist and proceeds to drive them around town, going from ATM to ATM, to empty their bank account of cash and make charges on their credit cards. Once the gang is done with their victim, they dump them on the street a bit worse for wear but usually alive. Also on the increase are virtual kidnap scenarios. The target victim is tricked into believing a family member or a loved one is being held through various deceptions and threat of violence or blackmail. This is done to extract a quick ransom before the scheme falls apart. The Philippines is home to a diverse kidnap sector, from local criminal gangs to transnational militant groups, varying in size and operational capability and differing significantly in their ideology and motives. In addition to traditional kidnap cases, the country has also witnessed a notable rise in virtual kidnappings in 2015. Kidnappings vary in modus operandi from opportunistic to well-planned and sophisticated operations, often involving victim surveillance and information-gathering phases before the abduction occurs. In Manila, criminal syndicates are known to hire part-time target spotters, such as staff at the Manila International Airport to supply intelligence of potentially wealthy tourists (particularly Chinese nationals and first-class travelers) and businesspersons. Virtual kidnapping is experiencing a significant growth across the Asia Pacific, including China, India, Taiwan, and Singapore (NYA International, 2015).[1] Also falling into this category of kidnapping are cases where the victims are abducted and then sold for use as labor for sexual exploitation.

Type 2: No Money, No Politics

Type 2 kidnapping has two variants. The first is the increasingly common parental abduction of children. The second variant of this type of kidnapping involves the abduction of persons, normally children, by strangers. In the first instance, situations of international parental kidnapping are reported in the United States all too frequently. It is common for the removal of a child to occur during a heated or emotional marital dispute, in the early stages of separation or divorce, or in the waiting period for a court custody order or an agreement. International parental kidnappings of US children have been reported in countries all over the world, including Australia, Brazil, Canada, Colombia, Germany, India, Japan, Mexico, the Philippines, and the United Kingdom.

Child victims of international parental kidnapping are often taken from a familiar environment and suddenly isolated from their community, family, and friends. They may miss months or even years of schooling. The child may be moved to multiple locations in order to stay hidden or out of reach of the parent remaining in the United States. In some cases, the child's name, birth date, and physical appearance are altered or concealed to hide identity (US Department of Justice, 2015).

In the second instance, stranger abductions are given a great deal of publicity, such as the case of three young women, Michelle Knight, Amanda Berry, and Georgina "Gina" DeJesus, who were kidnapped by Ariel Castro in Cleveland, Ohio, between 2002 and 2004. These girls were subsequently imprisoned in Castro's home until May 6, 2013, when Berry escaped with her six-year-old daughter and contacted the police. These are known as stereotypical kidnappings by strangers, and as fearsome as they may seem, because of their randomness and involvement of rape or homicide, children taken by strangers or slight acquaintances represent one-hundredth of 1% of all missing children. The last comprehensive study estimated that the number was 115 in a year (Finkelhor, 2013).

Type 3: Money and Politics

Type 3 kidnapping involves political motivation and demand for ransoms or other material items such as weapons. Such kidnappings are undertaken by revolutionary, separatist, or terrorist groups who wish to gain publicity for their cause as well as funds for their political activities and armed struggles. Between 1991 and 1998, the Revolutionary Armed Forces of Colombia—People's Army (Fuerzas Armadas Revolutionarias de Colombia—Ejército del Pueblo, or FARC-EP) collected an estimated US$1.2 billion from ransom payments. The FARC-EP called these kidnappings *retentions* to raise war taxes for their revolutionary causes.

Prior to 2006, when the Algerian Salafist Group for Preaching and Combat essentially became Al-Qaeda in the Islamic Maghreb (AQIM), kidnappings and attempted kidnappings occurred roughly once a year. But after 2006, the operational tempo of kidnappings in the Sahel quickened, with about three to five operations conducted per year. According to US Treasury Department Undersecretary for Terrorism and Financial Intelligence David Cohen, al Qaeda earned approximately US$120 million in ransoms from 2004 to 2012. Cohen added AQIM had become the most proficient kidnapping unit of all of al Qaeda's franchise groups. Typically, the group prefers to kidnap more than one person. Having multiple hostages allows the captors to kill one or more of them to ratchet up pressure for the ransom of the others. Guarding multiple hostages requires more resources, but Belmokhtar has plenty of human resources, and the additional ransom makes guarding them worth the extra effort. Holding multiple hostages also enables the kidnappers to make political statements—often connected to outrageous demands. In the Tigantourine attack, much attention was paid to the militants' demands to the US government to release Sheikh Omar Abdel Rahman, also known as "the Blind Sheikh," and Aafia Siddiqui, a Pakistani neuroscientist convicted of terrorism charges. But again, such demands are not unprecedented (Stewart, 2013).

Type 4: Politics, No Money

Kidnappers who engage in this type of abduction have only political motivations and are not seeking material gains. The kidnapping of Beirut, Lebanon, Central Intelligence Agency (CIA) Station Chief William F. Buckley is a classic example of a type 4 kidnap scenario, politics, no money went tragically wrong. On March 16, 1984, Buckley was abducted off the street outside of his apartment in Beirut as he was going to work. The group that kidnapped Buckley, Islamic Jihad, was an early precursor to Hezbollah. Buckley was interrogated and tortured by his captors for information about agents and other intelligence assets in Lebanon. He died while in captivity, sometime in 1985.

In the 1970s and the 1980s, the Italian terrorist group Brigate Rosse (Red Brigades) used kidnapping as an element of their strategy to destabilize and disarticulate the institutions of the bourgeois state. Fifteen of their known kidnappings were for demonstration/political purposes and only two for self-financing. The kidnapping of Italian prime minister Aldo Moro on March 16, 1978, by the Red Brigades ended tragically later that same year in his execution by the group. In Yemen, there was an upsurge in kidnappings involving foreigners during the late 1990s and up through 2011. The underlying reason for many of these kidnappings were tribal grievances about central government policies and what they perceived to be uneven distribution of national resources. There is a distinction between terrorist hostage takers in Syria or Lebanon and criminal KFR crews operating in Mexico or Colombia. While the former is interested in publicizing the abduction and the hostages, for the sake of publicity, the latter group is more interested in anonymity and strictly monetary gain. It is important to understand the difference, because—as the abductee—knowing in advance that, barring rescue by US Special Forces, you are likely to be executed very publicly and painfully or are alternatively a pawn in ransom negotiations between a third party and your kidnappers is crucial to informing what you need to do.

TIP OF THE ICEBERG: KEEPING KIDNAP THREAT TRENDS IN PERSPECTIVE

Accurate statistics worldwide on KFR are difficult to obtain for several reasons. So many cases go unreported or are inherently underreported. The first thing that kidnappers tell the victim's family or company is something like this: "Do not inform the police, or your employee will be killed." If the matter is resolved quietly, without involving the authorities, then it is as if it never happened. Secondly, incident classifications of kidnaps vary from country to country. Key themes driving KFR in 2015, for instance, recur in hot spot countries: militancy and conflict, failed or weak state security, corruption and criminality, and stretched national budgets associated with low oil prices. The year 2015 was also a story of continuation. Conflicts arising from the Arab Spring sustained kidnapping threats in Syria, Iraq, Libya, and Yemen. Kidnappings were characterized by their sectarian and political aspects as much as financial gain. Kidnappings in South Sudan and the Central African Republic (CAR) became severe following intensified civil conflicts. Kenya, Mozambique, Mauritania, and Uganda also worsened, contributing to Africa being in second place on the list of kidnap incidents by region. India and Bangladesh changed to high ratings, with localized criminals and Maoist rebels targeting domestic nationals. Islamist militants across the Middle East, Asia, and Africa continued to employ kidnapping as a revenue-generating activity as well as a weapon of war. In Latin America, although Venezuela's rating improved and Mexico reported decreases in kidnapping, both remain affected by corruption and underreporting of crime (NYA International, 2016a).

Top Severe Kidnap Threat Countries for 2016

1. *Libya:* A divided polity and the absence of any law enforcement underlined Libya's status countrywide as a severe kidnap threat environment for both domestic and foreign nationals. Islamic State (IS) militants gained a foothold in and around the central city of Sirte, perpetrating a number of mass abductions and subsequent executions throughout 2015. The kidnap threat will remain severe for the duration of 2017 owing to ongoing political divisions and current low price of oil, which will hamper any political and economic recoveries in the country necessary to establish even a basic level of security. IS will also seek to further enhance their presence in the country and attract recruits by perpetrating high-profile attacks and kidnappings (NYA International, 2016b).

2. *Afghanistan:* The risk of being kidnapped throughout Afghanistan remains a very high and constant threat. Over 100 Westerners have been kidnapped in Afghanistan in the last 10 years; a number of them have been British nationals in Badakhshan, Bamyan, Kunar, Kunduz, and near the border with Pakistan, but the kidnap threat is not isolated to these areas. The motivation and desire to undertake kidnapping in Afghanistan is likely to continue (UK Foreign and Commonwealth Office, 2016).

3. *Democratic Republic of Congo:* There is a high risk of kidnapping for ransom by armed groups, bandits, and elements of the Congolese armed forces in eastern Democratic Republic of Congo. KFR is particularly severe in areas north and west of Goma, North Kivu Province (near the western Ugandan border).

4. *Iraq:* With security forces overstretched in fighting ISIS in western and northern Iraq, kidnappings across the Shia majority south markedly increased in 2015. Powerful Shia militias were responsible for the kidnapping of dozens of foreign nationals, including US, Turkish, Qatari, Kuwaiti, and Saudi citizens. ISIS militants carried out hundreds of kidnappings targeting domestic nationals in areas under its control, with incidents primarily motivated by financial gain and ideology (NYA International, 2016c).

5. *Somalia:* The security situation in Somalia remains unstable and dangerous. Terrorist operatives and armed groups in Somalia continue to attack Somali authorities, the African Union Mission in Somalia, and other nonmilitary targets. The threat of kidnapping is considered severe (US Department of State, 2015a).

6. *South Sudan:* The lack of security force capability coupled with widespread lawlessness in Darfur and Kordofan enabled the abduction of numerous civilians and nongovernmental organization (NGO) personnel by various groups, including progovernment Janjaweed militia and the Sudan People's Liberation Movement–North. The kidnap threat in Sudan remains high in 2017 given the high degree of political instability, proliferating civil conflicts, and significant criminal activity (NYA International, 2016d).

7. *Yemen:* The severe threat from kidnap in Yemen was sustained by the complete breakdown in order amid the Saudi-led military campaign against the Houthi rebels. Although the majority of incidents in 2015 were politically motivated detentions carried out by the Houthi rebels, exposed foreign nationals continued to be targeted by a myriad of perpetrators. The kidnap threat in Yemen remains unchanged in 2016, driven by conflict and likely proliferating in areas most affected by violence. Various factors, including the Houthi rebels, the militant group al Qaeda in the Arabian Peninsula, and tribal militias, will operate largely unrestrained due to the continued weakness of the Aden-based government led by President Hadi. Foreign nationals will remain attractive targets, as their perceived high value can be leveraged to meet both political and financial demands in a complex conflict-affected environment (NYA International, 2016c).

8. *Central African Republic:* More than 200 people have been kidnapped in eastern CAR this year, already nearly double last year's level, in a wave of abductions blamed on the Lord's Resistance Army. The threat of kidnap in CAR is considered severe. The LRA has targeted the former French colony, which

is reeling from years of interreligious bloodshed. A history of military coups and rebellion in the CAR has caused a sustained economic crisis in the country and negatively impacted the national institutions' capacity to provide services to and protection for the population. The Department of State warns US citizens against all travel to CAR due to an unpredictable security situation subject to rapid deterioration, activities of armed groups, and violent crime. Indiscriminate violence and looting have occurred in CAR since the overthrowing of its government in March 2013. Sectarian violence is frequent and has resulted in thousands of deaths (US Department of States, 2015b; Reuters, 2016).

9. *Syria:* Amid the ongoing and increasingly complex civil war, the majority of recorded incidents in 2015 were sectarian in nature; however, it is likely that many involved financial demands. NYA International data show that 588 people were kidnapped in 2015, 84 of whom were released. ISIS militants were responsible for mass kidnappings targeting Assyrian Christians in northern Syria. The al Qaeda–affiliated militant group Nusra Front was responsible for the kidnapping of Kurdish civilians in the north east of Syria. ISIS and Nusra Front militants will remain active in carrying out kidnappings as the conflict continues with varying intensity. Increased military involvement by the West in the last quarter of 2015 has negatively impacted the oil-based revenue streams of militant groups. Therefore, it is conceivable that incidents of KFR in particular will increase as militant groups pursue alternative sources of revenue. The number of sectarian kidnappings targeting minority groups will likely remain high, particularly in the northeast (NYA International, 2016e).

10. *Nigeria:* The severe threat of kidnapping in Nigeria continued to be driven by Boko Haram's mass kidnappings in 2015. Abductions continued to be predominantly politically motivated, targeting high-profile domestic nationals. The 2015 elections were notably associated with a spike in abductions of symbolic individuals. There has, however, been an increase in wealthy, prominent victims, indicating a shift toward criminally motivated kidnappings. The line between piracy and kidnapping became increasingly blurred as wealthy locals were targeted across over 21 incidents. The threat of kidnapping remains severe in 2016. Ongoing Boko Haram operations in the region will maintain the current kidnap threat to foreign nationals in the northeast. Persistently high unemployment rates and poor prosecution rates will likely motivate more to resort to KFR as a source of funding. An increase in maritime-based militancy

in the south could result in an increase in KFR cases involving foreign nationals abducted onshore and offshore (NYA International, 2016d).

11. *Pakistan:* In 2015, Pakistan ranked among the top five global kidnapping hot spots. Political and criminal motives have driven most incidents nationwide, with terrorist groups continually responsible for abductions, particularly in Khyber Pakhtunkhwa and Balochistan. Local nationals were largely targeted compared to foreign nationals nationwide, and perceived high-net-worth individuals and their dependents were also especially targeted. Kidnapping is likely to remain a severe threat throughout Pakistan in 2016, with criminals and gangs largely responsible for incidents in major urban areas such as Karachi. Militant groups located in tribal areas will continue to pose a high kidnap threat to foreign nationals, despite reported security operations successfully undermining some terrorist operations in 2015 (NYA International, 2016f).

Regional Summary

Latin America

In 2015, the Americas saw a reduced proportion of global kidnapping incidents compared to previous years. Colombia's progress toward a peace agreement with the region's largest left-wing guerrilla group and security initiatives in Brazil have contributed to these improved results. However, Venezuela's rapidly deteriorating economy and Mexico's public distrust in authorities mean kidnapping remains a significant regional concern.

Mexico The number of reported kidnappings in Mexico decreased in 2015 compared to 2014. According to the secretary of the interior, Miguel Ángel Osorio Chong, the number of cases decreased by 27% and coincided with an additional decrease in disappearances. Throughout 2015, however, Mexico's authorities continued to be entangled in corruption scandals, indicating that the decreased number of reported kidnappings may be due to mistrust in policing, not fewer incidents. Kidnapping remains a significant threat in Mexico throughout 2017. Despite President Enrique Peña Nieto's short-term political victory of recapturing Joaquín "El Chapo" Guzmán on January 8, 2016, organized crime groups remain powerful and dominant perpetrators. Additionally, Mexico's high number of street gangs will continue to exploit the country's many overstretched and poorly resourced authorities, which will likely be reflected in repeated high numbers of incidents. Current reporting does not reflect the fact that the real percentage of kidnap victims

KIDNAPPING IN MEXICO

Sylvia Longmire, in her book *Cartel: The Coming Invasion of Mexico's Drug Wars*, writes that "Mexico is one of the worst countries in the world in which to get kidnapped. There are multiple criminal groups conducting kidnap operations, and many variations on the theme. Anything goes. The Mexican government's statistical information about kidnap-for-ransom (KFR) is inaccurate, and likely manipulated for perception purposes. It is estimated that 1-in-7 kidnap victims in Mexico will be killed, though realistically the exact number of incidents, types of victims, or average ransom demand is nearly impossible to accurately determine because only a fraction of incidents are reported to authorities or other organizations. This is mostly due to fear that corrupt local authorities collude with the kidnappers. Sometimes there can be a simple exchange of ransom for the victim, but in Mexico there is frequently bloodshed. While in Columbia kidnappers provide 'proof of life' by sending family members a photo of the victim holding the front page of a recently published newspaper, in Mexico the preferred method is to send the family an amputated finger" (Longmire, 2011). The drug cartels in Mexico, as well as second and third tier criminal organizations operating in the country, have expanded into the kidnapping business as a source of revenue—this is especially true as income from drug smuggling diminishes. While it is often thought that only the wealthy are targeted, this is not the case. Certainly being wealthy and ostentatious with one's wealth makes you a target in Mexico. However, kidnappers are frequently targeting midlevel executives/managers in companies, as well as migrants and independent businesspersons. One of the reasons midlevel executives are targeted is that there is a greater likelihood that the company will quickly pay the ransom, rather than bring in a high-priced negotiator, which is usually the case when a high-value target is abducted. It is estimated that at least 7 of every 10 kidnappings in Mexico never appear in the media.

Of all the security issues that plague Mexico, it is the abductions that strike fear and anger in Mexican citizens the most. Unfortunately, kidnappings in the country are on the rise. These increased by 33% in the first six months of Enrique Peña Nieto's presidency since he took office in December 2012. Between January and April 2013, 555 people were reported kidnapped compared to 417 incidents reported during the same period in 2012. On average, in 2013, at least 130 people were kidnapped each month, compared to an average of 109 the previous year. In 2012, 5.2% of the 2756 kidnappings reported resulted in the death of the victim. This is also a grim upward trend in Mexico.

this year could be much higher, as these accounts do not include express kidnappings. Express kidnapping is popular with street gangs and lower level criminals. The victim is snatched and thrown into the trunk of the car, then driven to various ATM's until their cash card is exhausted and the bank account is empty. They are then shoved out to the street. Besides not accounting for express kidnap incidents, mass kidnapping of migrants or unreported kidnappings are not included.

Colombia   The threat of kidnapping fell considerably in Colombia in 2015 following continued security improvements. According to official statistics, the number of incidents dropped by more than 30% in 2015 compared to 2014, due in part to FARC's decision to cease kidnapping. However, other left-wing guerrilla groups, such as the National Liberation Army, continue to use KFR to finance their operations.

The expected signing of a peace agreement between the government and the FARC in 2016 will likely reduce the kidnap threat in Colombia, since it will allow security forces to invest more resources into combating other left-wing guerrilla and criminal groups that use kidnapping as a source of revenue or scare tactic.

Venezuela   Further deterioration of Venezuela's economic situation increased the number of kidnapping incidents in 2015. Individuals of perceived wealth continued to be the principal target, although those of lower socioeconomic backgrounds were progressively targeted. Throughout the year, local media reported a number of incidents in which criminal gangs targeted highly protected people such as military personnel and politicians. The large urban concentrations and the border area in Colombia remained particular kidnapping hot spots in the country. The kidnapping threat in Venezuela will likely increase throughout 2016 as the economic situation continues to deteriorate. Similarly, a probable heightening of political tension throughout 2016 could also have an impact on the kidnapping threat, since it may reduce cooperation among political actors for implementing security policies.

Africa

The expansion of territory controlled by IS militants in Libya and Egypt has worsened the kidnapping threat across North Africa. The fragile security situation in the Sahel was also evident, with foreign aid workers targeted in Sudan and South Sudan and coordinated abductions by Islamist militants targeting foreign nationals in Mali and Burkina Faso. In Nigeria, the kidnap threat expanded at varying levels nationwide, with domestic nationals now increasingly targeted.

Kenya Both foreign and domestic nationals continued to face a high kidnap threat in border areas close to Somalia. Although reports are rare due to fear of reprisals, Al Shabab militants and criminal groups regularly conduct kidnappings near porous border areas. The kidnapping of a teacher on October 12, 2015, from a refugee camp highlights the high threat to NGO workers. Kenya's growing middle class were most at risk, as demonstrated by the August kidnapping of a footballer in Nairobi. The kidnap threat in 2016 remains high as the security situation is unlikely to improve due to high crime levels, presence of domestic Islamist extremist groups, and ongoing conflict in neighboring Somalia. Foreign nationals are likely to be increasingly targeted in 2016.

Asia

Kidnapping threats in Asia have varied and evolved between countries, with Afghanistan and Pakistan retaining the most significant threat from criminal and terrorist elements. In the Philippines, the Abu Sayyaf Group (ASG) has heightened the kidnap threat to foreign nationals in the south, and a potential rise in express and virtual kidnappings in China may stem from the growing use of social media.

India Kidnappings in India continued to illustrate the country's dominance as a global kidnap hot spot in 2015. Prominent threats originate from criminals planning intelligence-led abductions as they have demonstrated familiarity with their victims' habits and wealth for targeting. Indian nationals were mainly targeted for financial as well as political demands, most commonly observed in kidnappings by Maoist rebel groups in the east and northeast regions. India is likely to remain a top global kidnap hot spot in 2016, particularly given the continued high levels of poverty and corruption in law enforcement facilitating such crime. Express kidnappings were sporadically reported in 2015 and may similarly shape kidnap threats in major cities in 2017. While foreign nationals are generally exposed to low kidnapping threats, risks may increase in rural areas where militant groups are active.

Philippines As Southeast Asia's top kidnapping hot spot, the Philippines' kidnap threat extends nationwide with higher threats apparent in Manila as well as in Mindanao and Sulu. Insurgent and extremist groups such as the ASG and the New People's Army use kidnappings to achieve

THE EVOLUTION OF VIRTUAL KIDNAPPING

Years ago, criminals carrying out virtual kidnappings used simple tactics. They might wait at a Mexican bus station and spot an American's luggage name tag that included a home address and a phone number. If the tourist got on a nonstop bus for a five-hour trip during which there was no cell phone service, the criminals knew they had that window of time to execute the scheme by contacting family members in the United States, convincing them that their loved ones were in danger and demanding a ransom be paid by wire transfer.

Today, the schemes can involve accomplices in tourist hotels, telemarketing-style cold calls, money handlers, and phone techniques such as three-way calling that lead families and law enforcement to believe that victims have been physically detained.

Recently, virtual kidnappers cold-called hundreds of numbers in Texas—likely using directories and other phone lists—to target American physicians, banking that at least some of those contacted with family or connections in Mexico would fall for the scam.

"The FBI responds to all reports of U.S. citizens being taken hostage, whether virtual or traditional," said Special Agent Brian Wittenberg. "The virtual kidnappers are savvy and prepared, and one of our goals is to make sure the public is prepared as well." He added, "The criminals' tactics are constantly evolving, but the hallmark of any virtual kidnapping is always the same—preying on people's worst fears" (Federal Bureau of Investigation, 2014).

political motives or fund terrorist operations. While the vast majority of kidnap victims are domestic nationals, the ASG particularly targets foreign nationals for substantial ransom payments. The ASG will remain the main KFR threat in the Philippines. The abduction of three foreign nationals and a local national from a resort on Samal Island underlines the ASG's expansion of operations to the eastern part of Mindanao. The incident has also exposed the absence of security provisions and vulnerability of foreign visitors at popular island resorts around Mindanao (NYA International, 2016g).

International Patterns and Trends in Kidnapping

There are commonalities that can be observed when an experienced kidnap crew plans and executes an abduction. Every year, there are hundreds of thousands of abductions of all types. No one knows the precise figures; there are too many variables and much underreporting. Many are between two sets of criminals, so-called bad-on-bad kidnaps. Experts working in the field put the number of KFRs or political gain at around 40,000 a year. One of the strongest indicators of a high probability of kidnapping in a region or a country is a history of successful incidents in the recent past. This means the business model works. Kidnapping is a crime that evolves. With that said, there are some commonalities that can be observed internationally that fuel kidnapping.

The Gap between Rich and Poor and Failed States

The disparity between rich and poor is growing, and thanks to the Internet and the global media, everyone can see how the rich are living. It fuels resentment and desire for a bigger share. Also, countries that have no government or a government that is unable to exert its authority are a breeding ground for kidnapping and other crimes. Economic deprivation and high unemployment among people, economic deprivation, and a sense of desperation have planted the seeds of kidnapping as a way of getting money in poor communities. It can then become a way of life, even when legal options become available.

The Collapse of Communism and the End of the Cold War

The tension between the United States and the Communist bloc kept regional and ethnic power struggles in check. With that gone, some countries have lost their central authority, with various groups jockeying for power. There are many more states with weak or corrupt police.

A Weak Ethical Environment

With a tendency toward corruption, kidnapping is likely to be one crime among others in regions or countries where there is little respect for law, and officials and police turn a blind eye to offenses, or worse, play an active role.

Arab "Spring," Arab "Winter," and Islamic Extremism

The ending of authoritarian governments that ripped throughout the Middle East in 2011 and 2012 was initially heralded as victory for progress. As we have seen, however, the dismantling of the security apparatus in these countries along with very nascent opposition groups led to power struggles that were exploited by organizations with infrastructure and resources, such as the Muslim Brotherhood in Egypt, or the Iranian-supported Houthi's in Yemen, or Shi'a separatist groups in Bahrain. Internal armed conflicts that followed have broken down social order and, in the case of Syria, led to all-out civil war. The Arab spring has led to a dark Arab winter.

Islamists and other political extremists use kidnapping as a political weapon and as a means of financing their activities. Kidnapping blackspots (blackspots are considered areas where the crime of kidnapping is concentrated especially high)—especially express kidnapping—take place all over the world. In some countries or regions, it is endemic. In others, it occurs in waves. The proportion of KFRs in Latin America—mainly Colombia and Mexico—remains very high, slightly more than half the world's total, but the number of kidnappings is growing in the Caribbean and Africa, especially Nigeria. Countries where there is political instability, for example, those left unsettled after the Arab spring such as Egypt and Libya, bear watching (Dobbs, 2012).

A Closer Look: Kidnap for Ransom

Kidnapping is a broad topic. To understand it in more detail, I will focus primarily on kidnappings that are financially motivated and those that are politically motivated. Financially motivated kidnappings can be conducted by a variety of criminal elements. At the highest level are trained professional kidnapping gangs that specialize in abducting high-net worth individuals and who will frequently demand ransoms in the millions of dollars. Such groups often employ teams of specialists who carry out a variety of specific tasks such as collecting intelligence, conducting surveillance, snatching the target, negotiating with the victim's family, and establishing and guarding the safe houses.

At the other end of the spectrum are gangs that randomly kidnap targets of opportunity. These gangs are generally far less skilled than the professional gangs and will often hold a victim for only a short time, as in an express kidnapping (Stewart, 2013b).

Whether terrorists or organized criminal kidnap crews, most adopt a cell form of organization. The cell is the smallest element at the tactical level of an organization. Individuals, usually 3–10, comprise a cell and act as the basic tactical component for the organization. One of the primary reasons for a cellular configuration is security. The compromise or the loss of one cell should not compromise the identity, the location, or the actions of other cells. Compartmenting functions within organizational structure makes it difficult for an adversary to penetrate the entire organization. Personnel within one cell are often unaware of the existence of other cells and cannot provide sensitive information to infiltrators or captors. Terrorist or criminal kidnapping groups may organize cells based on family or employment relationships, on a geographic basis, or by specific functions such as direct action or intelligence. The terrorist group may also form multifunctional cells. Cell members remain in close contact with each other in order to provide emotional support and enhance security procedures. The cell leader is normally the only person who communicates and coordinates with higher levels and other cells. A terrorist group may form only one cell or may form several cells that operate in local or regional areas, across national borders, or among several countries in transnational operations (US Army TRADOC, 2008a).

Organized KFR crews, while of course not all the same, are generally divided into an operational cell and a support cell. This organizational structure basically holds true for terrorist organizations such as ISIS, FARC in Colombia, ASG in the Philippines, or Zeta-affiliated transnational criminal gangs operating in Mexico. The operational (kidnap) cell is responsible for the actual seizure. This cell must have the capability to overcome resistance by the target or the associated executive security protective elements and may be responsible for transportation from the kidnapping or the hostage-taking snatch site to a nearby rendezvous. While not always the case, a separate cell may have responsibility for guarding and sustaining the victim in captivity. Conditions for the victim may include isolation, interrogation, and torture (US Army TRADOC, 2008b).

The operational cells get logistical support from a support cell, which can include supplying food, vehicles, communications devices, newspapers, blankets, medicine, silenced weapons, anesthetic injections, restraining wire, electric stun devices, hand restraints, blindfolds, and vehicles. Multiple vehicles may be required to isolate the seizure site and assist with security while the operational kidnap cell exits from the immediate area. Often, the support cell is not given the details of the kidnapping operation, which effectively compartmentalizes information in the event members of the operational cell are arrested following an abduction or during the hostage release phase.

Target Selection Development Phase

Target selection begins with consideration by kidnappers of several potential individuals for abduction. The cycle that is used by kidnappers mirrors to a great degree to what is known as the *terrorist attack cycle*, which is target selection, planning, deployment, attack, escape, and exploitation. In a kidnapping, this means the group must identify a victim; plan for the abduction, captivity, and negotiation; conduct the abduction and secure the hostage; successfully leverage the life of the victim for financial or political gain; and then escape (Stewart, 2010a).

This particular phase is a generalized exercise where several potential targets can be surveyed, using open source information and casual surveillance methods. The objective of this phase is simply to narrow down a list of targets to one individual. During the target selection and initial planning stages, the group will conduct preoperational surveillance.

The purpose of this low-key surveillance is to determine the spectrum of a target's patterns of behavior such as the time the potential target(s) leaves for work, the route or the mode of transportation used, and the time they leave work and return home. Again, timing, route, and mode of transport are taken into consideration. Also, the kidnappers will take note of what type of security, if any, the target uses. This information is used to narrow the list of potential targets to *the one who presents the crew with the best opportunity for success*. This could be a combination of predictable patterns of behavior, net worth, habits of vulnerability, or other weakness that can be easily exploited. Once a target has been settled on, the focus of resources and labor shift to that specific individual.

Intelligence Gathering Operation

Once the team has focused on one target, they begin to gather as much intelligence on the potential victim as possible. This includes, but is not limited to, very detailed information developed over a period of weeks on how the target leaves his/her apartment or home and goes to their vehicle. Does the target drive, or is there a driver, or a motorcade? The travel route to and from work and home, the time of departure and arrival, the vehicles used, and the stops made are also gathered. Also, the team develops intelligence on the target's habits, marital status, and financial information. In this process, the team also gathers collateral intelligence on the target's family, friends, and work colleagues. Kidnap organizations in Mexico, for instance, will plan *months* in advance of the actual abduction, spending weeks watching their intended target to learn their daily routines, contacts, friends, routes to and from home, office, shops, and number of individuals around them.

Route Analysis, Snatch Location Selection, and Logistics

The intelligence phase of the operation is concluded once a solid profile of the target is developed. Planning for the execution phase begins. The location of the actual abduction is selected. The location of the kidnapping or the hostage seizure is selected for the optimum possibility of success. Daily personal and professional regimens may bracket the logical locations for a kidnapping. Three points of reference are the work place or office, the home or temporary residence, and the route between these normal daily sites. Some reports state that 90% of the crimes occur while the target is en route from one location to another and that 80% of the actual kidnapping occurs within 200–300 meters of the residence or the office (MacWillson, 1992). First, the target's routes are carefully analyzed with a view toward where the best snatch location should be. There are two key elements to this analysis. First, the location is selected in terms of the best exit route away from where the abduction is made. Second, the location is selected—usually—in a place where the target's vehicle or motorcade must slow down or stop. These vulnerable locations are known as *chokepoints* and, for professional security officers, are recognized as the most vulnerable locations for the principal they are protecting. A chokepoint can be either natural, such as a 90° turn requiring the vehicle to slow down, a stoplight, or a drawbridge, or human made, such as road construction, an accident, car breakdown stopping traffic, or other obstruction along the route. If the target travels by foot, then the identified chokepoint is usually an area that is isolated and allows for fewer chances of outside intervention by the police or others or multiple witnesses that can point the authorities in the right direction.

A crucial aspect of pre-event planning that is often overlooked or not given sufficient attention by amateurs is logistics. This includes seemingly mundane things, such as reliable transportation, good exit route planning and cover stories, safe holding location and backups, procurement of food and water in a nonalerting way, and methods of secure communication between the execution team and the support team, and ultimately with the outside in the negotiation phase. According to the legendary Carlos Marighella, the 1960s era communist revolutionary who is considered by some to be the father of modern terrorist tactics, "one must never neglect transportation and logistics. The importance of these is frequently underestimated. It is an error to leave this [planning] requirement to the final moment, or the eve of a tactical action. Transportation is an integral part of planning, and its requirements and acquisition should be the function of information, observation, and vigilance. The expropriation of vehicles must be carried out with rigorous care and precision. Equally important, vehicles must be maintained for proper use, and be repaired and bear phony license plates and registration papers. Transport failure risks the mission, and hurts morale. Therefore, those charged with the expropriation of vehicles should be carefully selected. This is no place for indecisive or vacillating individuals" (Marighella, 1985). Marighella (1985) also observes that route planning for the exit, or withdrawal, is more crucial in his view than the operation itself. Route planning must take into consideration possible alternatives should the original exit route be blocked, and consideration should be given to winding streets and indirect routes out of the operational area.

Abduction Operation

At the moment a kidnapping occurs, the abduction team has usually achieved tactical surprise and typically employs overwhelming force. To the previously unsuspecting victim, the abductors seemingly appear out of nowhere. But when examined carefully, kidnappings are, for the most part, the result of a long and carefully orchestrated process. They do not arise in a vacuum. There are almost always some indications or warnings that the process is in motion prior to the actual abduction, meaning that many kidnappings are avoidable. In light of this reality, let us take a more detailed look at actual kidnap itself (Stewart, 2010b).

The abduction operation typically focuses on three points of reference: work/office, home or temporary residence (such as a hotel), and route. As previously indicated, roughly 90% of kidnappings occur on the route between work and home, and of those, about 80% occur within 200–300 meters of the target's destination. Kidnappers have the advantages of surprise, choice of time, place, and conditions of the abduction. This is a critical time from the adversary's perspective, as they are executing on a specific scenario planned out in advance. Timing, for them, is crucial. Anything that throws them off as the abduction begins to unfold can lead to unanticipated consequences. The abduction, which can be explosively fast and relies on the element of surprise, essentially has two parts: initiation and capture. Within this sequence if you are situationally aware and are able to grasp what is unfolding, you have a very brief opportunity to escape from the situation. Specifically, if you are able to correctly identify and comprehend whether a person or a vehicle's (or both) movements and position indicate a dangerous situation is developing, it is vital to move—get off the "X." Attack recognition is a function of mental preparedness and situational awareness. If you are mentally prepared, having worked through scenarios and your reaction to those scenarios, then you will be prepared. The abductors may not have considered that you will bolt or ram their vehicle and wrench your vehicle into a sharp U-turn. Their objective is to capture and hold you hostage, so shooting or injuring you is a last, not a first resort for them. You have a real opportunity of escaping your abductors at this stage.

If you are not able to react and are physically surrounded and abducted, then resistance could result in serious injury. You need to keep your head and use good judgment in this phase.

Abduction Case Study: Victor Cortez

There is a case for creating a scene. On August 13, 1986, Victor Cortez, an agent for the US Drug Enforcement Agency (DEA) working undercover in Guadalajara, Mexico, was abducted and tortured for over 30 hours while investigating the earlier kidnapping and murder of fellow DEA Agent Enrique "Kiki" Camarena.

Cortez, recently recounting the incident for a group of law enforcement officers and associates in Houston, Texas, opined that his quick thinking on the street in the first minutes of the abduction likely saved his life (Schiller, 2014).[2] Cortez recalled that he and an informant with whom he was meeting were surrounded by Mexican police who were working security for narcotics traffickers in Guadalajara. When Cortez, who broke cover and disclosed his DEA affiliation, was nonetheless physically restrained by his abductors, he made a snap judgment to fight back. He recalled that he mentally slowed things down, and it cleared his mind. He had studied the Camarena abduction and knew that there were no initial witnesses to the slain DEA agent's snatch off the street. Cortez understood intuitively that his abduction was following the exact same script as the ill-fated Camarena kidnapping—so he fought hard and resisted his captors out on the street as long as he could. He knew that by doing so, he would attract attention and create witnesses to his abduction. Eventually, the captors subdued him but not before several bystanders indeed witnessed what was happening. One of the witnesses was the husband of a US consulate employee. Although he did not know Cortez, he did see the encounter. Later that same evening, when his wife told him that Cortez was missing, he related to her what he had witnessed. This resulted in a return to the scene of the abduction by fellow agents looking for Cortez, where other witnesses related what they had seen and were able to provide partial license tags of the vehicle Cortez was forced into. This vehicle was then traced to the police station where the abductors took Cortez and his informant. Cortez' situation was unique, in that he very quickly grasped the danger of his situation and acted accordingly—it turned out to be the right decision. In a classic KFR scenario, this might not necessarily be the right decision. In either case, Cortez' admonition to mentally slow things down and think through what was happening is very good advice. It substantially helped that he had a sense of what the scenario was and where it was going.

If you are kidnapped in a classic KFR scenario, your chances of surviving the ordeal are high. You represent monetary value to the kidnapper. This is only the case so long as you remain alive. The typical kidnapper wants to keep it that way. You can expect rough treatment and abuse—but you will remain alive. If you are captured and viable avenues of escape are cut off, your best defense and chance of survival is passive cooperation (Heard, 2015). Mentally, your frame of mind should be to live to fight another day.

Negotiation

Once you have been taken captive in a KFR operation, the negotiation phase begins. The negotiation phase has several stages, all of which are crucial to the kidnappers success and your survival. Your captors' nerves and adrenaline will be on edge during the early hours after your abduction because they need to safely get you to their hideaway, ensure you are secured, and begin preparations for initial contact with your family or company. While the negotiation process that will begin is essentially a business transaction, any resemblance to normal business transactions begins and ends with what is being negotiated: your price. As with business negotiations, there are a lot of moving parts. In this negotiation, however, there is a significant emotional pressure that the kidnappers will bring to bear on those closest to you (Wygand, 2007). To the extent that you are prepared to anticipate and shunt the emotional blackmail that will be brought to bear on your family, to someone that can negotiate competently on your behalf, you will be well served and increase the chances that your ordeal will be over sooner rather than later. Also, just knowing that you are prepared, while in captivity, brings peace of mind that is also important to your survival and ability to think clearly.

Different Types of Kidnapping Operations

Political Abduction

The classic KFR process, as previously described, provides a good model to understand the similarities and the differences between political and criminal kidnaps. There is intelligence gathering, route analysis, snatch location selection and logistics, and abduction operation. It is in the negotiation phase of the political abduction that political kidnap largely diverges from criminal kidnap. The motives for a criminal kidnap is business—money. In this regard, the kidnappers have a vested interest in keeping the incident below the radar of the authorities. It is no accident that one of the first instructions they give the negotiation team is "don't contact the authorities." The motives for a political kidnap are typically 180° the opposite in this phase. The kidnappers want the media to know that they are holding a hostage, and they want the world to know.

Kidnapping or hostage taking lends itself to ongoing media coverage. The media can develop story lines and seek to personalize the drama. As parallels to theater arise, the human aspects of triumph and tragedy can be shaped in many forms. Terrorists and national leaders can use this inclination of reporting to spotlight agendas and obtain conditional accommodations in front of a general public as well as coordinate for other covert arrangements (US Army TRADOC, 2008c).

Express Kidnap

The only similarity the express kidnap operation shares with its more sophisticated cousin, KFR, is the abduction. Aside from this, express kidnap relies on force and the victim's ATM access to satisfy the criminal motive of money. The criminals extort cash money, coerced withdrawals from ATMs, or immediate use of credit card accounts. This form of kidnapping can be just as dangerous as other forms of kidnapping.

Profiling and intelligence-gathering are done on potential targets, and there is route-planning to various ATMs. However, with street-gang level kidnap crews, this is a much more informal, shortened process.

Virtual Kidnap

Another form is virtual kidnapping. In this instance, the victim is not actually abducted and is unaware that a ransom has been demanded. Criminals select a period when a target is out of normal communication with a family, a business, or an organization. Kidnappers announce that they have kidnapped the individual and demand a ransom on short notice. Unable to confirm the whereabouts of the identified victim, a ransom is usually paid in this scam.

Tiger Kidnap

The tiger kidnap is a tactic popularized by the Irish Republican Army. In a tiger kidnapping, a close relation of a targeted individual is abducted. The targeted individual is then asked to carry out some action in order to secure the release of his loved one. Normally, this means committing a robbery, undermining security barriers, or conducting some other type of illegal act. Tiger kidnappings are rare and tend to be carried out by trained personnel operating at the behest of a larger criminal or terrorist organization.

MEASURES TO COUNTER THE KIDNAP THREAT

The principles used to develop a basic personal security plan are a very useful template for use in building a counterkidnap security program as part of one's personal security planning. These principles, planning, detection, delay, deterrence, and defense are, in the case of kidnapping, building blocks for the incorporation of disruption. This principle, while useful in other aspects of personal security, is particularly applicable to the threat of kidnap because it targets what the adversary depends on most about their victims, and that is their predictability.

Preparation Principle: Advance Planning Measures Specific to Kidnap

1. Know the threats in the area to which you are traveling before you go. Take time to make your own kidnap threat assessment. There are several excellent resources for this. The US Department of State's OSAC (https://www.osac.gov) is an excellent resource for security-specific information worldwide. It is worth the time and the effort to become an OSAC constituent and create a user account for the website. OSAC constituency is available to any American-owned, nonprofit organization or any enterprise incorporated in the United States (parent company, not subsidiaries or divisions) doing business overseas. One of the reasons that OSAC

is an effective source of security information is that it is a federal advisory committee with a US government charter to promote security cooperation between American business and private sector interests worldwide and the US Department of State. The office is led by an executive council of private sector organizations and the Bureau of Diplomatic Security, under the US Department of State. Information is shared via e-mail, telephone, and in-office consultations on a variety of security concerns, including crime, terrorism, contingency planning, and information security.

A second excellent source of intelligence is the British government's website (http://www.gov.uk/foreign-travel-advice). This is an open source that provides a very user-friendly, searchable database of 225 countries and territories worldwide. Each one has information specific to the location to include updates and summaries of the most current travel advice, safety and security information, terrorism, regions of concern and activities within the country itself, local laws and customs and their applicability to security/safety, entry information and health information, natural hazards specific to the country, and other pertinent data. Most importantly, specific POC information is provided. The US Department of States' website (http://www.travel.state .gov) is similar, providing an interactive map, graphics, and fact sheets for the region to which you are traveling.

Whether or not the kidnap threat is high where you are traveling, it is always a prudent measure to register your entry into the country with the nearest consulate, embassy, or interest section. This is free and can be done via the Internet prior to travel.

2. Establish a protocol with your wife, partner, or family in advance. The following are things that you should brief them on in advance:
   a. They will communicate with you only by Skype or an encrypted virtual private network channel or e-mail. There should be no social media posts of where you are, what you are doing, and when you will return.
   b. In the event that you are kidnapped, their role is not to negotiate with the kidnappers. This needs to be done by a third party who you trust can calmly negotiate on your behalf. The reason for this is that tremendous emotional pressure will be brought to bear on family/spouse, and they will usually not be able to negotiate rationally under these circumstances (Wygand, 2007).
   c. They will have a role, but not to negotiate or to communicate regularly with the hostage takers. They should be instructed that if contacted directly by kidnappers, they are to listen to

the abductors demands and not commit to anything over the phone other than to try if possible to secure a proof of life (see following section) that they have you and you are safe.

3. Designate a POC, preferably an attorney or a close friend whom you trust to competently negotiate on your behalf. Ensure that they understand this obligation and agree to it. Their contact information should be committed to memory, before you travel. In the event that you are kidnapped, this is the contact you should give to your abductors unless they insist on speaking to your family or spouse (if so, then being prepared in advance by prebriefing your spouse on protocol will ensure that the right procedure on your behalf is followed). This individual may be the interface with the kidnappers or will be the one who oversees the development of a negotiation strategy and team to handle this task.

4. Establish a set of safe questions and answers with your spouse or designated POC. These are questions to which only you know the answers. This aids in confirming proof of life and that you are alive. It also authenticates that the kidnappers negotiating with the team are the ones that are holding you and not someone else.

5. If you are traveling to a dangerous location, kidnap and ransom insurance is another step to take. While there are insurance policies that provide reimbursement, there are other considerations that deserve attention. Credible kidnap and ransom insurance policies cover unlimited expenses for the services of experienced crisis management teams, which include highly skilled professionals such as former CIA and Secret Service agents and ex-military police personnel. These individuals will be involved in negotiating your safe release. If a ransom is required, they are skilled at negotiating as little payout as possible, with safety as the top priority. If you purchase kidnap and ransom insurance, keep the purchase strictly confidential, since potential kidnappers may view such insurance as a source of ransom funds.

Since kidnap and ransom insurance is typically purchased from property/casualty insurance brokers, they must have adequate information to make sure that the coverage is appropriate. Here are examples of the information that is necessary to properly underwrite a policy:

- Your travel plans for the next 12 months; this helps determine patterns and possible exposures.
- The purpose of each trip you make; your goals in making the trip can often impact the likelihood of a kidnapping.
- Your familiarity with the destinations; this is a two-edged sword, since it often not only means that you understand the

risks involved in the area and will take measures to avoid them, but could also mean that you are well known in the area which could increase the chances of being kidnapped. Such information is helpful not only in the underwriting process, but also for a crisis management team.

It is also worth pointing out that the cost of kidnap and ransom insurance is modest. The premium for a US$5 million dollar policy for one year with nonhazardous travel that includes the services of a crisis management team is about US$2000. Premium costs for coverage for travel to high-risk areas are higher. Coverage is available for individuals and their family members, as well as corporations and their employees.

The possibility of a kidnapping is one of the bigger challenges faced by a growing number of US travelers, whether vacationing or on business. If the current pattern persists, we can expect that there will be more kidnap victims and payouts in the years ahead, even though many of these incidents never make the news.

6. Commit to memory critical numbers (spouse, POC at home, and local POC) in the event that you are released. You could be left on a deserted street or in a part of the city you do not know, with just enough money to make a call. It is good to have those numbers memorized in advance. To the extent possible, you want contact number(s) that you know will be manned 24/7 so that you will get another person on the other end of the line.

Detection Principle: Countersurveillance

If you are targeted specifically, a kidnap team will spend time—often a considerable amount of time—collecting intelligence on your movements and habits. You should understand that to physically surveil you, they must in turn expose themselves—however discreet they might be—to countersurveillance by you. Be aware of the déjà vu effect (see Chapter 2, Principle of Detection) in critical areas immediately around where you depart from (residence or hotel) or workplace. The kidnap planners will be following you to see what your behavior is when departing to or arriving from work. Look for the following signs, or "tells," that you are under surveillance:

- You note someone is watching you; you meet their gaze and they look away too quickly.
- You see the same car or the same individual more than once in a different time, location and despite a change of direction by you. Rule of thumb: If you see the same vehicle in a completely different part of town, chances are you are under surveillance.

- You see a vehicle that consistently follows your direction but studiously tries to remain behind other cars or moves to different lanes. When you accelerate, it accelerates. When you slow down, it slows down.
- You notice unexpected room service or towel service in the hotel. Office staff or hotel staff question you in the guise of polite conversation about your daily routine, where you go, where you work.

Principle of Deterrence: Crafting a Low, Unpredictable Profile

Being predictable in your movements and habits may translate in your mind to reliability, but in a high-threat kidnap location, it can be a gift to kidnappers who are planning to abduct you.

1. Developing the *habit of unpredictability* is probably one of the most important countermeasures you can adopt in your personal security plan. Actively change your time of departure for work, and make an effort to seek out different routes and modes of transport into the office. Randomizing your route, time of departure, and mode of transportation go a long way toward mitigating your risk of kidnap.
2. This also applies to workout schedules, dining out, that evening cigar or cigarette outside of the hotel, or other habits you might develop over time. Assume you are under surveillance and make it as difficult as possible for your adversaries to build a predictable profile of your movements. They will ultimately focus on an easier target, if you make it hard enough.
3. Go dark on social media: In this day and age, the concept of the street means a lot more than just the physical space to which you travel, walk around in, and stay while on a trip. It also means cyberspace and your presence in it. The tools are available today on the web to mirror and broadcast every move we make in the physical space, in cyberspace. It is a great convenience to our friends and family—and it is a significant vulnerability that is exploited by kidnap adversaries. In the target selection phase of a KFR operation, kidnappers are developing profiles of many targets. Just as they can hone in on you as a target on the street if you are predictable and obvious in your movements, they will certainly be able to develop a targeting profile of you via the Internet if you constantly broadcast your itinerary on social media. Checking into the airport, the hotel, a local restaurant, or a tourist attraction via Facebook or Twitter may be entertaining for friends and family

back home, but it also creates a virtual track of you on the ground. Kidnappers typically settle on the easiest target—do not make it easy for them by broadcasting your movements on social media. If you are headed to a high kidnap threat location, resist the temptation to post photos and movements on social media—switch them off. Communicate with family only via Skype, e-mail, or phone. This lowers your virtual profile and can significantly help lower your physical profile.

4. Like electronic media, make sure that any correspondence, bills or receipts, or other pieces of information about you are shredded. A determined team of kidnappers will resort to dumpster diving to develop information about you.

5. Studiously avoid putting corporate tags on your luggage or wearing corporate logo shirts. This serves to advertise that you are traveling on business and come up on the radar of kidnappers—who routinely utilize targeting sources in airports and hotels. You become an attractive target because you represent corporate deep pockets in terms of potential ransom payments.

6. In high-risk countries such as Yemen, Afghanistan, Libya, and others, avoid traveling by road inside the country. Travel by air instead. This will ensure you avoid kidnapping hot spots.

7. Be deliberate about your transportation, especially if you do not yet have a vehicle. Ask your hotel or business manager to call a taxi service. For any extended travel around the city or the region, hire a driver selected by the hotel, your business manager, or a trusted business partner in the country.

8. Avoid wearing expensive suits in an area where it just does not blend. Take the time and the effort, if you have been at a formal business meeting, to change out of more expensive clothing and don clothes that blends with the environment, especially if you are going to be out at cafes or markets.

9. Use good judgment. Bluntly put—do not allow yourself to become inebriated in public or at a nightclub. Furthermore, be aware that in some countries, a common kidnapping ploy is to use attractive women, typically prostitutes, to lure businesspersons to no-tell hotels (very common in Latin America). Both situations can make you a very attractive target for an express kidnap scenario or worse. If you are a team leader responsible for individuals in a location where there is the threat of kidnapping, set the rules with them on this score and lead by example.

10. When you choose a rental car, deliberately pick a common model/make, neutral color, no black out windows. If you have the option of choosing a car that is a bit worse for the wear and dirty, even better.

Principle of Delay: Slowing Down the Abduction

Ultimately, abductors must break from cover and converge toward you. Your ability to correlate the abductor's movements and successfully put objects in their path to delay their actions sufficiently for you to escape is a factor of how situationally aware you are and how well you recognize and confirm the threat. Certain indicators will give away abductor's intentions. They will attempt to engage your full attention, with one approaching and asking for directions or change, anything to distract your attention. It could be an attractive girl or guy or a group of kids asking for money or candy (they will have been paid off in advance). While you are looking one way, the attackers will converge from a different direction. Watch for this, and as it begins to occur, do the following:

1. Move: Get off the "X" and run. An important part of keeping situationally aware is knowing where your exit direction is should you need to escape.
2. Put objects between you and your adversary: If you are in a car, keep other cars between you and them. There is safety in numbers—move into a crowd and keep moving.
3. Look for objects to shove over as you run; fruit stands, trash bins, glass: These objects will require your pursuers to slow down or divert to get around them, and it gives you critical time and distance.
4. Remember, just as with Victor Cortez in Mexico, as you do this, you are creating witnesses: At some point, your attackers will break off the pursuit. Keep moving.

Principle of Defense: Survival Strategies in Captivity

If you are surrounded and caught, the smartest strategy is to stop physically resisting. The kidnappers want to get you under control and out of the area as fast as possible. Resistance might get you a broken nose or worse, and this is not a condition you want to deal with in captivity. Following are additional considerations to keep in mind from the moment of abduction, into your captivity:

- You will likely be hooded and shoved down onto the floor panels of the vehicle. Remain calm and mentally alert. Breathe and employ all your senses. Geo-orient yourself—ask yourself what you last saw and the direction that the kidnappers proceeded. Count the turns, left and right. If you can see or get a glimpse out of a window, note whatever you can such as landmarks, iconic structures/buildings, signs, and infrastructure. Use your hearing to make note of changes in road texture, railroad tracks, bridges, and sound. Make note of any unusual odors such as industrial odors, cooking food, spices, and livestock. Note subtle changes in temperature, as the countryside can be slightly cooler and the air fresher than the city. If your ears pop, consider the change in altitude—you may be headed into a mountainous region.

- Prepare yourself mentally for captivity of at least several weeks. Keep your thoughts in the here and the now. Surviving an abduction is as much, if not more, about keeping your spirits up and mentally strong as it is about staying physically well.

- Shortly after being confined, your kidnappers may come to you for your family's contact information. If you have prepared in advance, this is where you give them the contact number for your trusted POC that can negotiate on your behalf. That is the ideal situation. They may bluntly insist on family contact information—if this occurs, give them your spouse's number—do not hold back information or it will prolong your abduction. Again, if you have prepared in advance, you will have a good sense of what your spouse's response will be and how she will handle it. This will give you some peace of mind, which is a small victory you will need to keep your spirits up. Your captors will try to manipulate you and lower your self-esteem. They will tell you that your family, your negotiators, your company has forgotten you and do not care about you. This is designed to subdue you mentally. Do not believe it—it will help you considerably if you have made careful preparations in advance.

- If you need medicine for asthma or other conditions, speak up politely—let your abductors know. It is in their best interest to keep you in good health.

- Be prepared to provide proof-of-life answers to your abductors when they ask. This authenticates them to your negotiation team and confirms you are alive and well.

- Create a routine while in captivity and rituals. Do exercises, keep your mind busy, play chess in your mind, or mentally work on your memoirs. Try to maintain a regular sleep pattern and eat whatever is given to you.

- Try to develop a rapport with your captors. Avoid controversial topics such as politics or religion; keep the topics on day-to-day activities, weather, and sports. Use humor; it very much humanizes you. This can potentially save your life if things go sideways.

- Do not offer to help with negotiations. You do not want to contradict what the negotiation team's representative is offering. Do not offer to speak with the family over the phone. If they want you to speak with them, they will provide you a script. Do not try to be clever and pass along a duress message. If you deviate from the script, they will know it.

- Do not ask stupid questions such as, "Why am I being held?" That can open Pandora's box: political oppression, inequality, injustice, etc. You are powerless to change conditions, and you should say as much if it comes up.
- If you had a laptop or a smartphone with you when you were abducted, assume that they are compromised.
- Expect your kidnappers to interrogate you regarding your access to bank account information.
- Try to keep track of time; estimate the time of day. Use your senses to develop an idea of time, space, patterns, and your captor's routines.
- You should be prepared to escape, but do not do so unless you believe your life is in imminent danger.
- Always be prepared for your release. You will note changes in the demeanor of your captors, and (if you have not been allowed) you might be given the opportunity to bathe and shave prior to release. This is a vulnerable time for your captors, so be prepared.
- Be ready for a police rescue. The more time that the kidnappers negotiate, the greater the chance they will be identified or located. If the police raid the location, do not run away. The smartest thing you can do is lie down, spread your arms, do exactly what the police tell you to do. They may not be polite and not immediately recognize you as a hostage.
- If you are released, follow the kidnapper's instructions to the letter—listen to them carefully. If you are dropped off in a deserted area, wait until your captors are gone before orienting yourself. They may have told someone where you are, so wait awhile before leaving.
- If you are given some money for a taxi or to make a telephone call, do not tell the taxi driver or the individual in a bar/restaurant what has happened to you. Just call, advise where you are, and sit tight until you are picked up. If you have planned in advance, you will have memorized a 24/7 number that you can call, to be sure someone knows you have been released.

RECOVERING FROM KIDNAP

Freedom almost always brings a sense of elation and relief. However, adjusting back to the real world after being held hostage can be just as difficult as abruptly leaving it. Upon release, many hostage survivors are faced with transitioning from conditions of isolation and helplessness to sensory overload and freedom. This transition often results in significant adjustment difficulties.

Released hostages need time to recover from the physical, mental, and emotional difficulties they faced. However, it is important to keep in mind that human beings are highly resilient and can persevere despite tragedy. Research shows that positive growth and resilience can occur following trauma. Hostage survivors may feel lost or have difficulty managing intense reactions and may need help adjusting to their old life following release (American Psychological Association, 2016).

Any kind of trauma—and a violent crime is a type of trauma for the victim—involves a collapse of the person's feelings of security. Apart from the suffering of the direct victim, the entire family structure is also affected. Violent crimes are negative events that usually happen suddenly, generating fear and helplessness, threatening people's physical or psychological well-being, and leaving victims in an emotional state that they are unable to deal with using their normal psychological resources. Apart from the suffering of the direct victim, the entire family structure is also affected. The most common psychological consequences in victims of crimes like kidnapping involve the permanent modification of personality traits (such as emotional dependence, suspiciousness, or hostility) that persist for at least two years and lead to a deterioration of interpersonal relationships and performance at work (Koleoso and Akhigbe, 2013). Reactions to this kind of stress can be delayed. Numbness can be left behind once the elation of being free has worn off. This is a sign that you need to deal with unresolved feelings from the ordeal, which can also manifest as chronic indications of stress, disturbed sleep, bewilderment, dejection, anger, guilt, and fear. As part of a proactive program for recovery, the hostage survivor might want to consider seeking help from a licensed mental health professional, such as a psychologist, who can help develop an appropriate strategy for moving forward.

EXECUTIVE PROTECTION: KEY ELEMENTS OF A PROGRAM

Executive protection refers to those security measures taken to ensure the safety of very important persons or other individuals who could be exposed to elevated personal risk because of their employment (high-ranking military or diplomat), celebrity status, wealth, associations, geographical location, or any combination of these various factors. There is a close relationship between personal security, executive protection officer, and close protection that should be clearly understood if you are the individual developing security programs within your organization. Personal security is intrinsically an individual concern—it is about your feelings regarding your own safety and security. By natural extension, a program built around good personal security habits and instincts directly addresses these feelings, making you confident in your responsibility to yourself and, by extension, to others. You are able to wisely balance the threat, the risk, and the right measures to address risk-based scenarios. You will have internalized an attitude of awareness—observation as opposed to just passive sight. Personal security means that you adopt certain sets of protocols and procedures into programmatic form to reduce the personal risk of kidnap, terrorism, cyberattack, assassination, and any other threat that might arise.

A successful personal security program, as previously alluded to, is the foundation for extending personal competence into executive protection competence. Protecting an individual is a very different discipline from securing a facility. A top executive not only cannot be locked down but also, unlike a building with a single gate, access control, duress alarms, and CCTVs, can be exploited in indirect ways such as through family members. Confidence in your own security plan gives you the right attitude to resolve the inevitable challenges that will occur in the more complex world of close protection. This is crucial. As the executive protection specialist, you are the overriding protective countermeasure to your principal when he or she is away from the comforting security of corporate headquarters or well-secured residence. Your personal security program, and instincts, must be unimpeachable if you are to be an effective instrument of protection to an executive asset. Stated differently, no matter how well trained and effective you appear to be on paper as a close protection specialist, if your personal security instincts and habits are unrefined or nonexistent, you will be a liability to those you are chartered to protect.

Program Development: Step 1—Risk Assessment

Building a solid executive protection program requires that you gain a realistic understanding of the scope of threats, vulnerabilities, and risks that you and your company executives are facing. This is accomplished by commissioning a risk assessment. Chapter 9 provides a very reliable and comprehensive assessment method for you to follow if it is not possible to commission an outside analysis (even if you do invest in a third-party assessment, the risk principles outlined in Chapter 9 will give you a set of good guidelines around which you can gauge the quality of an assessment you have commissioned or questions you might have for an outside security consultant.) If you are not capable or comfortable doing the assessment yourself, it is well worth the time and the investment to hire an outside security consultant to execute this process. They will give you an objective focus on the most important issues around which your protection program should be designed.

The risk assessment contains specific elements that must each be capably fleshed out. Identify your asset(s), conduct an impact analysis, and identify relevant threats to your asset and their vulnerabilities. Identify the individuals who are critical to your organization (assets), assess the impact to the corporation if they are lost and examine the risks that each of those people faces. Is there a history of threats against any of these individuals? Do they travel regularly to dangerous places? Once you have determined who your assets are and what threats are relevant, you need to know everything about their public and private lifestyles. This is called *creating a principal profile*, and it requires the executive's full cooperation. You need to know everything about his/her work and home lives—everything from detailed information about his/her home, his/her family's habits, and any organizations and clubs he/she frequents. It is also important to investigate how easy it is for outsiders to get information on your principal and his/her family (Duffy, 2005). Develop risk statements, or scenarios, based on fact. A risk statement, which will accompany the list of prioritized risks to your asset(s) in a risk register, should be couched in terms such as the likelihood a specific asset (your principal) will be impacted by the successful exploitation of an identified vulnerability by a specific threat event–actor pair. Obtaining data to develop answers to those questions will yield a valid, relevant scenario against which you can design countermeasures to mitigate the risk.

Program Development: Step 2—Protection Plan

A well-done risk assessment lays out specific risks against which a deliberate program can be designed with risk mitigation strategies. This is part of the master planning process. Your plan should be a detailed roadmap that translates risk-based, prioritized decisions into an effective protective security design. Mitigation measures might include the development of protective intelligence and analysis capabilities, surveillance detection programs, residential physical and technical security measures, or specialized security driver training. This program management approach ensures intelligent design decisions, targeted allocation of resources toward countermeasures, ongoing project management structure including ongoing stakeholder engagement strategies, program delivery and execution, training requirements, budgeting, reporting, and documentation.

Program Development: Step 3—Stakeholder Engagement: The Human Factor

Whether it is physical security, cybersecurity, or personal protection, there is one constant: Security is more often than not viewed skeptically by corporate management as a cost center and, depending on the client, a nuisance. It is important to engage with corporate stakeholders from the outset (actually, from step 1 onward and in parallel with the program development process) in order to *recruit* and secure their support. The focus of your engagement is to help corporate management realize and embrace the value of the executive protection program. To do so, it is your job to help the penny drop with management in terms of identifying with the need for executive protection. One way to achieve this is to offer an alternative view to the assumption that security is just a cost center. Not only appeal to their heads, but also appeal to their hearts. One addresses the bottom line; the other engages their personal interest.

The appeal to the head approach includes emphasizing productivity and regular threat reporting summaries, for example. The appeal to the heart includes engaged, dynamic security awareness and training programs.

An executive protection program can produce increased productivity for the executive. Increased productivity is achieved through off-loading of the minutiae of travel/coordination onto the executive protection officer. That can be expressed as X number of hours per day/per week of the corporate principal's time to focus on business, which in turn can be mapped to monetary terms.

It can also be effective to boil down the protection program's efforts into a quarterly executive summary that lists the perceived threats and the steps taken to mitigate them. Robert Siciliano, a personal security expert who has advised British Petroleum and Best Western, refers to it as cultivating a healthy paranoia in your executive populace. "They should be aware of the risks they face and always informed of the worst-case scenarios." The more that executives know about the role of their protection detail, the better they will understand their role in helping the protection professionals keep them safe.

Of course, executives can come to view these conversations about lurking dangers as scare tactics. That is why it is critical that the chief security officer (CSO) responsible for developing and managing the executive protection program and not the individual security provider manage this communication. "I wouldn't try to talk my CEO into taking karate or judo," says one security executive for a Fortune 50 company in the aerospace industry. "But I think it's important that they're aware or sensitive to what's going on [within their peer group]. Threats or activity against other executives are a good opportunity to tweak them about security."

Also, CSOs should have answers ready for the executives' most common concerns about security in their lives. Take the following, for example:

- Can I trust them? In a culture where everyone seems to be angling for a book deal, top executives are loath to have a stranger listening to their phone calls and observing the details of their daily lives. Executives have to be able to rely on their discretion.
- What about my personal life? Most executives want to leave their work at the office. If a security detail during off-hours is necessary, CSOs can minimize complaints by ensuring that the protection personnel keep a low profile. Video surveillance technology and alarm systems can keep the security professionals at a comfortable distance.
- Will this slow me down? Executives concerned that security will be cumbersome can learn how the organizational prowess of their protection personnel can make everything run more smoothly.

The appeal to the heart can really link the need with desire and engaged interest for an executive protection program. Give your executives a little training of their own, with role play-based training courses that include self-defense, surveillance, and similar techniques. Some take defensive driving courses and learn what to do if attacked by armed assailants and what they should do if they are being watched (Duffy, 2005). It will make them better partners.

Program Development: Step 4—Planning Process Document

Draft and present a planning process roadmap. This document, accompanied with a presentation, should include the following:

- Executive summary that distills key risk and protection plan elements identified in the initial risk assessment and master planning stages: Express risk findings in declarative, bulleted statements that posit likelihood levels, asset impact levels, vulnerability exploitation identification, and threat actor–event pairs. For example, "The risk assessment identified a very high likelihood that the principal could be abducted en route to regional offices in [city] by known armed professional kidnappers affiliated with XYZ criminal group exploiting identified vulnerabilities in principal's route and mode of travel. This would result in severe loss to corporate leadership, potential for injury or death to principal, and severe harm to company reputation."

- In the executive summary, protection plan elements are tied directly to identified risks. It is very important within the report to show that there is a risk-based antecedent that directly justifies each proposed measure in the protection plan.
- Statement of purpose/objective for the executive protection program.
- Corporate background (values, vision, history, growth): The background should not be a cut-and-paste exercise taken from a corporate brochure. Write this background section with a view toward how elements of the company's background and direction could or will take the principal(s) requiring proposed executive protection into high-risk areas out of business necessity.
- Program benefits: This is where you will articulate your alternative view to the assumption that security is just a cost center, as alluded to earlier. List these benefits and, to the extent possible, tie the benefits to return-on-investment calculations and cost-benefit data if you have them.
- Success factors/key performance indicator.
- Program design: This will include a listing of individuals and positions requiring protection, where and when protection will be (and not be), levels of protection required, and how it will be delivered. This could include the following:
  - Close protection requirements: These would consist of, for example, identifying what principals need protection and if families are included, scheduling protection, locations, foreign travel, or special events. It is very important not to leave spouses and children out of security planning. The principal may be well protected, but if the family is not, then they are a significant concern since they represent a vulnerability in terms of forcing cooperation out of the executive by simply holding the family hostage and threatening harm to them.
  - Technical requirements: These would include things such as vehicle armoring, driver security training, communications needs (tactical very high frequency/ultra high frequency, encryption, repeaters, etc.), duress alarms, CCTV, or radio frequency identification tracking capabilities on private corporate assets such as vehicles, boats, or aircraft.

- Physical security requirements: These would include residential or special event security measures addressing issues such as standoff distance, access control—layering defensive measures—perimeter security, gate controls, barriers, crime prevention through environmental design measures, lighting, access control, blast protection, and alarms and video (CCTV) monitoring. Also for armored vehicles, an interior release latch within the trunk should be installed in the event of an abduction where the principal is forced into the trunk. There should be a process in place for vetting and selecting domestic help, gardeners, and gate guards[3] as well as executive or critical residences in high-threat areas. Of particular importance are the design of safe rooms within the residence, where a principal and family members can retreat in the event of a home invasion by terrorists or kidnappers. The author has had personal experience, on two occasions, in retreating to safe rooms under duress. Both occurred in Africa—one was a well-organized home invasion by a criminal gang in the middle of the night who ransacked part of the home and stole high-value items, killed the watchdogs on the premises, and disabled the annunciators while inside the home. The second was during a wartime situation during which time rebel forces had overrun a military base adjacent to the residence. In this instance, fighters overran the compound and threatened to invade the residence because of an active generator and security lights. At the very minimum, considerations for residential safe room selection and construction include the following:
  - Location: This is the first and, in my view and own experience, most important. Once the intrusion is detected, time is a luxury you do not have, particularly for unhindered movement within your residence. It can be in the dead of night or under gunfire and yelling that accompanies close combat and a compound invasion. Either way, it is frightening and confusing—you need to have a simple, direct way to safety. Ideally, master and guest bedrooms should be located in one area of the residence that can be closed off immediately so that family (or guests) can be kept together and not be separated. Separate areas only heighten the possibility that you, family members, or guests will cross paths with the intruders.
  - Construction: Safe rooms can be very sophisticated and expensive. The basic considerations once a location is chosen is the door (at minimum a solid-core door with

a deadbolt lock, with hinges on the secure side), a room that is slab to slab (floor to ceiling walls with no plenum space), and no windows. An interior bathroom, a walk-in closet, or similar works well.

- Provisions: The safe room should have a medical kit, water and some basic rations, and communications capability in order to call for help. In Africa, I also provisioned my safe room area with oxygen masks that could be used in the event of fire and a weapon—in one instance, a .357 revolver and the other a Winchester pump shotgun loaded with 00 buckshot. I personally recommend the shotgun, for the simple reason that ratcheting a shell into the chamber has a distinctive sound that intruders recognize—it is an effective deterrent measure.

• Intelligence and countersurveillance: These would address requirements for protective intelligence reporting/advance intelligence, survey, and analysis capabilities and counter-surveillance or surveillance detection measures outside of special events, residence, or work/business locations. A countersurveillance program is an absolute must for any company with operations within high kidnap threat locations or terrorist threat countries. It is an invaluable tool that disrupts a key planning element of kidnap operations, which is surveillance to assess arrival/departure schedules of potential kidnap targets. This program essentially takes the security guard position, and turns it inside out. Countersurveillance programs must be initiated carefully and require a professionally developed communications plan.

• Operations center and response requirements: These are a crucial element to the success or the failure of an executive protection program. A 24/7, staffed operations center capability is needed for quick response to emergencies such as an attempted abduction or attack; accident; home invasion; suspicious incident, person, or activity; or a terrorist attack, coup, or revolution in the country that threatens the life and the safety of the principals involved.

• Team structure: This would entail job descriptions and qual-ifications, team hierarchy, and communications within the corporation (to whom they report to for administration mat-ters, and operational matters).

• Training: This would lay out training for entry-level, super-visory, and advanced Executive Protection (EP) special-ists including course names and requirements and a career development path. Training would be aligned with corporate human resources policies and procedures.

- Procurement and budgeting: The case will be made based on cost analysis, for proprietary executive protection staff, full contract executive protection, or a hybrid model (proprietary supervisors and contract staff).

Program Development: Step 5—Implementation

Step 5 is about putting your executive protection strategy plan into action. No matter how small or large your program is, it needs to be managed closely and continuously to ensure that the main objective—protection and safety of the principals identified—is executed smoothly. The initial phase of implementation is important because this is where expectations as to whether the protection program is worth it (or not) are set between the principal and his or her executive protection team. Confidence building is done through careful assignment of professional, discreet, capable protection professionals. Their quiet confidence and demeanor will go a long way toward selling the program. Keep the following considerations in mind as you implement your plan:

- Selection of an individual who is charged with moving the plan forward with the principals and overseeing the supervision of executive protection agents: Emphasis should be placed on a smooth, nondisruptive implementation unless there are identified circumstances requiring drastic implementation; if that is the case, they need to be communicated and accepted by the principal in advance. Otherwise, the change can be an unwelcome shock to the system. Better to anticipate this in advance and deal with it rather than be caught in a reactive, defensive position. Phasing in protective measures is most easily done in the initial stages during special events and travel (Limoges, 2014). Once this is done, then it can be eased into the principal's daily routine.
- Ensuring that there is an independent mechanism developed to check and verify how well, or poorly, the plan is being implemented: The progress of the program will develop expectations on the part of principals and stakeholders. The ongoing challenge shall be meeting the expectations that the program sets with how service is delivered. This is always an aspect of executive protection that needs consistent attention. The best advice is to make it a point to have deliberate conversations between team members, and especially with additional executive protection staff members who are brought on-board on an interim

or subcontract basis, about how the principles are serviced. The goal of this conversation is to maintain a single philosophy about how the job is performed and what standards exist (Limoges, 2014).

- Building in program feedback mechanisms for principals, executive protection agents, and others so that you can receive prompt notification when something goes wrong or right.
- Making sure that drills and tabletop exercises are done on a regular basis.
- Maintaining an ongoing threat and risk assessment process: Threats change, assets change, and vulnerabilities change. Monitoring the program through continual assessment ensures that the protection methods selected are appropriate for the situation, properly implemented, and—should circumstances on which the initial program was based change—modified as needed.

SELECTED THREAT ACTOR PROFILE: THE MIND-SET OF A KIDNAPPER

A recent BBC Interview of a Mexican cartel kidnapper provided a rare glimpse into the soul of kidnappers themselves (Spata, 2016). The kidnapper's perspective offers a useful perspective into the personality profile of criminals who turn to kidnapping for ransom as a way to earn a living. There are general traits that are the hallmark of kidnappers for ransom. They come from communities or families that molded them into criminals—raw, poverty-stricken neighborhoods or communities where the authorities were the enemy; drugs and drug use was common; child abuse, broken families, domestic abuse and violence; gangs, generations of poverty; little to no opportunity to move up and out of the environment; an either–or choice in life. The sexual or physical abuse that they use with those they have abducted reflect the sexual and physical abusive environments from which they come. The kidnapper painted a picture of a tortured cycle in which young men like him who "look normal," but are "sick in the head," embrace a business that is addicting but ultimately leaves their lives "f—ed." "Kidnapping someone in Mexico is very easy, and it's a faster way of getting cash than drugs. You can earn anything up to $2 million. It's like being a rock star—you get anything you want—so it's very hard to give up. But at the same time there's always a sadness in me and the two things together drive me crazy." This succinct self-description mirrors what experts say are individuals who live and remain on the fringes of society, unable to hold down a steady job for long. They are a product of a failure of nurture, rather than nature. Their disregard for laws and social mores stems from an environment that is lawless and raw; they utterly disregard another's dignity or rights because they have survived to adolescence or adulthood through sheer survival and looking out for themselves above all else. Feelings of remorse, or guilt, are not present because the same remorseless, unapologetic pain was inflicted on them from childhood; it is a character flaw programmed into their personality from an early age. Conflict or adversity is handled through violence; it is all that they know. They can be sadistic, but when captured much like the school yard bully, weak and easily intimidated (Wright, 2009). They fold immediately when pressured. Abductees say that their abductors can swing between extremes—being almost apologetic at times but escalate rapidly to violent behavior when they feel threatened or out of control. A woman whose daughter was kidnapped in Venezuela by a professional crew noted, while discussing ransom with the kidnappers over the phone, an usual change in tone by the abductor. While she was in a tense conversation with him, he suddenly asked her to hold on— while he took a call on another phone from his own daughter. "Papa's working," the kidnapper said. "Don't worry."

For him, this was just business (Inskeep, 2013).

REFERENCES

Akhigbe, K. O., and Koleoso, O. N., "Psychological and psychiatric considerations in a kidnapped-gor-ransom victim: A clinical case study," *IOSR Journal of Dental and Medical Sciences* 10, 5, http://www.iosrjournals.org (September–October, 2013), pp. 1–5.

American Psychological Association, "Adjusting to life after being held hostage or kidnapped," http://www.apa.org/helpcenter/hostage-kidnap.aspx (2016).

Dobbs, P., "Kidnap and ransom today," Hamilton: Catlin Group Ltd, http://www.catlin.com/flipbook/kidnap-and-ransom-today/files/inc/342692550.pdf (October, 2012), p. 8.

Duffy, D., "The six things you need to know about executive protection" *CSO Online*, accessed March 2, 2016, http://www.csoonline.com/article/2112401/infosec-staffing/the-six-things-you-need-to-know-about-executive-protection.html (April 1, 2005).

Federal Bureau of Investigation, "Virtual kidnapping: U.S. citizens threatened by Mexican extortion scheme," https://www.fbi.gov/news/stories/2014/november/virtual-kidnapping/virtual-kidnapping (November 4, 2014).

Finkelhor, D., "Five myths about missing children," *The Washington Post,* https://www.washingtonpost.com/opinions/five-myths-about-miss ing-children/2013/05/10/efee398c-b8b4-11e2-aa9e-a02b765ff0ea _story.html (May 10, 2013).

Hanbury, R., and Romano, D., "Adjusting to life after being held hostage or kidnapped," *American Psychological* Association, http://www .apa.org/helpcenter/hostage-kidnap.aspx (July, 2013).

Heard, B. J. *Kidnapping and Abduction: Minimizing the Threat and Lessons in Survival,* Boca Raton, FL: CRC Press (2015), p. 40.

Inskeep, S., "For Venezuelans, kidnappings are simply business as usual," *NPR,* accessed March 7, 2016, http://www.npr.org/sections/paral lels/2013/06/06/188925079/For-Venezuelans-Kidnappings-Are -Simply-Business-As-Usual (June 6, 2013).

Limoges, E., "Implementing an executive protection program," Domestic Estate Management Association, Orlando, FL, accessed March 4, 2016, http://www.domesticmanagers.com/implementing-an-executive -protection-program (2014).

Longmire, S., *Cartel: The Coming Invasion of Mexico's Drug Wars,* Reprint edition, New York: St. Martin's Press (October 18, 2011), pp. 85–87.

MacWillson, A. C., *Hostage-Taking Terrorism: Incident-Response Strategy,* New York: St. Martin's Press (1992), p. 165.

Marighella, C., *The Terrorist Classic, Manual of the Urban Guerrilla,* Chapel Hill, NC: Documentary Publications (1985), p. 88.

NYA International, "Analysis: NYA International—Spotlight on the Philippines," http://www.krmagazine.com/2015/11/20/analysis-nya -international-spotlight-on-the-philippines (November 20, 2015).

NYA International, "Global Kidnap Review 2016," *Crisis Prevention and Response,* http://www.nyainternational.com/sites/default/files/nya -publications/160203-NYA-January-Kidnap-Review.pdf (February 3, 2016a).

NYA International, "Global Kidnap Review 2016," *Crisis Prevention and Response,* http://www.nyainternational.com/sites/default/files/nya -publications/160203-NYA-January-Kidnap-Review.pdf (February 3, 2016b), p. 6.

NYA International, "Global Kidnap Review 2016," *Crisis Prevention and Response,* http://www.nyainternational.com/sites/default/files/nya -publications/160203-NYA-January-Kidnap-Review.pdf (February 3, 2016c), p. 4.

NYA International, "Global Kidnap Review 2016," *Crisis Prevention and Response,* http://www.nyainternational.com/sites/default/files/nya -publications/160203-NYA-January-Kidnap-Review.pdf (February 3, 2016d), p. 7.

NYA International, "Global Kidnap Review 2016," *Crisis Prevention and Response*, http://www.nyainternational.com/sites/default/files/nya -publications/160203-NYA-January-Kidnap-Review.pdf (February 3, 2016e), p. 5.

NYA International, "Global Kidnap Review 2016," *Crisis Prevention and Response*, http://www.nyainternational.com/sites/default/files/nya -publications/160203-NYA-January-Kidnap-Review.pdf (February 3, 2016f), p. 10.

NYA International, "Global Kidnap Review 2016," *Crisis Prevention and Response*, http://www.nyainternational.com/sites/default/files/nya -publications/160203-NYA-January-Kidnap-Review.pdf (February 3, 2016g), p. 11.

Red 24, "Top 10 kidnap countries named by Red24," https://www.red24 .com/uploads/top10kidnapcountriesbyred24_02042012.pdf (April 2, 2012).

Reuters, "Kidnappings by Kony's LRA spike in Central African Republic," http://www.businessinsider.com/r-kidnappings-by-konys-lra-spike -in-central-african-republic-group-2016-3 (March 3, 2016).

Schiller, D., "Decades later, former DEA agent haunted by torture in a Mexican Jail Cell," *Houston Chronicle* (November 30, 2014).

Spata, C., "Cartel member explains what it's like to be a professional kidnapper," *Complex Life*, accessed March 4, 2016, http://www .complex.com/life/2016/03/bbc-interviews-cartel-kidnapper-mexico (March 11, 2016).

Stewart, S., "A look at kidnapping through the lens of protective intel- ligence," *Stratfor Security Weekly*, https://www.stratfor.com/weekly /20100519_look_kidnapping_through_lens_protective_intelligence (May 20, 2010a).

Stewart, S., "A look at kidnapping through the lens of protective intel- ligence," *Stratfor Weekly* (May 19, 2010b).

Stewart, S., "The unspectacular, unsophisticated Algerian hostage crisis," https://www.stratfor.com/weekly/unspectacular-unsophisticated -algerian-hostage-crisis (January 24, 2013a).

Stewart, S., "Kidnapping: An avoidable danger," *Stratfor Security Weekly*, https://www.stratfor.com/weekly/kidnapping-avoidable-danger (May 30, 2013b).

Turner, M., "Kidnapping and politics," *International Journal of the Sociology of Law* 26 (1998), pp. 145–160.

UK Foreign and Commonwealth Office, "Foreign travel advice, Afghanistan," https://www.gov.uk/foreign-travel-advice/afghanistan/terrorism (2016).

US Army Training and Doctrine Command (TRADOC), "Hostage-taking and kidnapping terror in the COE," https://fas.org/irp/threat/terrorism /sup6.pdf (December 5, 2008a), p. 5.

US Army Training and Doctrine Command (TRADOC), "Hostage-taking and kidnapping terror in the COE," https://fas.org/irp/threat/terrorism /sup6.pdf (December 5, 2008b), pp. 5–6.

US Army Training and Doctrine Command (TRADOC), "Hostage-taking and kidnapping terror in the COE," https://fas.org/irp/threat/terrorism /sup6.pdf (December 5, 2008c), pp. 5–17.

US Department of Justice, "International Parental Kidnapping," https:// www.justice.gov/criminal-ceos/international-parental-kidnapping (June 3, 2015).

US Department of State, "Somalia travel warning," https://travel.state .gov/content/passports/en/alertswarnings/somalia-travel-warning .html (October 1, 2015a).

US Department of State, "CAR travel warning" http://www.travel.state .gov/content/passports/en/country/central-african-republic.html (September 30, 2015b).

Wright, R. P., "Kidnap for ransom: Resolving the unthinkable," In *Kidnapping and Kidnappers*, Boca Raton: Auerbach Publications (January 22, 2009), p. 42.

Wygand, J., *The Secure Urbanite: Personal Security in the Asphalt and Concrete Jungle*, British Columbia: CCB Publishing (2007), p. 196.

ENDNOTES

1. This analysis has been republished with the kind permission of NYA International. It was originally published in the Global Kidnap for Ransom Update in October 2015.

2. On December 1, 2015, the author attended the public presentation by Victor Cortez to FBI Citizen's Academy in Houston, Texas and briefly met with Cortez.

3. A home invasion by a criminal gang experienced by the author in Africa, was made possible by a locally hired gate guard who used his knowledge of my movements and habits and the residence itself gathered over a period of months to assist the gang in the break-in.

CHAPTER 5

Patterns of Threat in the Environment

INTRODUCTION

The reality for business travelers abroad is that the criminal or the terrorist violence that so often captures the headlines is frequently not so obvious on arrival in a dangerous country. Life does go on in hostile third-world environments, and quite often, the relatively normal pace of outward life belies the actual danger that lurks beneath. Do not be fooled by an outward appearance of normality or quiet. In violent, dangerous places, it has been my experience that the maxim should be that there is 90% boredom and 10% sheer panic. Use that quiet time to plan for and manage the eventuality of panic. No matter where the conflict zone is, there is always some element of predictability to the violence.

There is an old cliché that is so often heard—"he (or she) was caught in the wrong place, at the wrong time." The implication to this throwaway line is that violence is random and unpredictable. Sometimes, it is—it is hard enough for professional analysts to predict terrorist attacks, let alone the person on the street. However, I do not believe that one needs to be inevitably caught or trapped in a wrong place/wrong time event. Yes, it happens and there is such a thing as plain bad luck. However, preparation and informed awareness can give you a crucial edge in detecting and avoiding victimization in such an event. You can, with effort, make your own luck. In Mexico, for example, express kidnapping—a favorite street crime—becomes a real possibility once a business travelers' profile is raised to the point where they become a target. More often than not, the principle threat that business travelers and employees of a company inside Mexico will face is a common street crime such as pickpocketing or being robbed, mugged, or express kidnapped. These criminal events are not random, unpredictable episodes of violence. If one unpacks the details of an express kidnap scenario, for instance, there are distinct patterns to the ultimate act of violence—the abduction and the exploitation of the victim. The victim plays a key role—typically, their own behavior signals their vulnerability. For the criminal threat actors, it is very much a case of right place and right time.

Violent criminal acts do follow certain conditions, trends, and patterns that I have observed in many third-world environments in which I have lived. In fact, these conditions and trends are evident in developed countries as well. Much of this is common sense, but nonetheless, it bears repeating since paying attention to these patterns can reduce your risk.

COVER OF DARKNESS

Good things of day begin to droop and drowse, while night's black agents to their preys do rouse.

William Shakespeare
Macbeth, act 3, scene 2

From time immemorial, the cover of darkness is a condition that has been exploited by criminals and leaves one prone to heightened risk. Criminals, by nature, prefer the cover of darkness in order to hide their movements and intentions. Burglars and break-in crews will gravitate to residences where the lights are completely off and appear deserted. In the third world, more often than not, the majority of cases of highway banditry occur at night. In many countries, local militia or soldiers will rent out their rifles, along with a few rounds of ammunition, to criminals who set up impromptu roadblocks at night to rob travelers or hijack vehicles.

In Northern European and Scandinavian countries, the long, dark nights in the winter months mean higher rates of burglary, robbery, and vehicle crime. Recorded public disorder, vandalism, and physical and sexual assaults typically peak on weekend nights and follow the pattern of nighttime socializing. There is a link between nighttime drinking in and around licensed bars and serious confrontational violence between gangs or groups of young people (Tomsen, 2010).

Recently, in the United States, there was a difference between behaviors by individuals involved in racial protests in Ferguson, Missouri. In daylight hours and after dark was a study in sharp contrast between relatively peaceful behavior and violent criminal behavior. The cover of darkness, the fear of darkness (Walrond, 2016),[1] and the accompanying rise in the potential for violence are a predictable pattern that should be anticipated and used as an element in a personal security plan.

ALCOHOL, DRUGS, AND THE ENVIRONMENT

History is replete with examples of the consequences of combining alcohol, a lawless environment, and a group of intoxicated humans. In 1669, the infamous buccaneer Henry Morgan threw a party on his flagship, the HMS *Oxford*, for a group of French pirates whose help he needed to attack the Spanish port of Cartagena. Everyone ended up drunk on rum, and a few seriously inebriated sailors lit a fuse that ignited explosives on the ship and blew it up. One of the most dangerous aspects of the American Wild West throughout the mid-late 1800s occurred in the frontier towns such as Dodge City, Abilene, or Cheyenne. Young cowboys, fresh off the cattle trails of Texas and Oklahoma, were primed with whiskey and had a paycheck in their pocket and a six-shooter on their hip. This lethal combination led to stringent gun control laws at that time in these towns, prohibiting firearms from being carried within city limits.

There has always been a clear association between alcohol, drugs, and violence. When this association is imposed on a lawless environment, it can be lethal and constitutes a very real threat to your personal security. Consider these statistics, drawn from the relative safety of the United States, a developed, first-world country with professional, trained police:

1. There is clear evidence of the association between violent or aggressive behavior and alcohol consumption:
   a. 86% of homicide offenders were drinking when arrested.
   b. 37% of assault offenders were drinking or intoxicated when arrested.
   c. 60% of sexual assault offenders were intoxicated.
   d. 57% of men involved in marital violence were intoxicated.
   e. 27% of women involved in marital violence were intoxicated (Roizen, 1997).

   The conservative estimate is that at least 42% of violent crimes reported to the police in the United States involved alcohol consumption (Gustafson, 1994).
2. There is clear evidence that alcohol can encourage aggression or violence by disrupting normal brain functions that would otherwise restrain impulsive behavior.
   a. Social cues are misjudged, leading to an overreaction to a perceived threat.
   b. Attention span becomes so narrowed that there is no thought given to future consequences of an immediate violent impulse. There is a substantially diminished sense of context (Cook and Moore, 1993; Miczek, 1997).

3. It has been shown that intoxication, alone, does not cause violence. However, it can be the catalyst that leads to critical mass that subsequently sparks the violent act. There is typically a fissile element that, when mixed with the alcohol, fuels the aggression (Pernanen, 1991; White, 1997). These elements can include but are not limited to the following:
   a. Violent lifestyle
   b. Violent upbringing
   c. Delinquent peer group (Jessor and Jessor, 1977)
   d. Lack of parental authority, supervision, or role model
   e. High testosterone levels (Dabbs, 1991; Virkkunen, 1994)
   f. Desire for revenge or vengeance

As noted earlier, the data from these studies were drawn from the comparatively safe environment of the United States. Placed into the context of a hostile third-world environment, the instance of alcohol- or drug-fueled violence is substantially more dangerous. Upon arrival in Kampala, Uganda, in 1985, the author was briefed about the pattern of alcohol abuse that roughly began after sunset and reached its peak between 10 and 11 p.m. There were at least five armed camps within the city, all aligned with various tribes and clan leaders, all fighting against then rebel leader Yoweri Museveni's National Resistance Army (NRA). The soldiers—many were no more than 12–13 years of age—were stationed at roadblocks all around the city. Some of the roadblocks were semipermanent; however, some would be impromptu affairs thrown up by a squad of drunk adolescent soldiers intent on looting or worse. As the drinking increased, gunfights would break out between the woefully underarmed police and the soldiers or between individual soldiers. On my first week in the city, at 7 p.m. in the evening, a firefight broke out between two soldiers at a residence near that of the then vice–president of the country. Both were drunk and in a jealous rage over a woman. Their indiscriminate shooting ended with one of them being shot. He was left in the roadway until after curfew the next morning. This was common throughout the civil war and unfortunately continued for a time after Museveni's NRA rebels took control of the city. A particular problem, which is unfortunately common to several conflict zones, is the use of orphaned adolescents as soldiers. In Uganda, they were called *Kadogo soldiers* (Muhumuza, 1995). *Kadogo* is a Swahili word meaning "little one." The tragedy of these young soldiers aside, at roadblocks, they were often the most dangerous and unstable element. The teenaged Kadogos were drunk, drugged, and hardened killers. Their reactions could be unpredictable and often lethal—more than one hapless traveler was shot at a roadblock manned by these child soldiers because the driver made a sudden move or argued or someone in the vehicle did so.

FIGURE 5.1   A Khat dealer in souk (marketplace) in San'a, Yemen showing a customer the day's freshest-cut leaves. (Photo by the author, September 2010.)

Likewise, in Yemen, the widespread use of the drug khat—combined with the dangerous environment—can result in dangerous consequences. Khat leaves contain a natural psychoactive substance that is amphetamine-like in its effect and very potent when the leaves are fresh (Figure 5.1). It is addictive, and khat chewers can become short tempered and irritable as the night progresses.

Roadblocks in Sana'a to or from the airport and around key parts of the city are regularly manned by soldiers who chew khat to stay awake and alert. When tensions within the capital are high, as they usually are, a soldier overly stimulated with wads of khat and an itchy trigger finger can spell trouble. The use of this drug is endemic throughout Yemen as well as East Africa, Ethiopia and Eritrea, and parts of Saudi Arabia.

BROKEN WINDOWS

"You know my method," declared Sherlock Holmes to Dr. Watson. "It is founded on the observation of trifles." Sir Conan Doyle's thoughts about deductive reasoning are woven throughout his stories featuring the great fictional detective. The premise of this kind of reasoning, when applied to personal security, is to observe one's environment and reason backward to a logical conclusion about meaning. Applied to the broken windows theory first introduced by James Q. Wilson and George L. Kelling in March 1982, it provides you with early indicators and warnings of a dangerous environment. Wilson and Kelling explained it this way: "Consider a building with a few broken windows. If the windows are not repaired, the tendency is for vandals to break a few more windows. Eventually, they may even break into the building and, if it is unoccupied, perhaps become squatters or light fires inside. Or consider a pavement. Some litter accumulates. Soon, more litter accumulates. Eventually, people even start leaving bags of refuse from take-out restaurants there or even break into cars" (Kelling, 1982). The broken windows theory is a criminological theory of the norm-setting and norm-signaling effects of urban disorder and vandalism on additional crime and antisocial behavior. The theory states that maintaining and monitoring urban environments to prevent small crimes such as vandalism, public drinking, and toll jumping help to create an atmosphere of order and lawfulness, thereby preventing more serious crimes from happening.

As applied to personal security, it is—as astutely pointed out by Mr. Holmes—a method of observing the trifles and arriving at logical conclusions about the security of your environment as you move through it. While law enforcement and physical security philosophies are forward looking and focused on fixing the broken environment in order to improve security, personal security philosophy dictates a backward-looking approach to make reasoned deductions on the broken environment vis-à-vis potential threat and risk. A neighborhood that exhibits neglect is sending you a message. The abandoned home on the corner with broken windows and a door off of its hinges is telling you that there are vandals, vagrants, squatters, and thieves in the neighborhood seeking shelter for nothing and lacking respect for boundaries and ownership. Most criminal actors are willing to shift from property crime to personal crime in an instant. Vacant, boarded-up businesses signal the absence of economic activity or one where the risk of crime outweighed the benefit of trade. Viable economic activity is the sign of a healthy environment. Absence of it is a big warning indicator. Gang graffiti spray painted on stop signs, schools, mailboxes, and other institutional fixtures indicates the presence of an organized street criminal element marking out their turf. They are setting criminal boundaries and, by extension, mean to enforce those boundaries with violence. In most instances, these clues cumulatively add up to indicators that the environment that you find yourself in is unsafe and of high risk.

It is important to understand that what might constitute a broken window environment in one culture does not necessarily apply to another. In many peaceful third-world environments, the first impression can be that one has arrived in an overcrowded city with a collection of broken-down hovels, potholed roads, and open-air markets. Typically, the key element to look for in this instance is the presence or the absence of open markets and a vibrant sense of trade and traffic. Conversely, in the third world, a key indicator of a deteriorating security (and political) environment is the increase in street prostitution coupled with very young children begging for money or food or the recent release into the general population of individuals kept in mental health institutions. The latter case was an ominous precursor to the plunge into civil war and chaos that I witnessed firsthand in Liberia in the early 1990s. Liberian President Samuel Doe released hundreds of mental health patients onto the streets of Monrovia during his tenure as a president. A society that cannot sustain a healthy economy and look out for its citizens is one that is on the road to disintegration and collapse.

Gangs and Gang Activity

Gangs may consist of a few individuals with little organization who commit minor crimes to highly organized groups with numerous members involved in sophisticated transnational crimes and criminal enterprise. Gangs form for many different reasons—including profit through criminal activity, territorial claims, protection, culture, or community history. Being able to recognize and distinguish gang graffiti from simple street art, understanding what gang it is attributed to, or recognizing and marking gang tattoos and their significance is a valuable skill to develop as part of a personal security plan. You may find yourself in a taxi or a rickshaw in the developing world, and being able to take mental note of the tattoo on your driver's hand or the scrawled gang symbology on a crumbling ghetto wall can potentially give you an advance warning of whose territory you are traversing and the gang member taking your taxi down a detour that you did not anticipate or want.

The gangs that commit most quality-of-life crimes that affect communities and neighborhoods are criminal street gangs. The criminal street gangs are often organized through a structure of subgroups known as sets or cliques. Their formation is sometimes based on the characteristics of more national or internationally recognized gangs whose perceived notoriety makes them appealing for copying. These local gangs are usually not directly associated with the nationally recognized gangs but are highly influenced by them. They often adopt derivatives of their names and use their indicators such as hand signs, symbols, colors, and graffiti. There are also some local street gangs who form with very little to no influence from nationally recognized gangs and develop their own characteristics and indicators.

To a gang, graffiti serves to establish its presence, to establish its turf or territory, to warn of impending danger or threats, and to put down rival gangs or issue a challenge. The gang language includes the use of numbers as symbols or numbers that correspond to letters of the alphabet. It provides a kind of shorthand or code for gangs.

The following are 23 criminal gangs (13 international and 10 national/ US centric), including the countries, the cities, and the big city districts in which they operate that could potentially present a threat to you:

1. *Gang name:* The Mungiki
   Gang type: Street gang/national
   Location: Kenya
   Description: Operating in the Mathare, Kayole, Murang'a district, and Ruai slums of Nairobi, the Mungiki is extremely violent gang syndicate that stands strong at about 100,000 members. Every resident of the slum pays a variable sum of money to the organization, in exchange for protection against theft and property damage. In addition, the gang mans public toilets and charges a fee for use of the facilities. In the past, its members have been known for their signature dreadlocks and a practice of bathing in blood. More recently though, they have been associated with numerous beheadings and forced female circumcisions as they assert themselves in the political arena.
   Gang identifiers/signs/symbols: Unlike most gangs who identify themselves by either clothes or body markings, the Mungiki have opted for something a little more representative of their ideals—a severed human head on a stick.

2. *Gang name:* Mara Salvatrucha (MS-13)
   Gang type: Street gang/national
   Location: North and Central America
   Description: MS-13 is considered one of the most violent gangs in the world. It was started in California in the 1980s when a group of Salvadorians fled the civil war in their country. Since then, it has grown to over 70,000 members with operations throughout North and Central America. Members of MS-13 distinguish themselves by tattoos covering the body and often the face, as well as the use of their own sign language. They are notorious for their use of violence and a subcultural moral code that predominantly consists of merciless revenge and cruel retributions. They have been known for acts of extreme and unprovoked violence, which often include gruesome dismemberments, even against women and children.
   Gang identifiers/signs/symbols: MS13, MSX3, Mara Salvatrucha, Devil's pitchfork, Muerte Santika, M hand symbol, Locos Salvatruchos

3. *Gang name:* Russian mob/Russian mafia/Solntsevskaya Bratva
   Gang type: Transnational crime syndicate
   Location: Russia; Ukraine; Hungary; Czech Republic; United States; Israel; United Kingdom; France; Benelux; Spain; South Africa; and other parts of Europe, Africa, and Australia
   Description: The Solntsevskaya Bratva, also known as the *Solntsevskaya Brotherhood*, is usually considered to be the largest faction of the collection of loosely organized crime syndicates known as the *Russian mafia*. Russian mafia groups sit on the other side of the organizational spectrum from Yakuza. Their structure, according to Frederico Varese, a professor of criminology at the University of Oxford and an expert on international organized crime, is highly decentralized. The group is composed of 10 separate quasi-autonomous brigades that operate more or less independently of each other. The group does pool its resources, however, and the money is overseen by a 12-person council that meets regularly in different parts of the world, often disguising their meetings as festive occasions (Matthews, 2014). Widely known for their practice of killing not only their rivals but also all their associated family members, the Russian Mafia brings new meaning to the word *cold-blooded*. Their reach is global, and if you ever want to do business in Russia, you can be assured that at least 20% of your company's profits will end up in their pockets if you value the lives of your family members.

   Actual information available about the Solntsevskaya Bratva is limited. What is known, however, is that the group's leader and founder, Sergei "Mikhas" Mikhailov, fashions himself more as a businessman than a mafioso. It is believed that the group controls hundreds of legitimate businesses throughout Russia and beyond. However, despite being involved heavily in legitimate business, the Solntsevskaya Bratva have no qualms about using murder and violence to achieve business ends and eliminate competitors.

   The Solntsevskaya Bratva are also involved in virtually every aspect of the Russian underworld and operate criminal rackets running the gamut of traditional mafia activities, such as prostitution, extortion, bribery and blackmail, credit card fraud, human trafficking, arms dealing, stock fraud, money laundering, and even online scams and hacking.

   The influence and the power of the Solntsevskaya Bratva extend well beyond Russia's borders. This gang has powerful influence in the United States as well, particularly in Chicago, San Francisco, Miami, Grand Rapids, and New York.

Gang identifiers/signs/symbols: There is a very strong and storied culture of tattoos used in Russian criminal gangs that dates back at least 200 years if not longer. In the 1930s, Russian criminal castes began to emerge, such as the Masti (suits) and the Vory v Zakone or Blatnye (authoritative thieves) and with that a tattoo culture to define rank and reputation (Wikipedia, 2016). The following are some of the more common Russian criminal tattoos:

a. *Stars*— Stars indicate an authority. It is placed on the shoulders or the knees ("I kneel to no one"). The eight-pointed star denotes rank as thief in law depending on where it is placed.

b. *Cat*—The cat is a traditional sign of a thief, often with a hat (from *Puss in Boots*). The abbreviation KOT stands for "native prison resident," or often the letters K, O, and T (kot; cat) indicate a chronic prison inmate.

c. *Lenin or Stalin*— Lenin or Stalin is often tattooed on the chest, partly from a belief that a firing squad would never follow orders to shoot such an image.

d. *Orthodox Church*—The Orthodox Church indicates a thief; usually a chest tattoo, with the number of cupolas indicating the number of convictions.

e. *Suns*—Rays can be used to indicate number and length of sentences served.

f. *Skull*—A skull indicates a murderer. Following the abolition of the death sentence for murder in 1947, the number of murders rose significantly, with an extra 10-year sentence being no deterrent to prisoners already sentenced to life.

g. *Cross*—The traditional thieves' cross is usually tattooed on the chest. This was very common.

h. *Ships*—With full sails, ships can indicate someone that has fled from custody, a gulnoy or a gulat, or that a wearer is a nomadic thief who travels to steal.

i. *Dragons*—Dragons indicate a shark or someone who has stolen state or collectively owned property.

j. *Spider*—When facing up, the spider denotes an active criminal; facing down, it denotes one who has left the lifestyle.

k. *Medals*—Medals can indicate rank or, if done in pre-Soviet style, contempt for authority.

l. *Eagle*—An eagle traditionally indicated a senior authority figure; if the eagle is carrying someone, it can indicate a rapist.

m. *Hooded executioner*—A hooded executioner indicates a prisoner who has murdered a relative.

n. *Bells*—Bells can indicate a long sentence with no chance of early release, a long sentence served without parole for being uncooperative to the authorities, or, if on the right shoulder, it can indicate a thief who stole from church.

o. *Images of the Madonna with Child*—Images of the Madonna with Child (St. Mary and the infant Jesus Christ) mean "prison is my home" and act as a talisman or a criminal lifestyle from a young age.

p. *Eyes*—When on the stomach, they indicate that the owner is gay, or when on the chest, they can indicate that they are watching over you. When on the buttocks, they can indicate a passive homosexual.

q. *Circled A*—A circled A (done in the style of a finger ring) indicates an anarchist.

r. *Circle with a dot inside* (as finger ring) known as the *roundstone*—A roundstone indicates an orphan or the saying "Trust only yourself" (Figure 5.2).

s. *Skull inside a square* (as finger ring)—A skull inside a square indicates a conviction for robbery.

t. *Quincunx*—A quincunx indicates one who has done extensive time, from the saying "the four walls and I" or "four guard towers and me" (четыре вышки и я, chetyre vyshki i ya).

u. *Snake entwined with a woman*—A snake entwined with a woman indicates a passive homosexual, especially if tattooed on the back. It is often a forced tattoo.

v. *Forced tattoos*—There are tattoos that are forcibly applied to signify demotion such as informer or conviction of sexual crimes. Someone with a forced tattoo has been expelled from the thieve society, in the Russian criminal hierarchy.

  i. "Informer" (ssuchenye).
  ii. "Enemy of the People" ("ВРАГ НАРОДА").
  iii. "Kulak" ("Кулак").
  iv. "I am a Bitch" ("сука").
  v. Beauty marks or dots on the forehead indicate a bitch who has sided with the prison authorities. Tattoos beneath the eyes indicate a passive homosexual and, by the mouth, indicate a passive partaker in oral sex. On the chin, they indicate a rat who steals from other prisoners. Red card suits, diamonds and hearts, on the back indicate a passive homosexual.

4. *Gang name:* Los Zetas
   Gang type: Transnational criminal organization (TCO)
   Location: Mexico—Tamaulipas, Nuevo Leon, Coahuila, Veracruz, Tabasco, Campeche, Yucatan, Quintana Roo, San Luis Potosi,

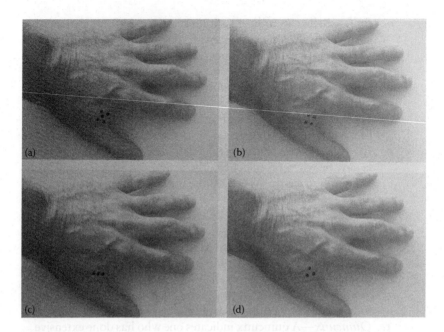

FIGURE 5.2 Dot tattoos are one of the most common recognition symbols used among cultures or the criminal underworld internationally. (a) The five-dot tattoo is known as the *quincunx* and has been used as a recognition symbol in gypsy culture or for a criminal's time spent in prison (four dots are the four walls of prison, with individual in the center). (b) The four-dot tattoo can signify blood in, blood out by gang members and is used by the Norteños (Nuestra Familia) Hispanic prison gang. (d) A three-dot triangle has many meanings. Sailors completing their first voyage often get it—it is termed *hobo dots*. In Latino gangs, it means *mi vida loca* ("my crazy life"). Among Asian gangs, it means "I need nothing." In German prisons, it means "know nothing, see nothing, hear nothing" (variant in Southern Turkish tribes is "hear nothing, see nothing, tell nothing); in Greece, it is a signal of an adherent to anarchist beliefs and ideals. (c) Three dots in a row are used by the Sureños Latino gang—each dot respectively stands for SUR. (Photo by the author.)

> Chiapas, Puebla, Tlaxcala, Hidalgo, Queretaro, Chihuahua, Guerrero, Oaxaca, Guanajuato, Zacatecas, Aguascalientes, and Michoacan; State of Mexico; United States; and Guatemala
> *Description:* Los Zetas is a Mexican criminal syndicate, considered by the US government to be "the most technologically advanced, sophisticated, powerful, ruthlessly violent, and dangerous cartel operating in Mexico." Their brutal tactics, which include beheadings to terrorize their rivals and intimidate

them, torture, and indiscriminate slaughter, show that they often prefer brutality over bribery. Los Zetas are Mexico's largest drug cartel in terms of geographical presence, overtaking their rivals, the Sinaloa Cartel. Los Zetas also operate through protection rackets, assassinations, extortion, kidnappings, and other activities. The organization is based in Nuevo Laredo, Tamaulipas, directly across the border from Laredo, Texas. As of December 2015, Los Zetas has begun identifying itself as *Cartel del Norte*, which translates to "cartel of the north."

Gang identifiers/signs/symbols: Z, Z 100%, Santa Muerte (saint of death), military tattoos, firearm tattoos (pistols or crossed automatic rifles), logos, or stickers on vehicle window such as Ferrari logo and John Deere tractor logo

5. *Gang name:* 18th Street gang
   Gang type: TCO
   Location: Central America, United States, Mexico, and Spain
   Description: The 18th Street gang, also known as Calle 18, Barrio 18, La18, or Mara-18 in Central America, is a multiethnic TCO that started as a street gang in the Rampart area of Los Angeles, California. It has been said that on average, every day, someone in Los Angeles County is assaulted by an 18th Street gang member. Although they are rivals with the Bloods (no. 9), Crips (no. 23), and MS13 (no. 2), over the last 10 years, the 18th Street gang has racked up a kill count over three times as high as any of their rivals.

   Gang identifiers/signs/symbols: the color blue, 18, 18th St, 10 5 3, XV3, XVIII, and Diez y Ocho

6. *Gang name:* The Triads
   Gang type: TCO
   Location: China, Hong Kong, Macau, Taiwan, Vietnam, Korea, Japan, Thailand, Malaysia, Philippines, Indonesia, Singapore, United States, Canada, Australia, New Zealand, United Kingdom, France, Spain, Netherlands, Belgium, South Africa, and Russia
   Description: The Triads is a massive Chinese crime syndicate, which can trace its beginnings to the seventeeth century, that is actually a conglomerate of gangs that has over 2.5 million members all over the world. While each branch has its own customs and practices, the Triads as a whole are known for their very organized structure and intense, bloody rituals. Triads currently engage in a variety of crimes from extortion and money laundering to trafficking and prostitution. They also are involved in smuggling and counterfeiting goods such as music, video,

and software as well as more tangible goods such as clothes, watches, and money.

Gang identifiers/signs/symbols: Highly elaborate, stylized Chinese characters and triangles incorporating mythic animals such as dragons or phoenix and tigers. Triads also use an elaborate hand signal communication protocol for entry into secret meetings or sites or as recognition.

7. *Gang name:* Camorra

   Gang type: TCO

   Location: Italy, United States, Canada, South America, Australia, and parts of Europe

   Description: The Camorra is an extremely influential and violent faction of the Italian mafia. While the Camorra members do not have a centralized leadership, this only makes them more robust. The Camorra is believed to be a loose affiliation of around 111 Camorra clans, which, in total, have over 6700 members.

   Leading Italian mafia expert and investigative journalist Roberto Saviano believes that the Camorra members are the most influential faction of the Italian mafia, based on their numbers, level of influence, economic power, and the level of violence that they use in pursuit of their goals. In addition to their criminal activities, they also control a large number of legitimate businesses throughout Italy.

   While the Camorra members are involved in virtually every type of criminal activity imaginable, they are especially notorious among locals for their extortion of local businesses. The price of not paying is often arson or death. Because of their use of bribery and violence to influence local politicians and law enforcement, Camorra clans can wield tremendous influence over the areas that they control.

   Gang identifiers/signs/symbols: Tattoos of ace of clubs, gun, knife/knives, knuckledusters, rosary with flaming heart, crown of thorns, heart pierced by knife, skull, Rolex watch or Rolex Crown tattoo, "Bodo," "Non toccare la mia famiglia" (Do not touch my family), "Rispetto, lealtà, onore" (Respect, loyalty, honor), and crossed pistols

8. *Gang name:* Yakuza

   Gang type: TCO

   Location: Japan, United States, and Korea

   Description: Yakuza is a blanket term for Japan's organized crime groups: the country's mafia. They were traditionally federations of gamblers and street merchants, but while the yakuza like to tout their history as going back hundreds of years, the oldest continuous group is, as author Kazuhiko Murakami estimates, probably the Aizukotetsu-kai, in Kyoto, founded in the 1870s.

While many yakuza groups started as loosely run gambling associations, they really came into their own in the chaos after World War II, first running the black markets, providing gambling, and entertainment—even managing some of Japan's top postwar stars and singers—before moving into construction and real estate and engaging in extortion, blackmail, and fraud (Adelstein, 2015).

Members of this Japanese gang are required to cut all ties with their family and pledge complete loyalty to their gang boss. In Western media, a practice often associated with the yakuza has been *yubitsume*, or the cutting off one's finger as an act of apology. This practice is actually so prevalent that when four-fingered British cartoons such as *Postman Pat* were introduced in Japan, the government considered adding an extra finger to avoid scaring little kids.

Gang identifiers/signs/symbols: Koi, cherry blossom flowers, red flower with black and white flaming, dragon, angry hangman, eagle, and geisha (among other highly stylized themes)— distinctive full-body or half-body suit tattoo

9. *Gang name:* Agberos (Area Boys)
   Gang type: Street gang/national
   Location: Nigeria
   Description: Agberos is a loosely organized group of teenagers and abandoned youth that roam the streets of Lagos, Nigeria, that has been known for its practices of extortion and drug violence. Although not nearly as ruthless or well organized as many other gangs on this list, they are still widely feared for their seemingly unprovoked attacks on innocent bystanders, and as their members age, they will likely become a much more sophisticate criminal organization. Their coercive and persuasive requests, petty crimes, and sometimes violent offences by the so-called *area boys* to acquire resources, generally cash in the urban main business and crowded areas, have disturbed the civil society and defied the civic authority.
   Gang identifiers/signs/symbols: Some have stars, teardrop tattoos, and crosses

10. *Gang name:* Wah Ching
    Gang type: Transnational criminal gang
    Location: United States, Hong Kong (China)
    Description: Wah Ching is a Chinese American triad society (secret society) and street gang also known as *Dub C* originating

in San Francisco, California, during the early 1960s. At the time, Wah Ching was organized into one enormous gang. Wah Ching controlled most of the criminal vices throughout the San Francisco and Los Angeles Asian American communities. Wah Ching members' clothing ranges from casual to business attire, making it hard for officials to distinguish them from other citizens. Although the origins of this international gang are disputed, there is one thing that is for sure—they are good at making money. Although they have been known to resort to extreme violence, they typically only use it as a means to an end. Most of their operations are focused around money laundering and financial crimes in Los Angeles and eastern Asia.

Gang identifiers/signs/symbols: Marks; scars; cigarette burns; three, five, and nine dots; quarter burns; cross burns; scratch marks; slash marks; coining; "TTTT"; animal tattoos; and teardrops

11. *Gang name:* United Bamboo (Zhu Lien Bang)
    Gang type: TCO
    Location: Taiwan, United States, Australia, and Europe
    Description: United Bamboo is a Taiwanese gang consisting of around 10,000 ethnic Chinese gang members and their associates. The United Bamboo gang began as an assassination machine backed by Beijing during the Communist takeover of China. They used violent tactics in order to silence dissidents, although their violence is now being plied for human trafficking activities, extortion, illegal prostitution and gambling, and drug smuggling. While they are based out of Taiwan, they have influence throughout the Pacific Rim, having notoriously murdered journalists as distant as California.
    Gang identifiers/signs/symbols: N/A

12. *Gang name:* Primeiro Comando da Capital (PCC)
    Gang type: Transnational criminal/prison gang
    Location: Brazil, Paraguay, and Bolivia
    Description: Found throughout the Sao Paolo prison system in Brazil as well as its numerous favelas (slums), the Primeiro Comando da Capital (PCC) gang is known for kidnapping, extortion, and its ability to instill fear. In May 2006, it managed to put the entire city of Sao Paolo under siege for almost a week while gang members brutally killed police officers and burned government buildings. Even though no more attacks have happened, police reports point out that behind the scenes, PCC is getting stronger and bigger. They are already operating in almost every Brazilian state and commanding minor gangs in those places. International activity, in other countries of South America, is also taking place.

Gang identifiers/signs/symbols: Chinese taititu (yin yang) symbol

13. *Gang name:* Jamaican Posses

    Gang type: International criminal gang

    Location: Jamaica, United Kingdom, United States, and Canada

    Description: Known to have an affinity for high-powered assault rifles, the Jamaican Posses (also, there is the Jamaican Shower Posse that is connected to the Jamaican Labor Party) is a loose affiliation of Jamaican gangs that are well connected in the island's government and heavily feared for its practice of ritualized killing that often involves laundry irons, butchers knives, and even vacuum cleaners. In the United Kingdom, these gang members are referred to as *Yardies* and are principally found in the Greater London neighborhoods of Brixton, Harlesden, Tottenham, and Hackney. The posses are violent drug trafficking crews, with an affinity for violence and killing.

    Gang identifiers/signs/symbols: Different ghetto neighborhoods within Kingston, called *garrisons*, are identified by graffiti with names such as Egypt, Mexico, Angola, and Gaza.

The following are US gangs with transnational ties:

1. *Gang name:* Crips

   Gang type: Street gang/national

   Location: United States

   Description: The Crips are a primarily African American gang. They were founded in Los Angeles, California, in 1969. What was once a single alliance between two autonomous gangs is now a loosely connected network of individual sets, often engaged in open warfare with one another. Its members traditionally wear blue clothing, a practice that has waned somewhat due to police crackdowns on gang members. The Crips is one of the largest and most violent associations of street gangs in the United States, with an estimated 30,000–35,000 members. It has been involved in murders, robberies, and drug dealing, among other crimes. They are bitter rivals with both the Bloods and numerous Latino street gangs. The Crips are known for wearing the color blue and carrying out extreme acts of violence.

   Gang identifiers/signs/symbols: The color blue, Crip, Locs, cuz, C hand sign, pitch fork up, three-point crown, six-point star, 6, and 3

2. *Gang name:* Aryan Brotherhood (Brand, AB)

   Gang type: Prison gang/organized crime syndicate/national

   Location: United States

Description: The AB is responsible for roughly one-fourth of prison murders in the United States; if you want to be a member of this gang, you must kill or assault a fellow prisoner. It is a practice known as *blood in, blood out,* so anyone who tries to leave the gang usually ends up dead or in the hospital as well. The AB has focused on the economic activities typical of organized crime entities, particularly drug trafficking, extortion, inmate prostitution, and murder for hire.

    Gang identifiers/signs/symbols: ABT (Aryan Brotherhood of Texas), TAB (Texas Aryan Brotherhood), I, II, XXX (Straightedge Extreme Skinhead), HH (Heil Hitler), swastika, double lightning bolts, and shield with sword

3. *Gang name:* La Nuestra Familia
   Gang type: Prison gang/regional
   Location: Northern California
   Description: La Nuestra Familia (Spanish for "our family") is a criminal organization of Mexican American (Chicano) prison gangs with origins in Northern California. While members of the Norteños gang are considered to be affiliated with Nuestra Familia, being a member of Nuestra Familia itself does not signify association as a Norteño. Some law enforcement agents speculate that the Nuestra Familia gang, which operates in and out of prisons, influences much of the criminal activity of thousands of Norteño gang members in California. The gang's main sources of income are distributing cocaine, heroin, marijuana, and methamphetamine within prison systems as well as in the community and extorting drug distributors on the streets. In fact, La Nuestra Familia is said to have started when a member of La eMe stole a fellow Latino's pair of shoes. This gang is known for requiring extremely strict allegiance, and it takes over two years to be fully initiated. Once you are in, though, there is no turning back.
   Gang identifiers/signs/symbols: Red bandannas, 14, XIV, and N, sombrero with machetes, and four-dot tattoo, meaning "blood in, blood out"

4. *Gang name:* Latin Kings
   Gang type: Street/prison gang
   Location: United States nationwide, in predominately Latino neighborhoods in US cities, Puerto Rico, Canada, Peru, Mexico, Spain, and Cuba
   Description: Widely considered to be one of the best organized Latin gangs in the world, the Kings have a highly detailed constitution that includes traces of Marxism, Confucianism, and Christianity. Although they are not as violent as many of the

other gangs on this list, they do engage in a fair share of illegal moneymaking activities including contract killings.

Gang identifiers/signs/symbols: Black and gold/something red, ALKN (Almighty Latin King Nation), ALQKN Almighty Latin King and Queen Nation, LK (Last Kings), pitch fork down, five-point crown, Amor de Rey, ADR (amor de rey/king kove), five-point crown or star, pitch fork down, 5, and Kingmaster-ALKN

5. *Gang name:* Mexican mafia
   Gang type: Prison gang
   Location: US federal prisons and California state prisons
   Description: The Mexican mafia is a loose ally of the Aryan Brotherhood; it is a West Coast prison gang that is known to be heavily involved in the business of drug trafficking. The Mexican mafia is also known as *La eMe* (Spanish for "the M"). Despite its name, the Mexican mafia did not originate in Mexico and is entirely a US criminal prison organization. Sureños, including MS-13 and Florencia 13, use the number 13 to show allegiance to the Mexican mafia. M is the 13th letter of the alphabet. Law enforcement officials report that La eMe is the most powerful gang within the California prison system. Government officials state that there are currently 155–300 official members of the Mexican mafia with around 990 associates who assist La eMe in carrying out its illegal activities in the hopes of becoming full members.

   Gang identifiers/signs/symbols: EME (*E* backward), M, Mano Negra, Black Hand of Death, La eMe, and M&M

6. *Gang name:* Black Guerilla Family
   Gang type: Prison gang
   Location: United States
   Description: A very politically motivated organization, one of the Black Guerrilla Family's objectives upon being founded in 1966 was to overthrow the US government. They have numerous allies on both coasts including the Crips and the Bloods. Their main rivals, however, are the Aryan Brotherhood and the Mexican Mafia.

   Gang identifiers/signs/symbols: Crossed sabers; machetes; rifles; shotguns with the letters "B G F" or the numbers "2.7.6.;" and black dragon

7. *Gang name:* Almighty Black P. Stone Nation
   Gang type: Street gang
   Location: Chicago-based/United States
   Description: A Chicago street gang with heavy Islamic influences. Its leader, Abdullah-Malik (born Jeff Fort) actually had ties to Muammar Gaddafi and had met with him on several

occasions. Although they were not known specifically for violence, they have often been targeted by the Federal Bureau of Investigation due to their high-profile activities. Considered by law enforcement authorities to be Chicago's most powerful and sophisticated street gang, the Black P. Stone Nation (BPSN) finances itself through a wide array of criminal activities and is part of the large Chicago gang alliance known as the People Nation. The BPSN originated and is based on the south side of Chicago in the Woodlawn neighborhood. As of today, the gang has a strong presence in northwest Indiana communities of Gary and Merrillville with a growing presence in Portage, the northern area of Crown Point, as well as the western area of Hobart.

Gang identifiers/signs/symbols: five-point star, pyramid, eye, crescents, initials BPS, and number 7 (7 = G for God/Allah)

8. *Gang name:* Hells Angels

Gang type: Transnational outlaw motorcycle gang

Location: Worldwide (425 charters in 50 countries)

Description: With an extensive international reach, this biker gang is well known for its ruthlessness. It should also be noted that while most mafia groups or criminal organizations engage in illegal activities with the objective of turning a profit, Hells Angels reverses that notion. They believe that violence and lawlessness are an inherent part of living the life, and any money made of their activities should simply be used to perpetuate that lifestyle. They are a "one-percenter" motorcycle club whose members typically ride Harley-Davidson motorcycles. The organization is considered an organized crime syndicate by the US Department of Justice. In the United States and Canada, the Hells Angels are actually incorporated as the Hells Angels Motorcycle Corporation.

Gang identifiers/signs/symbols: H. A., red and white, and 81, winged death's head, Support 81, Route 81, 1%, AFFA (Angels Forever; Forever Angels), and Filthy Few

9. *Gang name:* Bloods

Gang type: Street gang/national

Location: United States and Canada

Description: Known for wearing the color red and their intense rivalry with the Crips, the Bloods were originally a set or faction of the Crips. After breaking off, they were outnumbered 3:1, which caused them to resort to extreme acts of violence for which they are still known today.

Gang identifiers/signs/symbols: five-point star or crown, 5, and pitchfork down

10. *Gang name:* Texas Syndicate
    Gang type: Prison gang
    Location: Texas-based/United States
    Description: A relatively smaller gang with few allies, the Texas
    Syndicate is not to be underestimated. Unlike other Hispanic
    gangs, it is closely allied with Mexican immigrant prisoners.
    One of the gangs that it is allied with, however, is Los Zetas,
    and the syndicate has been known, along with MS-13, for car-
    rying out many of the Zeta's contract killings within the United
    States.

    Gang identifiers/signs/symbols: no gang color, TS, S super-
    imposed over a T, longhorn symbol, longhorn head, "ESE TE"
    (Spanish for "TS"), and 20 19 = T S

NATURAL DISASTERS

Natural disasters such as hurricanes, tornadoes, earthquakes, or other
natural hazards can severely disrupt the physical and social environments of communities. While at first blush, these kinds of disasters
appear to bring utter chaos, tragedy, and disorder, a closer look at the
rise and the decay of these kinds of events reveals predictable patterns
that, if understood in context, are very useful for the development of
personal security planning. Studies show that crimes of different types
occur at (roughly) five different stages of a disaster event, coinciding
with the development of different kinds of vulnerabilities corresponding
to each stage of the event (Thornton, and Voigt, 2010).

While this is a useful model for analyzing the dynamics of hazard
events and cascading threat events that follow, it is not as applicable
to some disasters as others. This model presupposes that crime(s) will
occur if three key elements converge in time and space: the availability
of suitable targets (i.e., property to steal or individuals to victimize),
the absence of capable guardians (police, neighbors, or technologies of
surveillance), and the presence of motivated threat actors (Cohen and
Felson, 1979). A disaster event changes local routine behaviors and
increases the likelihood that motivated offenders will identify suitable
targets in the absence of capable guardianship. Vacated (or insufficiently
guarded) residential and commercial properties represent suitable targets. With this assumption in mind, five distinct phases unfold during
a disaster event. These phases and the unique vulnerabilities that they
create (opportunities for criminal actors) are as follows (Kuo, 2012):

1. Warning phase: The warning phase, depending on the disaster event, can provide advance notice to individuals potentially

impacted by a storm or an event that is minutes, days, or even a week in advance. For instance, hurricane-tracking models provide days of advance notice of a storm's track, velocity, and landfall. On the other hand, a tsunami warning may only provide hours of notice, and a tornado, only minutes before impact. While early warning can result in an orderly evacuation of homes and businesses from a community, it also provides advance intelligence to potential threat actors of unoccupied businesses or residences. The type of crime that can be expected to occur in this phase, particularly if there is insufficient law enforcement response available, is residential or business burglary. If you happen to be in the position of remaining behind, the risk of you encountering someone breaking into your location can go up.

2. Impact phase: The impact phase describes the actual event itself. The event can range from seconds or minutes in duration (earthquakes or tornadoes), to hours or days (hurricanes, wildfires, volcano eruptions, floods). In either case, law enforcement response capability is usually handicapped because they are themselves sheltering from the event, and the initial shock of the impact knocks out communications, roads/transportation, or lighting—all things necessary for law enforcement to act effectively. Any time that an effective law enforcement response is incapacitated and an opportunity presents itself, capable threat actors will exploit the vulnerability. The type of crime that can be expected to occur in this phase is armed robbery and looting. This can include forced breaking and entering into hotel rooms, homes, or businesses.

3. Emergency phase: The emergency phase can overlap with the impact phase, depending on the event type. For example, in a hurricane or a flood, both impact and emergency responses can occur depending on fluctuations in the intensity of the event. In a tornado or a tsunami, the two phases are necessarily distinct from each other given the nature of the event. In this phase, local, state, and federal response authorities can be disorganized and fully engaged in responding to life-threatening emergencies. Law enforcement response, although less incapacitated in terms of mobility, is ineffective due to lack of resources. Armed robbery and looting remain viable types of crime in this phase, as well as a rise in sexual assaults (usually of women) and cyberlooting and—depending on the emergency—the rise of sham relief organizations on hastily activated websites.

4. Recovery phase: This can be a uniquely dangerous time following a disaster event. In this phase, depending on the scope and

the type of disaster, housing projects can be left abandoned for days and temporary housing sites go up to accommodate survivors, temporary workers, volunteers, and day laborers. The types of crime that accompany this phase include the prevalence of sexual assault, armed robbery and murder, burglary, and home invasion. Also, depending on the country that you are in, there will be an increased level of food insecurity and the desperation that accompanies this condition as the social fabric of an environment that lives hand to mouth in the best of times quickly unravels (this becomes even more acute if the international response is delayed or muted). As recovery response delays lengthen, individuals who are usually not given to criminal behavior can resort to violence in order to get the resources that they need for their families or themselves. Individuals acting under these circumstances can be particularly unstable and dangerous.

In Thailand and Sri Lanka following the tsunami of 2004, the security during this phase deteriorated drastically. Rapes increased dramatically in the refugee camps, and organized criminal groups exploiting the chaos of the disaster used the opportunity to abduct and sell children and vulnerable women into human trafficking networks. Bands of thieves roved the communities most affected, stealing jewelry off of corpses, as well as targeting residences, resort cottages, and hotel rooms.

In Haiti, following the earthquake of 2010, over 4500 hardened criminals escaped from the island's main penitentiary. Gangs of these former prisoners terrorized neighborhoods and temporary settlement camps, charging in with machetes to steal food and water. They held up sidewalk vendors at knife or gunpoint and gunned down unfortunates who encountered them— just for small amounts of cash.

5. Reconstruction phase: In this phase, contracts are let for reconstruction and work. The rush to recover often brings with it unscrupulous contractors who take money in return for shoddy or incomplete work or no work at all, as well as false claims filed for relief and insurance funds.

A rule of thumb to remember is that in areas where the baseline of criminal violence or insecurity is high to begin with, the social consequences of the natural disaster are not unnatural in their consequences. Previously existing social inequities or fissures will only be exacerbated. Communities characterized by residential instability, low socioeconomic status, and poor collective efficacy (social networks that represent the willingness to participate in social control) have impaired capacity to informally control crime. Disaster events aggravate social conditions that cause social disorganization and crime. Natural disasters can fracture community cohesion, impairing a community's ability to respond to and sanction antisocial conduct or crime.

CIVIL DISORDER AND RIOTING

The events of the Arab Spring in 2011, the Occupy Movement in 2012, and Black Lives Matter and the violent riots in Ferguson, Missouri, and Baltimore, Maryland, all have one thing in common: a massive, angry upheaval of humanity on the street with an axe to grind. Whether it is a stampeding mob from a sporting event gone sideways or a mob led by an agitator with an agenda calculated to incite the masses to violence, getting caught in the middle of an angry, often panicked, and unstable herd of human beings can invoke feelings of sheer terror.

It is important to understand that civil disorder and rioting are not random acts of violence, but have their own dynamic and specific characteristics. They can be spontaneous events, such as a celebration riot that gets out of hand. This often happens in sports event riots; the causes can range from a team's victory, a defeat, a bar fight, or a sports promotion that gets out of control. They can also be protest riots, such as the Arab Spring, the recent street riots in Ferguson and Baltimore, or anarchist-driven anticapitalist/antiglobalist riots in European cities. These are people who gather to protest a political, a social, a cultural, or an economic issue.

Civil disorder events have distinguishable phases and patterns that signal what is about to happen and the direction that the event will take. It is very useful to know these in advance, should you find yourself entangled in one of these uprisings. Before the mob is born, there is a crowd. The first phase is crowd gathering. This can be a peaceful, almost festive stage where people casually gather to recognize a common cause: the victory of their team or a peaceful protest of some political issue. It can be lively, the chants can be provocative and noisy, but the crowd's behavior does not progress past this stage. There is no confrontation. If there is a preplanned route, the route is followed and no one deviates from this route.

If the crowd is not channeled and it grows, the potential for mob action grows with it. This is the second phase. If you are in the crowd when this occurs, there is a distinct feeling of aimlessness in the crowd; no one knows exactly where they are going. There is a lot of loitering without purpose. Chants are sporadic, not organized. Typically, this can be the calm before the storm.

The third stage is the shift from a crowd to a mob. A mob is distinctly different from the crowd, because it is motivated by anger, fear, and panic. Typically, two types of facilitators fire the crowd into a mob. There are social facilitators who focus the chants and give them passion, heat, and volume. One might remind the crowd of some overriding injustice, such as of an arrest or of a killing. Then, there are physical facilitators. In the antiglobalization riots in Europe for instance, these were hooded anarchists who pried up heavy paving stones and heaved them at the police line, striking the riot shields or even horses brought in by antiriot police. The police, as human as the unruly mob on the opposite side of the line, were as on edge as anyone. The difference is that they have batons, tear gas, water cannons, and guns. An agitated mob will, sooner or later, provoke an eruption of violence from the police side of the line. The chaos that ensues can be and often is lethal.

Depending on the nature of the mob and the discipline of the police forces brought in to quell the mob, the riot itself can be slow to grow and erupt into violence or it can be extremely rapid and disproportionate. The Soviets were infamous for responding to street unrest with tanks, and they did not hesitate to run over any hapless protestor standing in the way.

The following are some sensible measures that should be considered, to preempt and counter the threat of common street violence abroad:

- *Personal security training* for employees and executives traveling or relocating to a high-risk country or region on how to increase situational awareness, secure personal belongings and improve observation/assessment skills (street smarts): This kind of training mitigates the appearance of vulnerability, prosperity, or inattentiveness that can attract criminal threats on the street.
- *Training in both defensive and offensive (maneuver and escape) vehicle operation/driving* to build skill in recognizing potentially developing situations in advance and build confidence in how to handle the situation: This includes road trip/route planning and security measures.
- *Advance research for the traveler* to know routes from the airport to the hotel or to a restaurant and to plan travel on safer roads (such as toll roads) versus less-secure routes.
- A list of *emergency contact numbers* preprogrammed in mobile phones.
- Knowing what *activities, people, places, and situations to avoid*
- *Learning the language* to increase awareness of the verbal communications taking place around you and to comprehend street signs and locations: If language training is not possible,

a minimum knowledge of the location, the culture, and the key phrases to recognize as trouble indicators and to use when help is needed will provide a level of protection and comfort.

REFERENCES

Adelstein, J., "The Yakuza: Inside Japan's murky criminal underworld," *CNN*, http://www.cnn.com/2015/09/15/asia/yakuza-yamaguchi-gumi -explainer/ (December 16, 2015).

Cohen, L., and Felson, M., "Social change and crime rate trends: A routine activity approach," *American Sociological Review* 44(4) (1979), pp. 588–608.

Cook, P. J., and Moore, M. J., "Economic perspectives on reducing alcohol-related violence," *Alcohol and Interpersonal Violence*, NIAAA Research Monograph No. 24. NIH Pub. No. 93-3496, Rockville, MD: NIAAA (1993), pp. 193–212.

Dabbs, J. M., Jr., "Salivary testosterone and cortisol among late adolescent male offenders," *Journal of Abnormal Child Psychology* 19(4) (1991), pp. 469–478.

Gustafson, R., "Alcohol and aggression," *Journal of Offender Rehabilitation* 21(3/4) (1994), pp. 41–80.

Jessor, R., and Jessor, S. L., *Problem Behavior and Psychosocial Development*, New York: Academic Press (1977).

Kelling, G. L. and Wilson, J. Q., "Broken windows: The police and neighborhood safety," *Atlantic Monthly*, accessed February 15, 2016, http://www.theatlantic.com/magazine/archive/1982/03/broken -windows/304465/ (March 1982).

Kuo, S. S., "Not only injurious to individuals, but dangerous to the state: A theory of disaster crime," In M. Deflem (ed.) *Disasters, Hazards and Law* (*Sociology of Crime, Law and Deviance* 17), Bradford: Emerald Group Publishing Limited (2012), pp. 19–41.

Matthews, C., "Fortune 5: The biggest organized crime groups in the world," *Fortune Magazine*, http://fortune.com/2014/09/14/biggest -organized-crime-groups-in-the-world/ (September 14, 2014).

Miczek, K. A., "Alcohol, GABAA-benzodiazepine receptor complex, and aggression," In *Recent Developments in Alcoholism*, New York: Plenum Press 13 (1997), pp. 139–171.

Muhumuza, R., "A case study on reintegration of demobilized child soldiers in Uganda," Uganda: World Vision Uganda (January 1995), p. 2.

Pernanen, K., *Alcohol in Human Violence*, New York: Guilford Press (1991).

Roizen, J., "Epidemiological issues in alcohol-related violence," *Recent Developments in Alcoholism*, New York: Plenum Press 13 (1997), pp. 7–40.

Thornton, W. E., and Voigt, L. "Disaster phase analysis and crime facilitation patterns," In D. W. Harper and K. Frailing (eds) *Crime and Criminal Justice in Disaster*, part 2, Durham NC: Carolina Academic Press (2010).

Tomsen, S., "Violence, danger, security and the night time economy," Australian Capital Territory: Australian Institute of Criminology, accessed March 12, 2016, http://www.aic.gov.au/events/seminars/2010/tomsen.html (June 15, 2010).

Virkkunen, M., "CSF biochemistries, glucose metabolism, and diurnal activity rhythms in alcoholic, violent offenders, fire setters, and healthy volunteers," *Archives of General Psychiatry* 51 (1994), pp. 20–27.

Walrond, C., "Security and personal safety," (Te Ara Encyclopedia of New Zealand), http://www.TeAra.govt.nz/en/security-and-personal-safety (March 15, 2016).

White, H. R., "Longitudinal perspective on alcohol use and aggression during adolescence," In *Recent Developments in Alcoholism*, New York: Plenum Press 13 (1997), pp. 81–103.

Wikipedia, "Russian criminal tattoos," accessed March 12, 2016, https://en.wikipedia.org/wiki/Russian_criminal_tattoos (2016).

ENDNOTE

1. Darkness increases fear of crime. A nationwide survey held in 1980 and 1981 found that more than one in two women reported not feeling safe walking alone after dark compared to around one in eight men. A quality-of-life survey in the 2000s found that, nationally, 18% of men and 36% of women generally felt unsafe walking after dark.

CHAPTER 6

Hotel and Residential Security

INTRODUCTION

In a more innocent era, hotel security quite often consisted of a hotel detective quietly ensconced in the lobby. This was the case not only in the United States but also internationally. Hotels were not the locus of international terrorism. Since 9/11, a series of bloody attacks on iconic or luxury brand hotels abroad have changed the way that security is perceived, prioritized, and implemented—internationally. Speaking frankly, hotels inside the United States remain stubbornly trapped in that more innocent era. The sheer numbers of iconic and luxury hotels and resorts internationally that are the venue of bloody suicide bomber or armed assault attacks represent a growing trend in terms of strategy. Since June 2015, there have been 13 terrorist attacks on hotels and resorts worldwide. Most represent a shift toward armed-assault style tactics that include the taking of hostages. Terrorists replicate successful tactics used by other groups, so I expect that this kind of security threat—left stubbornly unchecked—is bound to come to a five-star hotel within a US city or state. We are not immune to this kind of threat, as the gradual increase of so-called lone-wolf attacks within the United States demonstrates. While this book's principal theme is focused on international travel and security challenges, this particular chapter is highly relevant to business travelers within the United States. The reason is simple: Physical and procedural security measures for hotels and resorts in the United States are at best an afterthought and, more often than not, glaringly absent. That means your attention to good personal security planning is your first and last line of defense. As with any situation, there are rare exceptions. Abroad, some hotel chains, over time, have become much more cognizant of physical security and invest capital to design in more robust security measures that provide guests an added layer of defense against the still-growing threat of terrorism, not in the United States.

With residential security abroad, large corporations and govern-ments operating in third-world countries have the resources to invest in physical security upgrades and hire a trained and relatively well-paid guard force. With that said, it is better not to make assumptions about the effectiveness of existing security measures or the competency of the guard force at your compound. Benghazi, Libya, was considered a critical threat risk. Other diplomatic missions wisely removed their personnel, given the threat in the country. It was a critical threat that was supported by the solid evidence of similar multiple attacks in the immediate vicinity. Professionals on the ground knew it. Why their judg-ment and experience were not heeded remains under investigation at the time that this book is being written. The process for physical security assessment and design at the US State Department is a good one, argu-ably world class. Likewise, in January 2013, the residential compound at the Tigantourine British Petroleum/Statoil Natural Gas Plant near In Amenas, Algeria, was considered well protected with security fences, armed military patrols, and long-range reconnaissance equipment, not to mention the hundreds of miles of inhospitable desert. Nonetheless, a determined and well-led team of terrorists infiltrated the Algerian's vaunted ring of steel, achieved complete surprise, held hostages, and killed 37 foreigners. In both cases, layered defenses broke down either because of willful negligence on the part of decision makers or because of inadequate threat and risk assessment processes. The harsh reality is that for all the talk of lessons learned, lessons are not learned. Mistakes are repeated. More often than not, residential security is—if you are lucky—limited to the gates, guards, and guns approach. The gate may be a rusty wrought iron affair that will not close properly; the guard, a local contractor who is there to open or close the gate; and the gun, an ancient rusted Kalashnikov or shotgun.

The reason that I point out these disturbing trends in hotel and resi-dential security is simply that as terrorists shift their strategy toward softer targets such as these, being secure is really up to you. Personal security in this regard means that you should know what to look for, whether it is a luxury hotel in downtown Kiev or Mexico City, a walled residential villa in Sana'a, Yemen, or a sprawling expatriate residential compound in Benghazi or Algeria.

Hotels and, to a lesser extent, residential compounds are not designed with high security in mind. They are built to accommodate the traveling public or the long-term expatriate. Aesthetics and comfort, not security and safety, are the principal design priorities. Reasonable experts can debate this—but, for all intents and purpose, this is the case.

However, as diplomatic missions are hardened into virtual fortresses around the world, and airports carefully scan every single item that the traveling public carries, from fingernail clippers to toothpaste, it is axiomatic that terrorists will focus their tactical plans against softer targets. As previously mentioned, they already have and this growing trend should be expected to continue and potentially accelerate. Hotels and resorts are attractive targets because they must remain public venues in order to remain in business (an exploitable vulnerability), mounting an attack takes less planning and skill than harder targets (threat capability), and for what they represent to many of the terrorist groups active today.

One of my favorite examples of spectacularly failed security tactics—designed and calcified into a strategy to fight the last war—is France's infamous Maginot Line. If you have not heard of it, it is instructive to know about it and—more particularly—its failure in terms of security design. This massive, thick concrete system of defenses was built along the border of France after World War I to prevent a German invasion of the country from ever occurring again. On the eve of World War II, German tacticians, knowing that it was impregnable, simply went around it. France fell within weeks. The Maginot line represents how otherwise smart engineers and designers can be utterly blinded by the efficacy of their solution, to the exclusion of what is going on around them or—in the case of the French—in Berlin. There is *real danger* in not stepping back to take stock of context, how it can or has changed, and instead abstracting your enemy into a calcified set of capabilities, tactics, logistics, and history, all for the purpose of building a set of data against which one measures solutions.

Do not be lulled into a false sense of security by the security theater outside of big hotels. These usually are an example of reactive security tactics that consistently fail. If I sound a little skeptical, it is because there are at least 80 examples since 9/11 of how, in one form or another, hotel and resort security utterly failed. Security practitioners in today's hotel and resort industry have an ongoing challenge in considering all of the valid scenarios that might be used to compromise their facilities and jeopardize the safety and the security of the guests. Unfortunately, the Maginot Line syndrome plagues both senior hotel management and the security officers themselves, who—often overwhelmed with the security challenges that they face in the private sector, fall back on what they believe will work best—either a risk avoidance strategy (protect everything in sight) or a compliance strategy that focuses on all the things that should be in place, without consideration of what ought to be in place. A good example of this was the counterterrorism security measure taken by a hotel security officer at the Le Royal Hotel in Amman, Jordan, following a series of hotel bombings by Abu Musab Al Zarqawi's al Qaeda in Iraq (the precursor to the current ISIS) in the city in 2006. The security officer promptly implemented screening measures of guests directly in front of the entrance's giant plate glass windows. A lovely red carpet was put down to the entrance and the exit of the screening device. This did nothing to diminish the fact that a bomber wearing a suicide vest—the modus operandi of all the previous hotel attacks—would not be deterred in the least by this very visible show of security, a display of security theater at its finest.

CONSIDERATIONS WHEN CHOOSING A HOTEL

In recent years, there have been some devastating attacks on high-profile luxury hotels, notably, the 2008 Lashkar-e-Taiba attacks in Mumbai, India, targeting the iconic Taj Mahal Palace and the Oberoi Trident hotels; the September 20, 2008, vehicle-borne improvised explosive device (VBIED) attack on JW Marriott Hotel in Islamabad, Pakistan (the bomber detonated nearly a ton of trinitrotoluene (TNT), obliterating the security barrier and much of the hotel); and, more recently, the attacks on luxury hotels throughout Africa principally consisting of assault-style tactics. If you have the choice, before departure, do your homework with the following considerations in mind.

Location and Layout Trumps Amenities, Convenience, and Proximity

In Sana'a, Yemen, the Swiss Mövenpick Hotel is arguably the nicest venue in the city. There is a sedate flow of well-heeled customers who stay in its rooms, eat at its restaurants, drink at its bars, and utilize its banquet and conference facilities. As one of the city's only real five-star hotels, it hosts conferences and dinner events. It is a gathering place or businesspersons from Yemen and other countries, diplomats, government ministers and their entourage, and very important persons (VIPs). From the standpoint of convenience, amenities, and proximity, it is absolutely the best place to stay. However, from the standpoint of security, it is absolutely not.

This hotel's well-appointed main facade also faces the main entrance of a Western embassy that is flanked on both sides by two sandbagged machine gun emplacements. Both guns are pointed in the vicinity of the third and fourth floors of the hotel itself. Anyone who has had the memorable experience of watching a sudden, close encounter between attackers assaulting a fixed position and soldiers who must quickly rouse themselves and bring their weapon to bear—on full auto—knows that some of those rounds will not be right on target. Succinctly put, the hotel's facade and rooms facing the embassy and the machine guns are an excellent backstop.

The hotel offers direct access to the city's main ring road. The standoff from that road was not paramount in the Swiss architectural designer's mind when placing the hotel where it is today. The entrance from the main road to the hotel's lovely glass entrance is a straight shot, slightly downhill, right into the ground floor. Yes, there is a roundabout. However, as with other physical security measures placed cleanly on a two-dimensional set of drawings by an engineer in an antiseptic office thousands of miles away around the normal flow of traffic, behavior, and topology, these countermeasures would not in the least deter an adrenaline-filled terrorist shouting his final words at the world at the top of his lungs as he piloted a TNT-filled truck into his target at full speed—a slight bump in the road that is probably not going to slow down the VBIED steered by someone on a mission. That said, it is a first-class hotel. What was lacking was context in the design.

Down the road, set back off the main road, is the venerable old Sheraton Hotel (Figure 6.1). The elevators, when they are working, still play music from the 1970s. It has clearly seen its heyday. But the setback from the main road is excellent, and the road getting to the front of the hotel winds around and is appropriately screened from view by vegetation, past a tripod-mounted 12.7 mm Dashka trained on the entrance. It is a sprawling facility with multiple entrances and exits, making escape easy. Whenever I am in Sana'a, I pass up the amenities, the convenience,

FIGURE 6.1 (a) Entrance to the old Sheraton Hotel in Sana'a, Yemen (in 2011). The standoff from the main road and the screening shrubbery made it far preferable to the more luxurious Mövenpick Hotel down the road. (b) Ancient Zumit Hotel, in Tripoli, Libya. Its obscure, low-key exterior, pedestrian-only access, and low-key profile made it the author's choice when staying for extended periods in Tripoli. (Photo by the author.)

and arguably the better luxury on offer at the Mövenpick and choose the Sheraton. Location and layout, for starters, put it in the win column.

It is a similar situation in Tripoli, Libya. Currently, it is too dangerous to visit, but when I did, my choice—based on location and layout—was an old boutique hotel (a former Caravanserai) called the *Ancient Zumit*. It is tucked away into the old medina or old city's warren of alleys and narrow streets that could not accommodate vehicles and is naturally designed for privacy and security—a two-story interior tiled courtyard, with a massive wooden door on the front and a discreet way out via an alley in the back. The location, the low profile, and the natural security were important considerations over some of the more upscale, but high-profile luxury hotels in the city such as the five-star Corinthian Hotel. The Corinthian, in fact, was attacked in January of 2015 by five terrorists affiliated with ISIS. The attack included a car bomb detonated in the hotel's garage, followed by an assault-style attack on the hotel itself and a protracted hostage situation. This attack only confirmed my own judgment when I visited Tripoli.

Realistic Expectations

Some guidance put out by security consultancies will insist that it is important that you ask in advance if the hotel staff has ever undergone security or emergency management training, if the hotel has an emergency evacuation plan, if the staff has had background checks, if there are security personnel, etc. If you are doing an advance assessment for the president of the United States or a high-level diplomatic delegation or your corporation's VIPs and a partner firm, by all means do so. That is part of your advance duties. My only advice in this regard is that you be very, very skeptical and take all assurances that you receive from the hotel with a grain of salt.

If it is for yourself, do not waste your time or the time of your firm in tracking down this information. Do not expect or assume high security standards. What might appear to be high security standards to hotel chain management could be, as is often the case, nothing less than a list of compliance checks with no real assessment work or analysis behind it. It is a hotel, not a nuclear weapon storage facility. Assume that the staff are not up to speed when it comes to security or emergency management training or that the hotel has ever even considered an emergency evacuation plan. If the local staff was vetted by the local security service, it is probably because they are working for the local security service. When the regional security officer comes around from Western embassies, the hotels have certainly told the local representatives that these standard operating procedures are in place. They check the box and get on with what hotels do best—get paying customers to fill their rooms. Assume none of the above.

This book is geared toward getting you prepared and capable of bringing your own set of security principles to the matter of hotel risk, starting from the moment that your taxi pulls into the entrance.

Hotel Arrival: Deterrence and Delay

As you arrive at your hotel, be cognizant of some specific physical security aspects. These mental notes as you arrive might dictate whether you want to remain at the hotel for long, and it should inform your room selection.

Standoff and Perimeter Security

How much standoff does the hotel have from the main road? For instance, if you are checking into the Phoenicia Hotel Beirut, you might consider selecting a room as far away from the front entrance as possible as there is no standoff at all from the front or the side of the building. On February 14, 2005, less than 300 meters from the entrance to the hotel, former Lebanese Prime Minister Rafik Hariri was assassinated by a 2200 lb. improvised explosive device that obliterated the former prime minister's six-vehicle armored motorcade, creating a crater 30 ft wide and 14 ft deep, and severely damaging several nearby buildings including the Phoenicia Hotel. That hotel had to close for three months while the damage was repaired. Vehicle bombs (VBIEDs) are one of the weapons of choice in Beirut and have been for years. Standoff is really important.

Is there a security checkpoint on the perimeter, and how effective is it? The presence of concrete barriers,; an S-curved entrance, other types of barriers such as bollard or wedge barriers, armed and *alert* guards, and security lights might influence whether you choose to keep a room overlooking the front entrance of the hotel or choose one as far away from the entrance as possible. Attention to detail on the perimeter, even if kept low key because it is a hotel, can be an indicator of how good or inadequate the hotel's security posture is.

Screening

Upon arrival at the entrance to the hotel, is your luggage taken away and screened separately? If it is, this represents a certain level of comprehension and consequent security awareness of the threats that exist where you have arrived. It is also, as with the quality and the level of security on the perimeter, an indication of the hotel's overall posture with security.

Are there metal detectors at the entrance to the lobby? Where are they positioned? If they are, as was the case with the hotel in Jordan, placed in front of plate glass windows at the entrance to the hotel, then you can surmise that security overall is about checking the box for corporate-standard compliance purposes. This should influence your decision in terms of room selection within the hotel.

Arrival to Check-In: Moving from Public to Private Space

In an ideal world, there is a nice, ordered line of guests in front of the check-in desk. In reality, there may be two or maybe three tired, stressed hotel employees trying to get rooms occupied as quickly as possible. There will be people checking in and checking out, all crowding up to the counter. In an ideal world, you do not care what room you are booked into. In reality, you have arrived in a third-world hotel without any meaningful security measures in place. At the check-in desk, you should have some very specific security concerns about how your communications with the desk clerk proceed and your room selection. These are the considerations that you must have in mind.

Communications: The Need to Know

When you check in, tell the clerk to simply write your room number on the envelope with the keys and give it to you. If they announce the room number to you, within earshot of other individuals, quietly request another room. If it is crowded, do not make a fuss about it at the desk. Handle this later. But do not remain in the same room. No one but you, and the immediate hotel staff, needs to know who you are and what room you are staying in.

Ask the clerk about house phone procedure. Specifically, guest phones within the room should not allow direct room dialing. In-house phones should be routed directly to the desk or the hotel operator, and requests for room contact should be by guest name and not room number. If this procedure is not in place, make note of it.

Also, ask the clerk about fire alarms, whether there are fire drills, and if there is a fire safety plan in the room. This is always a good question, because hotels that do not concentrate on security will quite often have a fire safety plan or protocol. The exits, the alarm system, and the announcements that accompany a fire safety plan can parallel a security incident—either way, this is useful information to get before moving into your room.

Room Selection

These are the considerations that you should bear in mind when selecting a room:

- Upper floors are safe in terms of crime, but—beyond the sixth floor—they are exceedingly risky for fire safety. You want a room between floors 3 and 6.

- If criminal threat is uppermost, stay away from rooms that are near fire stairs. Stairways provide an avenue for escape, meaning that rooms close to stairways, and guests, are a viable target.
- Ground floor rooms are vulnerable to entry.
- If you are checking into an older motel with doors that face directly onto a parking lot, try to get a room that opens into an interior courtyard rather than the parking lot. There are a number of reasons for this. Motel parking lots are notoriously dangerous, because they offer opportunity for vehicle break-in or theft. Since there is no control past a front desk, anyone can park and pretend to be a guest, leaving open the possibility of room invasion or room break-in and theft when you have gone out.

Moving from Public to Private Space: Front Desk to Room

Be cognizant of individuals who board the elevator with you and then get off on your floor. In any country but particularly in third-world countries, following check-in, I am very wary about anything that smacks of coincidence. If someone boards the elevator with me and there is no one else, I will always let them exit first and then stay on the elevator and "accidentally" go to a different floor, exit, and then get on a down elevator for the lobby. I will then reboard and go to my floor. It sounds elaborate, but this little procedure adds a layer of deception when moving from *public to private* space that can confuse a potential adversary and a layer of deterrence to your own personal security protocol. To the extent possible, I like to reduce my information profile. Even if invited, I decline to exit the elevator and implement this protocol.

The ideal situation is to have a clear, deserted path to your room. Use your judgment. If you see a familiar face when you get off the elevator, particularly after having used your deception routine, then get back on, go to the lobby, and immediately request another room on another floor. Otherwise, if there is normal traffic in the hallways once you have arrived on the floor where your room is located, just be cognizant of their direction (beware of individuals who change their direction and follow on your heels to your room).

An important part of personal security is fire safety and awareness. A guest could fall asleep with a lit cigarette and start a fire in his or her room. Or as what happened in the Istanbul JW Marriott attack in 2008, a dump truck filled with 1000 lb. of explosives could ram the security perimeter barrier and set off a natural gas leak that led to a raging inferno in the hotel itself. When moving through the hotel, keep in mind what kinds of fire safety measures are in place. In the third world, if you are in an international brand hotel, there is a decent chance that fire safety and code have been included in the construction and fitting of the hotel. Look for fire sprinkler heads and take note of the exits and how many doors away your room is to that exit. Make a note of it. Out of habit, I always test the door of the exit, to make sure that it is not locked (as a habit, I also use stairways within hotels, rather than the elevator).

In the Room

At the Room Entrance

- Check to ensure that your room has a solid-core wooden or metal door. The door should be self-closing and self-locking.
- Check the door's lockset. A recent incident with hotel electronic locks revealed a vulnerability that allows hackers to exploit the lock and gain entry to the room. In addition to the door's entry lockset, there should be a deadbolt lock with a 1 inch throw bolt.
- Check to see if there are pry marks around the doorjamb. If there are, request another room.
- The door should have a wide-angle peephole, a door chain, and/or a wishbone latch.

Initial Entry to the Room

- Immediately upon entry, lock the door behind you and perform a room sweep to ensure that windows, patio doors, or balcony doors are secured. The security sweep should start with the closets and then the bathroom, the balcony (if there is one), and under the bed.
- If there is an adjoining door to another room, test it to ensure that it is locked with a deadbolt lock.
- If you are forced to be on a ground floor, are low enough that access is possible from the ground up to windows or sliding doors, or are adjacent to another room where balcony access is easy, make certain that sliding glass doors and/or windows lock.
- Check to see if your room has a smoke alarm and a diagram outlining where to exit in a fire emergency.

While in the Room

- Do not open the door to someone who knocks, unannounced. If someone who appears to be hotel staff is waiting outside, ask them to wait and call to the front desk to confirm that the visit is legitimate. Typically, hotel operations staff should be able to contact housekeeping, room service, security, or maintenance staff to confirm that the visit is legitimate. If they leave, there is no problem—simply advise the front desk that you prefer to be notified by phone in advance of a visit to ensure that it is legitimate.

- When unpacking, it is important to be deliberate about where the items are placed in the room. If there is a safe, use it to secure valuables to include jewelry, electronics, wallet, etc. If there is no safe, ensure that your valuables are secured out of sight in your suitcase. If possible, bring along a small lock that can be used to secure the suitcase when you are out of the room. If your items are arranged deliberately, you can—with practice—detect if they have been moved or tampered with. It may just be housekeeping, or it could be someone else. Knowing is better than not knowing. It is a good security habit to develop.

In the Event of a Security Incident or a Fire

There are several things that you should do to prepare yourself for a rapid exit from the room. This is true whether there is a security incident and you are evacuated or if there is a fire. Either way, you need to be prepared to leave unnecessary things behind and have the things that are most critical at hand, so that you can take them and move when the time comes.

- If the fire alarm sounds, leave immediately. Take the stairs and not the elevator.
- Before turning in at night, put the room key, your wallet with credit cards, your ID (passport), and mobile phone on the nightstand next to you. If you have to move quickly, having these crucial items conveniently at hand will prevent you from wasting critical time looking for them before you go.
- If you encounter smoke, *get under it*! Get low and move to the exit.

In the event that you cannot get out of your room and are trapped by smoke and flame, do not panic. Consider the following steps:

- Shut off fans or air conditioning at the thermostat in your room.
- Soak some towels and stuff them in any cracks or opening around the door. Depending on what hotel you are in and the codes applied, the door is rated for at least 20 minutes and the walls themselves for a half hour.
- Call the front desk, the fire department, or any other number that you can while you can and let them know where you are and your predicament. Stay calm and advise them only of the specifics regarding your room number and situation. It is not the

time to get into a lengthy question-and-answer session regarding who will respond, when, and how.

- Wait at the window and signal with a piece of light-colored cloth or a flashlight.

In and around the Hotel

Situational awareness within the hotel environment itself, no matter how small the establishment, is important should an emergency arise. Whether it is a fire or a terrorist attack such as the one that unfolded in 2008 in Mumbai, the shock of an incident is very disorienting. Knowing what to do, and where to run, can make the difference between life and death. Preparation means focusing on the details of your immediate environment and committing them to memory. As noted before, but bears repeating, know where your exits are and how many doors are between the stairwell and your room. Check the doors to ensure that they work. These are just a couple examples of keeping aware of your environment.

All hotels, whether they are in the United States or international, typically have floor plans of the establishment posted on each floor—usually by the elevator. They should also have them posted inside your room, but this is not always the case. These floor plans indicate where you are with an X or an arrow and the fire escape route. Take a moment to study the diagram and commit it to memory.[1] Knowing your options for escape and evasion when the shooting starts, when the mob breaks in, or in the first minutes of disarray when part of the hotel is on fire or destroyed from a bombing must be a crucial part of your security plan.

Scouting out the premises of the hotel is next. What you are looking for includes alternative exits out of the hotel and into the street or other areas that can offer shelter. It is important to remember that in an emergency, employee-only areas into the back-of-hotel operation areas such as the kitchen, the laundry, or the loading dock are viable routes out. Take this into consideration when reconnoitering, and do not be afraid to exercise your curiosity. The worst-case scenario in the event that you find yourself in the bowels of the hotel's back-of-house areas is that you get lost.

RESIDENTIAL SECURITY

Both the US government and private corporations house employees in long-term residential villas or apartments while abroad. Depending on your situation, you might also be housed in a long-term residence or have the choice to select one. In the absence of a professional security staff in the country that can prepare your residence and security needs in advance of your arrival, these are some considerations that you should keep in mind for your personal security that can be found in good procedural and physical security.

Residence Selection: Security Preparation and Planning Measures

If you have the option to preselect a residence, there are some site selection considerations that you should keep in mind that will enhance your personal security. These considerations are as follows:

- Access: Access should take into consideration emergency response and consist of bidirectional entry and exit streets (noncontiguous) to the residence for emergency response.
- Public transportation adjacencies: Avoid selecting a residence adjacent to an elevated roadway and active waterway (uncontrolled bay/ocean front[2]).
- Avoid high-crime or gang-infested neighborhoods and those that have a history of terrorist activity or military activity.[3]
- Take into consideration neighbors to the residence. In addition to large commercial shopping areas or industrial processing and storage facilities, a location adjacent to a sports stadium, an event venue, or a popular public square, park, or market could expose you to large crowds and the attendant risk that poses.

Perimeter: Security Detection and Delay

If you are fortunate, the compound on which your residence is located will have a walled or a fenced perimeter that provides some setback and privacy. You should survey the perimeter both during the daytime and at night to assess any weak areas. Look for holes in the fence or a deteriorating fence that can easily be lifted from the ground, unlocked gates, untrimmed vegetation that overhangs the fence or a wall that can be used to climb over or used as cover, and poor or nonexistent lighting. If you find any of these conditions, get them fixed as soon as feasible.

Gate Guards: Deterrence, Detection, Delay, and Response

Guards are an excellent security countermeasure to invest in. With that said, they need close oversight and supervision to be effective. From experience, I can confirm that in the third world, your gate guards are probably hired by a local guard company, are poorly paid, and, more often than not, sleep on the job. The ones that do not are exceptional. Because the pay is low, gate guards are vulnerable to bribery by thieves or other potential adversaries looking for details about your habits, movements to and from the residence, and when the residence is empty. There is usually a guard supervisor that patrols at least once or twice a shift to ensure that the guard is alert and on duty. If there is no patrol, then look for a guard service that has one. If you have doubts, or problems with the guard, report this immediately and get the guard replaced. One thing to be aware of is a guard who is overly friendly and insists on helping you with groceries, luggage, or things such as this so that he or she can get close to you and your team and see what is inside the house in terms of valuables, entrances, exits, and potential vulnerabilities that can be exploited. This is valuable information to thieves. The quality that you should seek in a guard is the one who stays awake and alert, pays attention to his duties, and stays professional and away from you or your team. It does not hurt to tip a guard who shows those characteristics—but nothing more. From long experience, if I encounter a guard who exhibits the former qualities (overly friendly and familiar), I fire them immediately and get them replaced. Setting the right tone is, in itself, a good deterrent because word gets around that you are firm.

Canines

Canines on the premises are very useful and are an excellent deterrent to thieves and detection measure for you or your team. With that said, they should be kept close to the house, in an enclosure away from the perimeter after hours. Thieves will use poisoned food to disable or kill the dogs, before breaking in. Do not install small doggie doors for the pet, because they can afford egress into the residence by a small intruder (theft rings routinely utilize children as a means to get inside of a residence via small openings).

Exterior Lighting and Decorative Shrubs: Detection and Deterrence

There should be bright exterior lighting that is outward facing and placed strategically around the residence. If you are not allowed to use lighting because of light pollution or trespass complaints, it is likely because the external lights are not properly installed and the illumination angle is too high. Ensure that the lights illuminate key areas of your perimeter only. Trees or shrubs should be kept trimmed so that there is no cover afforded to a potential intruder. Illumination beneath these trees or shrubs is good, because it removes a dark hiding place.

Ground Floor Windows and Doors and Exterior: Security Delay Measures

Your ground floor windows and doors (front and rear, garage, and service doors) should all be solid-core wood or metal doors with good-quality locks and also deadbolt locks (top and bottom). Consider fitting ground floor windows with steel bars, bolted into the window frame itself. There should be window locks on all windows, and if there are louvered windows, these should be kept locked—especially on the ground floor. Keep fire safety in mind for bedrooms and safe havens—if there are exterior grills or grates, they should be unlockable or removable from the inside to allow emergency egress in the event of a fire. Locks should be installed on any exterior fuse boxes or external power sources.

Inside the Residence: Layering Your Defenses

With attention to detail outside of your residence in terms of where it is located, its perimeter, guards, and physical security, there are steps that you should follow to ensure that security outside is reflected inside the residence—both for yourself and your family or team.

Detection

There are two threat events that can occur within the residence—intrusion by a threat actor or fire. A burglar alarm with intrusion detection and motion detection should be employed to close off areas of the house that are unoccupied at night. If you have pets and also employ motion detection, they should move with you at night into the sleeping area of the residence, and occupants should be notified when the motion detection is switched on. In a high-criminal threat area, having this capability will give you time to secure occupants in the safe room and notify authorities in the event of a home invasion or a break-in. At the very least, utilize intrusion detection capabilities with an electronic alarm system after hours or when away. You should periodically test smoke and carbon monoxide detectors, and replace batteries if needed. Finally, place flashlights in several areas in the house. Check the batteries often.

Deterrence

Do not leave keys hidden outside the home—there is always the possibility that they could be found and used by an intruder to get into the residence.

Leave an extra key with a trusted neighbor or colleague. Cultivate a security habit of mind with your team or family. This includes the following:

- Locking doors even when you or your team/family members are at home
- Coaching family members and domestic help in the proper way to answer the telephone at home
- Keeping variance of daily routines; avoid predictable patterns around the house or the neighborhood
- Keeping an eye out for occurrences or individuals that are out of place or strange

If your family develops good security habits, this increases the overall security resilience of your presence in the country. Also, it will give you some peace of mind if you must go out of the city or the country on business, leaving them behind.

Delay: Importance of Establishing a Safe Room

Designate an internal room, install a two-way communication system or telephone, and furnish the safe haven with an emergency kit. It is highly unlikely that you would spend more than a few hours in a safe haven. However, the supplies listed below are suggested for your maximum safety (refer to Chapter 4 regarding considerations on how to select and secure your safe room).

The following is a list of possible safe haven supplies:

- Fire extinguisher
- Fresh water
- Five-day supply of food
- Candles, matches, and flashlight
- Extra batteries
- Bedding
- Toilet facilities
- Sterno stove and fuel
- Shortwave or other radio
- Medical/first aid kit
- Other items for your comfort and leisure—a change of clothing, books, and games

Respond

While at home, you and your family should rehearse safety drills and be aware of procedures to escape danger and get help. Keep at least one fire extinguisher on each floor and be sure to keep one in the kitchen. Show family members and household help how to use them.

SELECTED THREAT ACTOR PROFILES: PICKPOCKETS, THIEVES, AND THE WORLD'S OLDEST PROFESSION

Pickpockets and thieves actually use a lot of the same techniques for security that are outlined in this book. The difference, of course, is that their personal security is focused on not getting caught—just like you, they do not want to become a victim—of the law. Pickpockets, burglars, and thieves often work in teams and will use techniques such as preparation (practicing a technique or scenario, knowing the turf where they will operate and escape, researching where the authorities are), detection (watching and following a target, learning his or her habits, predictability, routine), distraction (a form of delay), and escape (a form of response).

On the street, pickpockets have several techniques that all rely on some form of distraction. There is the "bump and lift" (the thief bumps you coming from opposite direction, apologizes, but lifts your wallet at same time), the "bump, grasp, and slip" (while you are in a long queue at the airport, the train station, the museum, or the theater, the thief bumps you and apologizes while getting a grasp on your wallet. As you move away, he or she slips out), or the "pressure distraction" (the thief holds your arm, closest to your wallet, and as you focus on the pressure, he or she lifts your wallet). The oldest tricks in the book come from the world's oldest profession—prostitutes. Stories abound of tipsy or drunk marks encountering a hooker on the street, and as he/she distracts the mark, part of the prostitute's crew bumps him/her and steals his/her wallet, camera, or briefcase.

In terms of personal security, I have observed that prostitution—particularly street prostitution—is an indicator that you should pay attention to. The level of street prostitution in an urban area is directly proportional to a country's economic and security plight. The higher and more blatant the number of prostitutes, the worse the conditions are in the country or the city you are in—it reflects desperation. As a rule of thumb, I have always considered the level and the sheer number of street prostitutes as the ultimate canary in the coal mine in terms of a location's social deterioration, and the more of them that you see, hear (in Africa, they would literally hiss at you when going by in a taxi), or encounter typically means the more street and property crimes you will encounter as well. It is a pretty reliable threat indicator and pattern of risk to pay attention to. Prostitutes maintain a good network of criminal contacts and do not hesitate to exploit this. They are very resourceful and are often exploited by street gangs to case a victim, luring them to organized kidnap operations. Like street criminals, prostitutes in the third world are—unlike high-priced escorts in New York or elsewhere in western Europe—not in the profession by choice. It is sheer necessity—they come from abject poverty and will do whatever it takes to get money to feed their family.

Be aware of the pattern of criminal tactics used against you, such as a scenario unfolding before your eyes in a city park (if the sob story or drama playing out in front of you feels rehearsed, it is); seeing the same individual(s) more than once, like déjà vu, is not a coincidence, and, of course, if he or she just looks too good to be true—they are.

ENDNOTES

1. While taking a photograph of the floor plan with one's smartphone or camera is useful, there will not be time in an emergency to find the photo and study it. To the extent possible, study the diagram and remember it. This is true for many knowledge-driven requirements in this book. Committing things to memory develops good instincts. Carrying memorization around in your pocket on an iPhone is a poor substitute.
2. On January 8, 2016, and again on January 22, 2016, two separate terrorist attacks—one in Mogadishu on a popular hotel and the other on a beach resort in Egypt—were carried out by terrorists assaulting from the sea.
3. The author, along with colleagues, was pinned down in a residence that took direct mortar and small arm fire for several days during the civil war in Kampala, Uganda, because it was located immediately adjacent to a military camp.

CHAPTER 7

Cybersecurity on the Road

INTRODUCTION

Anyone who has ever had their laptop, smartphone, or other portable information technology (IT) device stolen can attest that the injury is significant and can have crippling consequences in one's personal life. What hurts the most is not the loss of the machine, it is the loss of the data. Today, we rely on the availability, the confidentiality, and the reliability of access to or the retrieval of our personal data more than ever—online banking, shopping, reports, personal and professional correspondence, and business contacts are all extremely valuable assets in our personal and professional lives and by extension to our corporate bosses and partners. Despite the tangible value of the data that we carry with us, many people take little or no real effort to protect it. There are competent, creative adversaries that rely on this and prey specifically on tourists or business travelers.

Your data or your company or government's data are extremely valuable in the wrong hands. While corporate proprietary information may be very secure within the layered enterprise security of your company's headquarters, it is very insecure inside your hotel room, the airport terminal, or the local coffee shop. These are all places where hackers who specialize in stealing data know you and where your information can be found.

DARKHOTEL THREAT

Kaspersky Lab recently published a report that described a WiFi exploit by hackers, called the Darkhotel group,[1] possibly affiliated with Korea. The hackers specifically targeted more than a dozen luxury hotels in the Asia Pacific region frequented by businesspersons and government officials. Over 70% of the victims' organizations were from Taiwan and Japan. Other businesspersons from Russia, China, Hong Kong, India, and the United States were also targeted. There are indications that these attacks are continuing. Darkhotel never goes after the same target twice; they perform operations with surgical precision, getting all the valuable data that they can from the first contact, deleting traces of their work, and melting into the background to await the next high-profile individual.

The hackers insert malware[2] on the hotel's wireless network before a guest arrives. This attack vector is used to employ a mix of highly targeted and botnet-type[3] techniques, infecting the hotel network. When specific executives such as chief executive officers, senior vice presidents, sales and marketing directors, or research and development executives from government or defense companies check in to the hotel, their laptop or other device is quietly exploited through the hotel wireless network. The botnets are used for surveillance (the hacker can see when a target has logged onto the hotel network with his or her room number and last name), a distributed denial-of-service attack (DDOS)[4], and/or downloading of more sophisticated information-stealing malware onto their victims' machines. The attacks via hotel networks have been under way for at least four years and are still ongoing, according to Kaspersky, but the Darkhotel group has been waging other forms of attack for at least seven years. Kaspersky believes that the attack, which originated in the Asian Pacific region, is occurring outside the region as well.

The attack takes place when the targeted guest logs into the free hotel WiFi network from their room. An alert is sent to the hacker since he or she already secured control of the hotel network. A popup alert, looking entirely legitimate (for instance, such as an update to Adobe Flash Player or something similar that is received all the time and quickly dismissed), is received. When the unsuspecting target clicks on the popup, it goes away—but this covertly installs malware which then goes to work. Darkhotel is considered professional, well organized, and methodical. They use a Trojan horse software program that has an information-stealing component and other malware to conduct reconnaissance on the targeted executive's machine, looking for audiovisual software, cached browser and e-mail passwords, and any other sensitive information. The attackers infect each victim only once and then delete any trace of their activity after they have pilfered what they want. Other types of attack methods used by the group are spear phishing and poisoning of peer-to-peer networks.

FOREIGN INTELLIGENCE SERVICE THREAT

In all foreign countries, the local intelligence services should be assumed to be hostile. It is nothing personal—it is just that they have the interests of their own national security and economic interests at heart and not yours. There is really no such thing as a friendly intelligence service, whether you are in Europe, or Canada, or some other country that is an ally of your country. To believe otherwise is naive. Between intelligence services, there are only cooperative relationships that last as long as what both get from the arrangement is mutually beneficial. That never lasts.

You become a target of interest to an intelligence service if there are indications, confirmed or suspected, that you have some direct access to an individual or information that the service also wants. You can also become a target of interest if you are engaged in some activity, either wittingly or not, that is perceived as inimical to the country's national security interests.

You should anticipate interest in your laptop and access to information on it upon arrival—whether there actually is interest, or not, is a moot point. Again, it is naive to hope that no one will want access to the laptop, so adopting an anticipatory perspective from the outset is prudent. The rule is that you have no reasonable expectation of privacy once you are on the road. For instance, in Russia, their federal law permits the monitoring, the retention, and the analysis of all data that traverse Russian communication networks, including Internet browsing, e-mail messages, telephone calls, and fax transmissions.

In many countries, particularly states of the former Soviet Union, the Middle East, China, and some African states, hotels have an obligation or are strongly encouraged to support the host government's intelligence and law enforcement services. That translates to surreptitious keycard access to your room; master combination to your room safe; notification when you are out; and possibly even prewiring the room with covert video, audio, and/or WiFi capture technology. When you leave the comfort of your home or the corporate office, you are fair game. The longer you remain in the country, in the same room, the more vulnerable you become.

The Honey Trap Threat

You and your data can also be exploited through good old-fashioned extortion or blackmail, specifically, sex. Typically, this attack unfolds when you are approached by an attractive woman or man who then persuades you to have sex with them (Figure 7.1). The act itself is recorded for posterity, and shortly after the act, you are approached with the video or the photos and a threat that you must cooperate and turn over data and information, in return for the extortionists keeping the incriminating evidence quiet. This tactic has been around since Delilah accepted 1100 pieces of silver to seduce Samson for the Philistines in ancient times and the Dutch exotic dancer Mata Hari coaxed secrets out of French

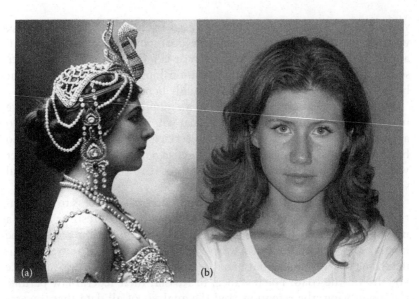

FIGURE 7.1   Two classic examples of "honey trap" agents. Dutch exotic dancer and spy, Mata Hari (a) targeted French officers during WWI using classic seduction techniques. More recently, Anna Chapman (b) worked for Russian Intelligence (SVR) as an "illegal" operative, and targeted officials in the US government using honey trap methods. (Courtesy of Wikimedia Commons, https://commons.wikimedia.org/wiki/File:Mata-Hari _1910.jpg; https://commons.wikimedia.org/wiki/File:Anna_Chapman _mug_shot.jpg.)

diplomats and politicians for German intelligence in World War I. It is a simple, elegant, and effective method. The former Soviet Committee for state security (Komitet gosudarstvennoy bezopasnosti) and, its successor, the Russian external intelligence service (Sluzhba Vneshney Razvedki [SVR]), developed this approach into a fine art. They train their officers in the craft of spotting, recruiting, and running "swallows"—beautiful young women or men (known as *ravens*), who are then directed against business or government targets of interest. While the Russians are best known for using this tactic, they are, by no means, the only intelligence service that employs this method of exploitation. The North Koreans make use of "flower girls," directing them against businesspersons. The Chinese also use honey trap techniques to extort business, banking, and research and development information (The Week, 2011).

Sexual or romantic entanglements can be used in one of two ways. One is to get incriminating video or photos of you, at which point you are confronted with the evidence and forced to cooperate. The second is more subtle. You can be seduced into accompanying someone to their room. While you are out, your room is surreptitiously entered and your electronic media are exploited. There are several ways in which an adversary will target your valuable information. Most of the time, it is via surreptitious entry into the room while you are out. A professional operative is able to do this without you ever having known he or she was there. This includes exploiting your electronics. Once inside your room, physical access is possible to your electronic equipment. It takes very little time to image your hard drive and even less time to read the SIM card on your phone.

Technical Threat

In the days of the Cold War, there was a protocol that Western intelligence officers followed that was informally termed *Moscow Rules*. This protocol was implemented whenever an officer was working and traveling inside the iron curtain or in any country that was cooperating with the Soviet Union. It was automatically assumed that, from the time that your plane landed, your movements, conversations, phone calls, or any electronic communications would be monitored. While the days of the Cold War are over, the threat posed by foreign intelligence services and their cooptees has not diminished. Foreign business travelers or diplomats remain viable targets for exploitation because of the value of sensitive information that they possess or their access to venues or individuals with critical information. It can begin at security and customs inside a country upon arrival. In Israel, for instance, a business traveler was instructed to switch on his laptop and then made to wait for a considerable length of time while his e-mails and documents were reviewed and presumably copied.

From a data security point of view, travel is inherently risky. The likelihood that private personal or corporate data can be compromised greatly increases the moment you board an aircraft.

Vulnerabilities

Certain professions, positions, or roles make you vulnerable as a target. You can be a target for blackmail by foreign intelligence services or private corporate groups seeking advantage if you are a government official with important access; a corporate executive; or a student from a prestigious university researching aeronautics, science, and other areas that may land them future sensitive government or corporate jobs in a work that is kept confidential from other countries. Certain behaviors, particularly when traveling, can leave you open to exploitation as well. These include the following:

- Work and exhaustion: When traveling you can be off guard, cutting corners due to urgency to complete tasks. You might be suffering from sleep deprivation, and you use time-saving behaviors such as password reuse. Ironically, it is the very productive high-intensity multitaskers that burn the candle at both ends who become irritated with anything that smacks of delay and open themselves up to attacks because they cut corners. Also, if you are tired and in a hurry, you are susceptible to phishing campaigns to get information.
- Stress: Security has become much more stressful. Hundreds of laptops, smartphones, and other devices are left behind at airports every week. These are the ones that are found, reported, and stored in lost and found for later retrieval. Quite a lot never make it that far.
- Distraction/high visibility: Your vulnerability to exploitation can begin before you even log on. In a crowded waiting area of a noisy bar in the airport, there are prying eyes that can discreetly shoulder surf and obtain valuable information.
- Convenience: Free WiFi connections in hotels, airports, or train terminals are often set up without the proper security setting in place. Most WiFi networks require you to sign in to a captive portal page before they will allow you external access. In many cases, it is the sign-in page itself that is malicious, and by the time the user has entered their surname and room number, they will have been delivered an exploit tailored to their machine. Bringing a virtual private network (VPN) up at this point plays directly into the attackers' hands, channeling the infection onto the enterprise network (Higgins, 2014).

Personal Cybersecurity Program for the Business Traveler

Develop a layered plan for cybersecurity that can be integrated into your overall personal security plan. The following are important considerations.

Established Secure Baseline of Information Security

If you have undisciplined, loose cybersecurity practices at home or even in the office, chances are these practices will be mirrored in your portable media and cyberpractices while on the road. Make sure you have, or can establish, a good baseline of cybersecurity practices at home, prior to travel. These steps would include, but are not limited to, the following recommendations:

- Home computer and network
  - Run patched, updated, and supported versions of software and operating systems.
  - Install antivirus and antimalware; enable auto-updates.
  - Disable Java; use script control browser plug-ins.
  - Use separate administrator and user accounts.
  - Secure wireless access points.
  - Open attachments from trusted senders only.
  - Use strong/complex passwords for accounts.
- Mobile devices
  - Where applicable, enable antivirus and device integrity. Do not use rooted devices.
  - Enable screen lock with password or PIN (at least six characters).
  - Enable device encryption.
- Storage
  - Disable autorun on all systems.
  - Enable antivirus for all removable media.
- Games and apps
  - Install from trusted sites only.
  - Disable location services.
  - Avoid entering personal information.

Preparation

- Try to obtain and use a blank or a clean laptop during your trip. Consider a company-owned loaner cell phone, laptop, and/or tablet to limit the loss of both corporate and personal data if the device is lost, stolen, or confiscated by officials.
- Make sure that you pack a small lock that can be used to lock your devices into your suitcase in a pinch (if a hotel or a room safe is unavailable or too small).
- Limit or minimize any data that you are taking such as a presentation or a draft document on which you are working.
- Limit removable media such as compact disks (CDs), digital videodisks, and thumb drives to what is required only for the trip. Perform a full device backup and secure with a strong password. Store the password in a secure location while you are away.
- Inform banks and credit card companies of your travel plans and include dates, locations, and any special instructions. International transactions are typically flagged as fraud, and purchases may be delayed or your card may be cancelled without advanced travel notice. Consider using virtual credit card numbers that offer one-time use and are disposable yet will display on the credit card bill. Pack only essential ID, credit, and debit cards. Leave the others in a secure location.

- Update data protection software such as operating systems, antimalware, antivirus, security patches, and others prior to departure. Install full-disk encryption on laptops.
- Use the US State Department website (http://www.state.gov) to prepare and familiarize yourself with destination country or region export control laws concerning sensitive equipment, software, and technology (that includes encryption). Security testing/hacker tools can be forbidden and illegal in some countries.
- Change all passwords on all devices and use different passwords on each.
- Configure automatic wipe settings to wipe the device's data after a predetermined number of pass code entry failures.
- Check online to see if there is a listing on the airport's website for their public Internet link service. Doing this in advance is of limited utility, if you a traveling through several international airports—however, doing it before travel will mentally make it a priority that you will follow through with it during the trip (see detection countermeasure).

Detection

- Pay attention to your surroundings. Do not look at important documents when sitting in a waiting area for a plane or a train—wait until you are alone and in private for that. Watch your IT kit (laptop, tablet, smartphone, and accoutrements) as closely as you would your passport. Be especially vigilant when your travel is for vacation and not business. Let your hair down, but do not let your guard down with it.
- Be wary of the security line exiting the airport (many third-world countries have an exit security scan) or transferring through an airport to another flight. Check with the information desk at the airport, if you did not do so before leaving home (preparation stage), to find out the name of its public Internet link service so you will recognize it when your laptop finds it on WiFi.
- In the hotel, put your laptop or removable media into a soft cloth FedEx envelope (untearable) and seal it and mark it with a pen, so you will be able to detect if it has been tampered with.
- Consider subscribing to a commercial credit monitoring service to identify daily alerts to credit report and changes to your public profile.

Delay

- If you always use the official access keys provided by the café, the restaurant, or the vendor establishment, this can add a layer of security.

- When using public WiFi, use trusted VPN connections as much as possible. If you do not have a VPN available, use secure hypertext transfer protocol-secure (HTTP) connections to the extent possible (type in *https* instead of *http* at the beginning of a uniform resource locator [URL]).
- It is best to allow no, or minimal, sensitive data on the device. If data does need to be physically carried, such as for a presentation, secure encryption should be used. However, it is far better to allow remote access through very secure means such as a Secure Sockets Layer virtual private network (SSL VPN), coupled with RSA key fobs, so data never reside on the portable device, but access is controlled. Remote access sessions should also require complex passwords to log in, and inactive sessions should be timed out.
- Do not reuse passwords for multiple sites.

Defense

- Obtain and use a privacy screen on your laptop, so that someone sitting next to you cannot look over your shoulder to see what websites you are browsing or what you might be working on.
- Do not loan your device to anyone or attach unknown devices such as thumb drives. Thumb drives are notorious for computer infections.
- Avoid transmitting sensitive information, such as work documents or credit card details over public WiFi spots.
- Disable WiFi when not in use. WiFi ad hoc mode or unsecure file sharing can enable direct access to your devices by an adversary. Use airplane mode on your smartphone or tablet media to disable or suspend all connectivity.
- Disable Bluetooth when not in use (or set it to "hidden" or not "discoverable").
- Do not leave your laptop unattended. Take it with you, to the extent possible, or store it in the hotel safe. For a worst-case scenario, secure it in your suitcase and lock it.
- With regard to gifts and conferences, be wary of free items such as vendor flash drives or other items that can attach to your media. They may have "added-value" features—a gift that, unbeknown to you, keeps on giving to the adversary.

Response

- Report lost or stolen devices as soon as possible to whomever it concerns. This might include your company, mobile provider, hotel, airline, insurance company, and/or local authorities. Local authorities have a better chance of finding stolen property if it is reported stolen *as soon* as you know that it is missing. Upon return, analyze the device to see what has happened on it. Then, wipe and reuse it. Return the loaner device(s).

- Have all devices, media, and thumb drives taken on your trip reviewed for malware, unauthorized access, or other corruption. Do not connect it to a trusted network until you have tested it for malware. If the device is found to be compromised, reformat it and rebuild it from trusted sources/media. Then, restore data from backups taken before the trip.
- After ensuring that your devices are secure and not compromised, change all business and personal passwords. If possible, change the passwords for things such as corporate accounts and banks, using a device other than the one you traveled with.
- Inform your bank or credit card companies of your return and review transactions.
- Continue to monitor your business and personal financial institution transitions for unauthorized or unapproved use.

IDENTITY THEFT ABROAD

In the early 1970s, when I traveled as a teenager throughout Europe with my family, it was something of a tradition for our father, the architect of our global travels thanks to hard work and saving on his part and also the famous Arthur Frommer's travel guidebook *Europe on $5 and $10 a Day*, to lose his camera, passport, and money. This happened more than once. Fortunately for my father, we were traveling in what was a safer time. Identity theft was almost nonexistent. The US Embassy reissued a new passport on the spot with no more than my father's drivers license as proof of his identity; his traveler's checks were a whole lot safer than carrying cash because ID and signature verification were required to cash it (unlike cash, if a traveler's check was lost or stolen, the issuing company will replace it), and the only photos lost were the limited ones taken on the 36-exposure roll of Kodak film on his camera, and although credit cards were beginning to catch on, it was well before the days of electronic exchange of personal information and automation. Identity theft was a crime that was in its infancy.

How times have changed. The frequency of identity theft has increased dramatically. Criminals use electronic means to obtain the personally identifiable information (PII) needed to carry out this crime. The threat is real as evidenced in some of the key findings from the US Department of Justice's Victims of Identity Theft report:

- ID theft cost Americans US$10 billion more than household burglary, motor vehicle theft, and property theft in 2012.
- 85% of fraudulent use involves existing accounts.
- 7% of persons aged 16 or older were victims of ID theft in 2012.
- 29% of ID theft that involved personal information took one month or more to resolve.
- 66% of ID theft victims report a direct financial loss (US Department of Justice, Victims of Identity Theft, 2012).

The threat actor's goals may include attempts to ruin reputation, cripple financial status, or create legal problems. The classes or the types of threat actors could include hacktivists (hacker activists), disgruntled former/current employees, cybercriminals, and nation states. Today's online connectivity fosters a proliferation of locations where PII may be retained and available. Additionally, personalized e-mail phishing attacks (spear phishing and whaling) are increasing in sophistication (National Security Agency, 2014). While America is one of the top victim countries in the world, Russia is considered the principal threat actor in terms of identity theft. Russian hackers are the world's biggest supplier of fraudulent credit card numbers and other PII. High unemployment rates have pushed thousands of software engineers and programmers into poverty, forcing them to turn to illegal activities in order to survive. The Russian mob has welcomed them with open arms, providing them with the equipment and reaping the benefits of their criminal work.

Eleven countries with the highest rates of identity theft in the world are a strange mix of wealth and poverty, but they have few things in common. All have strong economies and citizens who prefer to do their banking online, leaving enough trails for hackers to pick up and steal their identity (Jevtic, 2015). They are the following:

1. Mexico
2. United States
3. India
4. UAE
5. China
6. United Kingdom
7. Brazil
8. Australia
9. Singapore
10. South Africa
11. Canada

While you should always be vigilant with regard to your personal information, travel presents a unique and higher risk than when you are at home. The steps previously outlined in this chapter regarding personal cybersecurity measures while traveling should provide a good measure of protection to your PII. If you are being targeted for identity theft, there will be indicators such as unexplained charges or withdrawals from your bank or credit card accounts (this occurred to me about 10 years ago, in New York City) or a deluge of e-mails or calls soliciting you to make a purchase, you do not get your bills or other mail, merchants refuse your checks, debt collectors call you about debts that are not yours, you find unfamiliar accounts or charges on your credit report, medical providers bill you for services that you did not use, your health plan rejects your legitimate medical claim because the records show you have reached your benefits limit, the Internal Revenue Service notifies you that more than one tax return was filed in your name or that you have income from an employer you do not work for, you get notice that your information was compromised by a data breach at a company where you do business or have an account, or you are arrested for a crime that someone else allegedly committed in your name. You need to act fast—make it a priority. The following are the steps that you should take:

1. Cancel your credit/debit cards. With ATM cards, if you report the loss before someone uses your ATM/debit card, you have zero liability, but your liability increases in other instances. With credit cards, if you report the loss before your card is used fraudulently, you are not liable; if not, your liability is limited to $50.
2. Contact the major credit bureaus and initiate a fraud alert. An initial fraud alert is good for 90 days and extendable up to seven years. If someone else tries to set up a new account or take out a loan in your name, you will receive a phone call to confirm that it is you. Advise the credit bureaus that you want a copy of your credit report. Also, solicit additional information or advice that they can give you (Equifax: 1-800-685-1111, http://www.equifax .com; Trans Union: 1-800-916-8800, http://www.transunion.com; Experian: 1-888-397-3742, http://www.experian.com).
3. If your social security card was in your wallet (and now you know why it *never* should have been in the first place), call your local social security administration office and explain what happened. They will replace the card for free, but you will have to fill out Form SS-5 and present documentation (Danisewicz, 2013).
4. Contact your bank and other financial/investment institutions. They should offer to change your accounts, if necessary.

5. Subscribe to a credit monitoring service that monitors your credit and immediately reports significant changes in same, that is, large purchases, unauthorized purchases.

A stolen identity can be a cloak of anonymity for criminals and terrorists and a danger to national security and private citizens alike (Federal Bureau of Investigation, 2016). Identity thieves can use your personal information to open bank accounts or obtain credit cards in your name. Consider taking steps to protect yourself against future identity theft. Visit the Federal Trade Commission's identity theft center, an excellent site to help you deter, detect, and defend against identity theft. Collect and save paperwork related to your loss. If an arrest and a conviction are obtained in the United States, the judge will consider requiring the offender to pay you restitution. You may be asked to provide verification of the amount of money that you lost.

REFERENCES

Danisewicz, C., "Travel assistance 101: What to do if your wallet is lost or stolen while traveling," *On Call International*, accessed March 12, 2016, http://www.oncallinternational.com/blog/travel-assistance -101-what-to-do-if-your-wallet-is-lost-or-stolen-while-traveling/ (August 2, 2013).

Higgins, K. J., "Korean-speaking cyberspies targeting corporate execs via hotel networks," *Information Week DARK Reading*, accessed January 26, 2016, http://www.darkreading.com/vulnerabilities---threats /advanced-threats/korean-speaking-cyberspies-targeting-corporate -execs-via-hotel-networks/d/d-id/1317361 (October 11, 2014).

Jevtic, A., "11 countries with the highest rate of identity theft in the world," *Insider Monkey*, accessed January 26, 2016, http://www .insidermonkey.com/blog/11-countries-with-the-highest-rates-of -identity-theft-in-the-world-351940/ (June 6, 2015).

National Security Agency, "Identity theft and mitigations," *NSA Fact Sheet*, https://www.nsa.gov/ia/_files/factsheets/FactSheet_IdentityTheft ThreatAndMitigations_Unclassified.pdf (May, 2014).

Federal Bureau of Investigation, "Identity theft," *The FBI*, accessed March 12, 2016, https://www.fbi.gov/about-us/investigate/cyber /identity_theft (March, 2016).

The Week, "Beware China's 'honeytrap' spies," *The Week*, accessed March 20, 2016, http://theweek.com/articles/487543/beware-chinas -honeytrap-spies (February 3, 2011).

U.S. Department of Justice, Victims of Identity Theft, Erika Harrell, PhD. and Lynn Langton, PhD., BJS Statisticians, December 2013, NCJ 243779 (2012).

ENDNOTES

1. Alternatively called the *Tapaoux group*.
2. *Malware* is shorthand for *malevolent software*, and, indeed, that is exactly what it is. It is a broad term that encompasses various forms of hacker exploits such as viruses, worms, Trojan horses, keystroke loggers, rootkits, botnets, and spyware, for example.
3. Botnets are networks made up of remote-controlled computers or bots. These computers have been infected with malware that allows them to be remotely controlled. Some botnets consist of hundreds of thousands—or even millions—of computers. According to a report from Russian-based Kaspersky Labs, botnets—not spam, viruses, or worms—currently pose the biggest threat to the Internet. A report from Symantec came to a similar conclusion.
4. A DDoS attack can be used for several purposes. It can be used for extortion, to shut down a website or an individual's operation or to continue a business, or for cover for a different more malicious attack—its use in this regard is to distract or delay actions by the target.

CHAPTER 8

Shopping Malls, Sports Stadiums, Theaters, etc.
Soft Targets

INTRODUCTION

You might be browsing the fruit stand at a local market, having a morning cappuccino at a sidewalk café or the hotel restaurant, sunning yourself on a crowded beach or cheering on the local football team in a crowded stadium, or perhaps you have just dropped off your family at the airport, waving goodbye as they move toward the crowded morning check-in counter. Odds are, in ever-increasing frequency, you are innocently placing yourself or your family in the crosshairs of a terrorist attack.

In the five months since the November 15, 2015 Paris, France terrorist attacks that left 498 innocent civilians lying dead or wounded, there have been an estimated 34 or more terrorist incidents worldwide, resulting in 1800 or more casualties, specifically aimed at soft targets (Wikipedia, 2016).[1] A *soft target* is a location where people congregate in large numbers such as restaurants and cafes, hotels, resorts, theatres or sports stadiums, or the departure area of an airport. It is an area where there is no expectation by the public of a strong security presence. These kinds of attacks are likely to only increase. ISIS is expanding its reach into the West. While most of the soft target attacks still occur in developing countries in Africa and the Middle East, these operations serve to sharpen the tactical skills and strategies of terrorist planners. As we have seen, sooner or later, these attacks spill outside of the conflict zones in Syria, Libya, Iraq, and Nigeria and with deadly effectiveness explode onto the streets of European cities. Left unchecked, the United States will likely be next.

This threat is very real and growing. In January 2016, Rob Wainwright, the head of Europol, the Hague-based organization that coordinates European Union policing efforts over terrorism and organized crime, said ISIS had "developed a new combat-style capability to carry out a campaign of large-scale terrorist attacks on a global stage, with a particular focus in Europe" (Willsher and Walker, 2016). Barely two months later, Wainwright's prediction tragically came true in the twin assaults on the Brussels airport and metro. The armed assault tactics frequently used by Al Shabab to devastating effectiveness on hotels, restaurants, and shopping malls in East Africa are firmly ensconced in the modern Islamic terror tactical playbook. In recent times, these armed assault-style tactics were employed by the terrorist group Lashkar-e-Taiba in the Mumbai, India, attacks on several hotel venues in 2008. More recently, Al Shabab was responsible for the bloody 2012 attack on the Westgate Mall in Kenya and has since honed the tactic on hotels and restaurants in Mogadishu, Somalia. Islamic extremist terrorists, although only loosely affiliated in separate groups around the world, do pay attention to each other's successes and replicate what works. Increasingly, it appears that terrorists' level of planning for attacks are high, including dry runs before the actual attack. Weapons, ammunition, and explosives can be cached near the target for easy access in advance; there is demonstrated operation and communications security and—ominously—little to no interest in negotiation or keeping live hostages. The ISIS cell active in France and Belgium has shown a sophisticated level of tactical planning, with the logistics needed to obtain the explosives and the weaponry to execute the attack, and an ability for those who survive to recoup and continue planning further attacks.

Increasingly as soft target venues in large cities are hit, the ability of the police and the military to provide adequate security becomes taxed beyond their capabilities. It is one thing to provide security for iconic, high-profile targets. Maintaining a high level of security visibility on the street can only be sustained for so long. When your enemy shifts to places where people dine, find entertainment, or stay, the list of potential targets becomes endless. The attacks in France and Belgium were both successfully executed despite unprecedented levels of alert by the authorities. It would seem that the security theatre on consisting display of heavily armed police and military throughout a city is no longer a deterrent for terrorists, and that alone is a chilling prospect. It is a false sense of security, at best. When it comes to soft targets, personal security is ultimately your first and last line of defense.

PREPARATION

There are only two specific elements of preparation that you need to pay attention to before going to a soft target location. First is timing. Second is location and layout. With regard to timing—when you plan to go to the mall or the theatre or an event—keep in mind that there are distinct patterns involved with a terrorist team's selection of specific soft targets. One key element is that of timing. Terrorists want to achieve maximum publicity for actions. The denser the crowd, the higher the body count. They will choose the national holiday, the big event, the peak season. If you have some control over timing, you can build in an element of security deterrence by choosing time periods for shopping, travel, dining, sunbathing, etc., that are off peak or are before/after the morning and evening rush hours. The Westgate Mall attack commenced around lunchtime on a Saturday, when the mall was filled with shoppers. The Brussels airport attack commenced in the morning at the departure area ticket counter when it was certain to be crowded with travelers checking in for their flights. The Sousse beach resort attack in Tunis in 2015 occurred in peak tourist season, at noon when the beach was packed with sunbathers on their annual European holiday. To the extent possible, try to mitigate your risks by selecting off-peak season or rush hour travel and activity at the venue to which you are going. Think about avoiding crowded, packed places at Christmas, New Year's, Ramadan or Eid Al-Fitr, Passover, or Thanksgiving.

Secondly, look specifically at the location and the layout of your destination. The terrorist planning team did precisely the same thing, and you should too. They were planning an attack—you will be planning your escape. Try to obtain the layout of the venue so that you know where the exits are that can be used for an escape and the chokepoints you should avoid. In malls, make note of where the larger department stores are located as they have secondary exits or loading dock areas in back of house. At many resort hotels, the design is low-rise horizontal structures, which offer many access points in and out of the building. Resorts are often open campuses with minimal barriers and multiple access and egress points spread over acres of property, often near expanses of beach, water, jungle, mountainous terrain, and varied geological features. If you are not able study the layout of the venue before you depart, try to find a mall map or a map of the location once you get there and spend some time getting yourself clearly oriented with the exits, the major shopping stores, or the major landmarks within the campus or the venue. In particular, take note of elevator or escalator locations. Mark these areas and—very important—identify alternative ways around them, such as an emergency stairwell. As you proceed through the location when things are normal, always keep an eye out for alternate exits, public phones, WiFi hot spots, restrooms, guard or police stations, information booths, or first aid centers and clinics that in a contingency would provide support. In a resort, knowing where the alternative exits are and where the natural cover is located can be extremely useful knowledge in an assault-style attack.

If you visit a site repeatedly, practice entering and exiting by the safest route, so that you train yourself to it. If you must flee, do not get sucked into fleeing the way you came in just because it is the way you came in or get sucked in the direction that the crowd is moving. Comply with your prior evaluation of the safest exit in the preparation phase, unless a threat gets in the way.

DETECTION

One theme that is consistent throughout after-action reports of terrorist incidents is the survivor's admission that "something was not right (about the shooter, or the situation), but I dismissed it." Our instincts are that small voice that whispers in our ear that there is something odd or off about the situation. As mentioned earlier, watch for the absence of familiar and the presence of strangeness. That feeling, more often than not, is momentary and fleeting. However, you should learn to trust your instincts and follow through on them. Things that you should watch for include the following:

- Odd demeanor: Terrorists and criminals are typically not balanced human beings. They will often try to fit in in terms of how they are dressed and what they are carrying, but if you are paying attention—something does not fit or add up. At the Sousse beach attack, in Tunisia, the attacker was dressed for the beach, but his Kalishnikov rifle was hidden by a large beach umbrella he was awkwardly carrying. In a crowd of happy tourists on holiday, look for that one who is dressed like a tourist but whose demeanor is decidedly not happy but grim or detached. If he or she is a suicide bomber, they might try to look and act natural, but deep down it is very difficult to contain their anxiety or euphoria. According to a former Israeli intelligence officer, Major Avi Nardia, "You can see it in their face." That small observation says a lot. An individual about to commit a suicide bombing may display nervousness, profuse sweating, constant scanning for fear of being discovered, or the proverbial thousand-yard stare that one witnesses in soldiers who have been in combat and are still disconnected from utter horror of what they saw. In the suicide attacker's case, he or she is trying to psychologically disconnect from what they are about to do or may be under the influence of a controlled substance to numb his or her natural sensibilities. It is at this stage where you have the greatest ability to detect a possible attack (Wagner, 2016).

- Heavy, loose fitting apparel that does not make sense for the climate or the venue: It can be used to conceal a suicide vest or belt, or a weapon, or both.
- An unusually heavy backpack or bag.
- An unattended backpack or bag that someone sets down and walks away from: This happened with the Tsarnaev brothers at the Boston Marathon bombing in 2014, where both brothers set down backpacks concealing homemade bombs and walked away.
- A vehicle left parked and abandoned in a no-parking zone.

CONSIDERATIONS ABOUT THE THREAT

Before the twin attacks by al Qaeda on our US embassies in Nairobi, Kenya, and Dar Es Salaam, Tanzania, on August 7, 1998, the standard response protocol for a bomb threat was one designed with a very different adversary and set of tactics in mind. Bearing in mind threat actors of yesteryear that telephoned in bomb threats, presumably having smuggled in a bomb that was ticking away in the bowels of a building or parking areas, diplomats diligently cleared their desks of working papers and tucked them away in their safes, queued up at the nearest stairwell, and calmly filed out of the building to a waiting area some small distance away from the embassy. All were very deliberate, and all were very time consuming. The terrorists who attacked our embassies then and continue to attack the West today are singularly unconcerned about providing a warning. They might (will not always) praise their deity in a battle cry before activating their suicide vest or pressing the button in the car or the truck. For some kinds of attacks, there is little to no time for a response once the threat is identified.

The point is that as the threat environment has changed, you need to adapt and change with it. Unfortunately, glacially paced change is in the nature of large corporations or governments. Ultimately, following those tragic attacks, new procedures were issued regarding bomb threats that took the tactics of suicide truck bombers into account. The real issue, however, is the fact that the nature of the threat was already well known, yet nothing had changed. It took the shock of a terrible attack to nudge the leviathan that is our bureaucracy toward a new strategy. That in itself is tragic, and bureaucratic intransigence is a major risk factor that should be taken into consideration.

It is important to pay attention to the threat actors and the kinds of tactics they use in this day and age to assess how you will respond to an event. This is especially critical given the kinds of risks we, as individuals, must face today given the increasingly heavy emphasis by terrorists on soft target venues. Being prepared and alert can go a long way toward keeping you alive. The countermeasures recommended below are not a guarantee—a surprise attack is still a surprise, and there will always be limitations about what measures you can take. However, the difference between being unprepared and alert instead of clueless is in my view what gives you an edge that can keep you alive.

There are two threat event responses that we will describe. The first is the active shooter (or shooters) event, which will address the assault-style tactics increasingly being used by terrorists abroad such as in the 2015 Paris Charlie Hebdo attack; the November 2015 multiple Paris assaults; and the recent luxury hotel attacks in Ouagadougou, Burkina Faso, Bamako, Mali, and the Grand Bassam Beach Resort attack in the Ivory Coast. The second is the suicide bomber attack such as what we have recently witnessed in Brussels, Belgium, and the 2005 Amman, Jordan, luxury hotel attacks.

RESPONSE COUNTERMEASURE 1: ACTIVE SHOOTERS

The explosive, deafening sound of unexpected gunfire in close proximity is usually the first indication that you are in what is known as an *active shooter* scenario. It is at this moment, if you survive the first volleys from the attackers, that you must have a clear plan of action in place. There is a saying attributed to a Navy SEAL that sums it up very succinctly: "One does not rise to the occasion, but falls back to the level of their training." This is very true. During the US Civil War, in the shock of combat, many soldiers who died were found to have multiple lead balls rammed down into their musket barrel, loaded compulsively in the heat and the shock of battle. With little discipline or training, they fell back on fear in the situation and in the confusion never fired their weapon. Freezing up in the face of a threat event is a common and very human response to a threat event. This disassociation from what is unfolding is more likely to occur if you have no plan on which to fall back. It will get you, and those you may be responsible for around you, killed. While it may be understandable, it is not acceptable. The City of Houston, Texas, police department some years ago developed a simple but effective protocol for responding to an active shooter, assault-style attack. It is known simply as *Run, Hide, Fight*. It is a simple, elegant, and commanding way of responding. There are others, but in my view, they are too complex and didactic and, while fine for explaining in a classroom the dynamics of an assault and how to respond to it, utterly fail in terms of a portable and clear method for action when on the street. When shots ring out, you need trained instincts, not a complex thought process to guide your actions. Keep it simple. Following are the elements of this security response.

Run

This step is about escaping the situation. When the first volleys ring out, get off the X. Run!

Today's terrorists do not take hostages or negotiate. When the incident happens, it will be explosive and breathtaking in its rapidity. When an incident unfolds, you do not have the time or luxury to ponder your situation. You will fall back on your preparation, your training. That means knowing, intuitively, *where* to run to when an attack unfolds. Knowing your potential routes away from the incident, acting quickly, and moving down your chosen path of exit does two things: (a) as you move away from the gunfire your chances of survival increase (*remember, distance is your friend!*) and (b) being capable of acting in the moment (rather than freezing up) decreases the potential for confusion, panic, or procrastination on your part. There is no time to think when the incident begins—so advance mental preparation is crucial. Case in point: Many of the victims of the Nairobi Westgate Mall attack were killed because they were frightened into immobility. *These situations can pose hard ethical decisions.* Ultimately, it will be up to you. However, the best advice— although it may sound cold—is not to waste time coaxing an individual paralyzed by fear and crying to escape with you. This is not necessarily an easy decision, and I would make exceptions for family members. No one else. In the situation, the imperative is to move away from the threat as quickly as possible, so driving that point home forcefully is crucial to other individuals who are with you. Help the procrastinator snap out of it—if they cannot, then take the lead and leave them behind.

Chokepoints and Routes

Avoid predictable chokepoints. Elevators and escalators should be avoided at all cost. Both can lose electrical power and leave you stranded, or worse, you might be in that glut of panicked tourists or shoppers trying to get out all at once and risk being trampled to death or left in the terrorist's crosshairs because they, too, are hoping for victims coming to them on the elevator or the escalator. Take the stairs.

Keep moving. If you escape—keep moving away from the scene. Do not stop to take cell phone videos, pictures, or selfies. The last thing you want is to be caught between first responders and the terrorists. If you encounter additional shooters, immediately seek cover and concealment by staying low and out of sight. Remember that concealment is anything that will prevent an enemy from seeing a target—it will not necessarily protect you from incoming fire. Cover is anything that can both conceal you and deflect or absorb incoming rounds fired at you. Once you are in motion, commit to your action but keep your wits about you. If you must reverse or change course, remember that you still have two more options.

Hide

If you are unable to escape or come up against additional attackers while running and must change course, then you will have to find a place where you can shelter in place, barricade yourself in, and hide. Turn off the lights; turn off your cell phone, and if there are others with you, make sure they do the same. If you are at a resort location and know the layout of the campus, hopefully, you will have identified outside venues where you can seek cover or concealment. Do not get too comfortable in your relative safety because a determined adversary, given time, can find you. Your principal objective is ultimately to escape. However, finding a place to hunker down can temporarily deny the attackers access to you, while they seek out easier prey.

If possible, while in hiding, try to communicate quietly with police and emergency personnel, both to tell them what you are witnessing and to have a link with information from the outside. Remain cognizant of the source of the threat, if the attackers or the group of attackers is on the move and in what direction. Establishing and keeping in contact with police can be vital, particularly if you are not in the open and in a lockdown situation where your escape is determined by information you cannot know because it is outside your shelter. Keeping communication lines open, even if you are silent and just waiting for information to be given to you, lets police and rescue know where you are, which lets you know when it is safe to escape and by what means.

Fight

Fighting may be your only option. In both the terrorist attacks on the Westgate Mall in Kenya, in 2013, and earlier in the 2008 Mumbai attacks, the attackers had no desire to negotiate or take hostages. Killing was their principal objective. Confronted with an armed attacker and with no way to run or hide, fighting back to defend yourself—with whatever you have at hand—is your only option for survival. Your objective is to disrupt or incapacitate the attacker, and this can be done by turning the table on him or her and acting aggressively and smartly. Find improvised weapons such as a fire extinguisher, a chair, a heavy object, a book, or a paperweight and be prepared to strike or throw it at the attacker. If you are in a room with lights, turn them out. When the attacker bursts into your location, commit to your action. If there is a group with you, you should understand that a group en masse rushing against the attacker, combined with yelling and distraction techniques, is likely your best option. Remember, it is your life or theirs. A good example of this option against an attacker includes the two off-duty US servicemen who, with two other passengers, elected to counterattack and subdue a heavily armed terrorist attacker aboard a high-speed train between Amsterdam and Paris in August 2015.

Recovery

It is very important to know that first responders will likely be very focused on finding and engaging the attacker and will not be that friendly. Support their efforts. The police are trained to look at hands—"hands kill" is the old maxim. If you have a mobile phone or something else, put it away and keep your hands raised and fingers spread. Do not make sudden, quick movements to answer a call from your best friend or husband or wife. That can all be done later. Do not ask questions, and if you have a member of your team who feels compelled to launch into a tirade, burst into sobs, or ask questions, shut them up. Do just what you are told and proceed in the opposite direction of the first responders entering the threat area unless told otherwise. There will be time for venting, crying, or questions later.

RESPONSE COUNTERMEASURE 2: SUICIDE BOMBER

In a suicide attack, there is practically nothing you can do when the bomber detonates—the flash to bang is instantaneous. The key to mitigating *some* of your risk to exposure to a suicide attack is in the detection phase, and—if you do survive the blast—in the postattack phase. Understanding the tactics and the behavior of the threat actor is crucial, if you are alert, to the recognition and the action in the detection phase of an attack. Also, depending on your circumstances, there are choices you can make in terms of transportation, crowds, and the like that can increase your odds at survival.

Preattack Phase

As noted earlier, the act of killing oneself is not natural. Islamic jihadist terrorists have justified suicide attacks as martyrdom operations and go to great lengths to ensure that bombers know they will be elevated to the status of heroes in their community if they sacrifice themselves. Despite this assurance, there are behavioral tells and other indicators that you can spot, if you are observant: bulky clothing on a hot day, to hide the explosive vest; a very heavy backpack or piece of luggage; nervousness or sweating; or a distant look in the bomber's eyes, as they try to disconnect from what they are about to do—a glazed thousand yard stare. If you are observant, this stare is something you can catch because it is abnormal in an active crowd of people going on about their normal everyday lives. It falls in the category of strange.

Also, suicide attackers want to inflict as much damage as possible—this is inculcated in them by their trainers and commanders. They gravitate toward the largest crowd of people (such as what happened at the Brussels airport check-in counter) or the center of mass (the middle car of a bus or a train). To the extent possible, be aware of this and make your choices accordingly.

Detonation Phase

If you do have a brief indication that detonation is imminent, such as a glimpse of the device, or something that the attackers shout, the best advice is as follows:

- Duck and cover—Lay flat, as low as you can get. Most explosives used by suicide bombers are designed to burst in a flower bouquet pattern to throw the shrapnel horizontally between 2 and 6 ft. above the ground. This pattern increases the chances of hitting the human torso and head with shrapnel. Therefore, the best place to be in the event of an explosion is flat on the ground (Usmani, 2015).
- Keep your mouth open and breathe in small intervals—The most lethal aspect in an explosion is not shrapnel or heat, it is the blast overpressure. The blast wave travels at supersonic velocity and severely affects the air-filled organs like lungs, kidneys, and bowels. We naturally tend to take a deep breath and hold it in emergencies. However, this proves lethal in a bombing situation, since our lungs become like a pressurized balloon to be ruptured by the blast wave. The majority of victims in a typical suicide bombing die from internal bleeding in the lungs. Only 6% on average die from shrapnel wounds. Your chances of injury with empty lungs are far smaller compared to holding your breath.
- Reduce your lateral profile—While laying on the ground, try to lay on one side and use your arms to protect the exposed eye.

Postdetonation Phase

There will likely be no warning of an explosion. When the vest or device works, it is instantaneous—one second, all is normal, and the next, the air is filled with smoke and there is fire and debris. It is incredibly disorienting. You will not be able to hear; everything will be muffled. Once the device has exploded, the following measures are recommended:

- If you have survived and can move, cover your mouth with a handkerchief or clothing to reduce the enormous amount of dust and smoke you could inhale. Do not shout; you inhale a lot of dust when yelling.
- Leave the area of the blast as quickly as possible. Do not retrieve personal possessions, luggage, or other items. Do not immediately try to make phone calls. Your immediate objective is to put distance between yourself and the blast zone. There could be a secondary bomber targeting the crowd that comes in to help. Be aware and alert and get away from the blast scene.

SELECTED THREAT ACTOR PROFILES: THE JIHADIST SUICIDE BOMBER

How often, in the wake of a terrorist attack involving Islamic jihadist suicide bombers, do we hear terms such as *criminal monsters, crazed madmen, nihilists,* or similar epithets? Perhaps it is understandable, given the horrendous consequences of these attacks. However, as professionals in the business of security, we owe it to ourselves and the clients we serve to put aside the hyperbole used by politicians and others and take a closer look at the profile of suicide bombers—labels are the luxury of pundits, armchair analysts, and individuals who feel they must calm fears and soothe feelings. If we do not clearly understand the threat, we will never be able to develop an effective and successful countermeasure to that threat—randomly attached labels denote one's inability to fathom deeper reasons for the act of suicide bombing and do nothing to advance the understanding and the development of effective countermeasures. Typically, most suicide bombers run the gamut of psychological makeup—some may have had a criminal past (such as the Belgian bombers in March 2016), but their motives are far from criminal in nature, and it would be a mistake to label them as such, the criminality of the murderous deed they commit aside. Others have no criminal past, and in the majority of cases in the West, suicide attackers come from relatively successful—by outward standards—families. Still others from countries such as Libya, Algeria, or elsewhere are psychologically normal and deeply integrated into social networks and emotionally attached to their national communities (Hassan, 2009). Nonetheless, as Westerners, we seem unable to grasp why a healthy, outwardly successful, financially comfortable, seemingly normal young man or woman straps 10–15 kg of triacetone triperoxide (nicknamed Mother of Satan) to his or her body and with little hesitation activates the trigger. Why? The answer to that remains complex, but one plausible answer is that these individuals believe that their community is under threat. Within Islam, this community is called the *Umma* or the broader community of Muslims. One often hears from radical imams that "when the arm of the 'body of Islam' hurts, the whole body hurts." They are speaking of the Muslim Umma. Within Islamist extremist groups, the theme of injustice, of grievance to the larger cause of Islam, is regenerated constantly and coupled with the obligation to do something about it. Further, to fail in perpetuating justice, or jihad, is to bring shame to family, friends, and the community as a whole. This is a powerful motivating factor within Muslim communities, which is not so apparent or prevalent in the Western psyche or tradition. It is, however, a drumbeat in radicalized Islamist circles. The importance of the individual in Muslim communities is subservient to the whole—this is in their DNA. Martyrdom relies on the perception of selflessness for the cause and uses sunk costs motivation, that is, the martyr does not die in vain. Martyrdom implies that the person in question died for a cause or is willing to die for a cause. The symbolic impact of martyrdom varies across cultures, but within the field of radicalization, the act or the pursuit of martyrdom denotes the absolute value of a radical's way of life. Suicide bombing falls into the category of altruistic suicidal actions that involve valuing one's life as less worthy than that of the group's honor, religion, or some other collective interest. For the individual, participating in a suicide mission is not about dying and killing alone but has a broader significance for achieving multiple purposes—from personal to communal. These include gaining community approval and political success; liberating the homeland; achieving personal redemption or honor; using martyrdom to effect the survival of the community; refusing to accept subjugation; seeking revenge for personal and collective humiliation; conveying religious or nationalistic convictions; expressing guilt, shame, material and religious rewards; and escaping from intolerable everyday degradations of life under occupation, boredom, anxiety and defiance. The witches' brew that configures these purposes together varies and is an outcome of specific circumstances of the political conflict behind the rise of suicide attacks as a tactic and a weapon. Perceived injustice is stoked into a hot fire by extremists, and the dark consequence of this manifests in revenge. This is a strong motivator of suicide bombers. Revenge is considered a response to the continuous suffering of an aggrieved community. At the heart of the whole process are perceptions of personal harm; unfairness and injustice; and anger, indignation, and hatred associated with such perceptions. Men attach more value to vengeance than women, and young people are more prepared to act in a vengeful manner than older individuals. It is not surprising, then, to find that most suicide bombers are both young and male (Hassan, 2009). In September 2007, when American forces raided an Iraqi insurgent camp in the desert town of Singar near the Syrian border, they discovered biographies of more than 700 foreign fighters. The Americans were surprised to find that 137 were Libyans and 52 of them were from the small Libyan town of Darnah. The reason why so many of Darnah's young men had gone to Iraq for suicide missions was not the global jihadi ideology but an explosive mix of desperation, pride, anger, sense of powerlessness, local tradition of resistance, and religious fervor. A similar mix of factors is now motivating young Pashtuns to volunteer for suicide missions in Pakistan and Afghanistan. Finally, an Israeli study of several suicide bombers, whose missions failed because either their vests failed to explode or they were apprehended and prevented from activating their bomb, revealed some interesting psychological tendencies between the bombers themselves and their commanders. The bombers themselves tended to have lower egos and were intimidated by people in positions of authority. They are easily led. Organizers, on the other hand, had bigger egos, were better mentally equipped to handle stress, and for the most part unwilling to consider suicide martyrdom themselves. The profile described fits that of Germaine Lindsay, one of the London suicide bombers on July 7, 2005. Lindsay, who was married to Samantha Lewthwaite, was considered to be somewhat gullible and easily influenced. Lewthwaite went on to become known as the *White Widow* and is considered a lethal jihadist leader and recruiter both for Al Shabab and now ISIS.

REFERENCES

Hassan, R., "What motivates the suicide bombers," *Yale Global Online*, accessed March 20, 2016 http://yaleglobal.yale.edu/content/what-motivates-suicide-bombers (September 3, 2009).

Usmani, Z., "Common sense guide to survive a suicide bombing attack," *Linked in Pulse*, accessed March 14, 2016, https://www.linkedin.com/pulse/common-sense-guide-survive-suicide-bombing-attack-usmani (March 23, 2015).

Wagner, J., "How to survive bomb attacks," *World Wide Dojo*, accessed March 14, 2016, http://www.worldwidedojo.com/reality-based/how-to-survive-bomb-attacks (2016).

Wikipedia, "List of terrorist incidents, July–December 2015," https://en.wikipedia.org/wiki/List_of_terrorist_incidents,_July%E2%80%93December_2015 (April 12, 2016).

Willsher, K., and Walker, P., "ISIS targeting Europe for Paris style attacks," *The Guardian*, accessed March 2, 2016, http://www.theguardian.com/world/2016/jan/25/french-police-foiled-paris-terror-attack-bernard-cazeneuve (January 25, 2016).

ENDNOTE

1. Estimate derived from a listing of terrorist incidents worldwide from November 13, 2015, to March 26, 2016.

CHAPTER 9

Risk Assessment for Personal Security

INTRODUCTION

The purpose of formally assessing risk in the field of personal security is to develop an executive protection program (see Chapter 4) or to develop a plan for a project that either you or someone you are in charge of is executing with a team in a high-risk location. There are several different kinds of risk assessment methods used today in the field of security and business with varying degrees of complexity in formula, granularity, scope, and terminology. The right kind of risk assessment depends on the application—one size or formula does not fit all. In the field of personal security, my own view is that the simpler the method, the better. Unlike risk assessments done for sensitive government or industrial facilities, infrastructure, or business enterprise, the personal security risk assessment is focused mainly on one key asset—you or individuals for whom you are immediately responsible. For this reason, the personal security risk assessment that I describe here is very suitable for tailoring to a *micro* rather than a *macro* scale and scope.

The risk assessment process is the best way to design and implement a personal security program or security program related to personal security—such as an executive protection or a corporate traveler security program. This approach methodically guides your collection, selection, and evaluation of information to ensure that it is detailed, accurate, and relevant. It provides structure to what is an imperfect science at best—although there continues to be excellent strides made in perfecting it. More than any of the other disciplines within the overall field of security, personal security is fraught with subjective information and is thus very dependent on good judgment, instinct, experience, and timing. This method can be used when you are required to design a program to demonstrate to decision makers your justification for countermeasure selection, for estimation of threat and risk, and as a baseline for future analysis. It is especially important when resources are limited and can only be allocated toward critical needs. It is a hands-on process that requires you to interact with the requirements of your stakeholders, research and ask questions about the kinds of adversaries you or your team might face, and understand the kinds of weakness that might exist through questioning and evaluation. The importance of asking the right question to get the right information—and not throwing something up against the wall (next to my dislike of checklists is the hackneyed question, "what keeps you awake at night?") to see what sticks—is very important when conducting an assessment, whether it is complex or simple. At the very least, you need to know what it is that you are digging into and do a bit of research before the survey. It is important to order your survey's sequence to mirror the risk assessment process. The analysis process is iterative and repetitive for a reason: By overlapping the right stages, you will be able to uncover the right data that evolve into information and link to each element of the process, providing continuity. Taking a haphazard or hasty approach to risk assessment in order to get to a quick solution and "make a plan!" does yourself or your client or team no favors. Asset criticality and impact of loss mirror elements within vulnerability and threat, so each must be taken in specific order to ensure discipline in the method. This also ensures that you remain as objective and unbiased as possible, which is particularly important when conducting purely qualitative assessments that have subjective inputs.

The risk analysis method that I have adapted for personal security in this book is based principally on the analytical risk management (ARM) process.[1] It is purely a qualitative method that provides a good estimate of your risk. The examples used to populate the data fields within the following tables are only for illustrative purposes, to give you a sense of how the method works.

STEP 1: IDENTIFY ASSETS AND IMPACT OF LOSS

The logical first step in the risk assessment process is to identify the assets requiring protection. Essentially, that means identifying and methodically thinking through those things about *yourself* that require protection and security and by extension your team, VIP client, or otherwise. Thinking critically about yourself or team members as the critical assets means that there are several important elements that support your (or their) well-being. These are also assets. This could be you or your team's health (people); your laptops, mobile phones, and credit cards (equipment/ materials); your data, passport or travel documents, plans, and intentions (information); hotel or residence (facility); and business meetings, appointments, or leisure activity (activities/operations). Typically, risk assessments are organization driven and more macro in scale. One's credit card or medication might not make the list of critical assets. In the specific context of personal security, however, this microassessment approach focuses in on what would be, in another context, relatively minor asset categories such as your prescription medicine, credit cards, identity documents, laptop, and data. For you, or your team, these seemingly minor assets are very important or, in some cases, critical to your survival and well-being.

The questions you might ask to gather more information about critical assets are the following:

- What items are critical to your health?
- What confidential or sensitive business activities will be occurring at the location to which you are traveling?
- What material or equipment is critical to your business activities and functions?
- How important is your team to your mission or project?
- What would be an undesirable event for you or your team and what would you expect the impact to be?

Identify Undesirable Events and Anticipated Impacts

The next stage of analysis is to identify and list undesirable events that could directly impact you or your identified assets, for example, a kidnap event, a terrorist attack, an armed robbery, a theft, a media exposure, or an event or a condition that shuts down your ability to communicate (natural disaster, attack targeting critical communication infrastructure, or theft/confiscation of your mobile/sat phone). Simply put, they are events that result in an impact of loss to your assets or yourself. When applying this analysis to your trip, it requires you to think through each stage and mode of your travel when living and working in a third-world country, each phase of your day from when you depart from your hotel or residence, to work, and back. Identify, in a general sense, the kinds of threat events that could arise in the environment or along the path of your trip. These do not have to be specific, only generalized for the time being. However, this exercise is the first filter used to distinguish what should be a realistic risk to consider and what should not be considered (Table 9.1).

Value/Prioritize Assets Based on Consequence of Loss

With a list of assets and associated impact-of-loss statements, you can now assign qualitative numerical and linguistic ratings to each impact

TABLE 9.1 Example of Chart for Developing Asset, Event, and Loss Impact Statements

Assets	Undesirable Threat or Hazard Events—Loss Impact Statements
Yourself	Kidnap—Extortion, possible injury, death
Team	Suicide bomber—Significant loss of life
Blood pressure meds	Heart attack—Possible loss of life (hazard event)
Laptop	Hacked—Compromise of confidential information
Credit card	Identity theft—Compromise of bank account, credit
Passport	Theft—Roadblock arrest or detainment, travel delay
Hotel	Terrorist assault—Significant injury and loss of life
Residence	Earthquake—Injury and possible death (hazard event)
Leisure activity	Terrorist attack—Significant injury and loss of life
Meeting	Disclosure—Predictable location, attendance

statement and, based on these ratings, prioritize which assets are more valuable. Value is determined by the consequence of loss. For example, if you are kidnapped and subsequently injured or killed, that would quite naturally be at the top of the list. If you lose your passport, the consequence of loss would be potential inconvenience and delay in travel, or at checkpoints, but much less consequential as loss of life. The consequence of a purposeful or inadvertent meeting disclosure could provide adversaries valuable information to your location and schedule that could then be exploited in a kidnap or an attack event. This is an example of a cascading event and impact, which is important to keep in mind when assessing undesirable impact and consequence in risk. These judgments are initially heuristic (best-guess "feel," trial-and-error) estimates that *can and should* be changed as more data are gathered. However, this filtering process is a methodical way to order and prioritize your risk analysis (Table 9.2).

Impact on Business or Mission Function

1. The postulated threat event or incident would have minimal or no impact on my business or mission function(s).
2. A threat event or an incident might cause some slight degradation of one function of my business or mission but only temporarily.
3. A threat event or an incident would minimally degrade my business or mission, by causing failure of one function of the task.
4. A threat event or an incident would significantly degrade my business or mission, by causing multiple failures of task functions.
5. A threat event or an incident would cause my business or mission to fail.

TABLE 9.2 Example of an Impact Assessment Matrix

| Threat/Hazard Event | Asset | Impact Assessment | | | | | Rating | |
		Business or Mission Degradation	Health (Sickness, Injury, Death)	Reputation	Recoverability	Total	No.	Linguistic
Kidnap	You	4	3	3	5	15	75	Critical
Suicide attack	Your team	5	5	4	5	19	95	Critical
Hacker	Your information	4	1	2	3	10	50	High
Lack of drug supply	Your equipment/ material	4	4	4	4	16	80	Critical

Scaling Criteria for Impact

Total	Impact Rating	Impact Value
20	100	Critical
19	95	
18	90	
17	85	
16	80	
15	75	
14	70	
13	65	
12	60	
11	55	

(Continued)

TABLE 9.2 (CONTINUED)   Example of an Impact Assessment Matrix

	Scaling Criteria for Impact	
Total	Impact Rating	Impact Value
10	50	High
9	45	
8	40	
7	35	
6	30	
5	25	
4	20	
3	15	Medium
2	10	
1	5	Low

Impact on Health (Sickness, Injury, and Death)

1. The postulated threat event or the hazardous condition would have minimal or no impact on my health.
2. The threat event or the hazardous condition would lead to illness or minor injury from which I could recover.
3. The threat event or the hazardous condition would cause minimal degradation of my health over time or injury requiring medical assistance.
4. The threat event or the hazardous condition would cause significant degradation of my health in a short time or crippling injury requiring hospitalization.
5. The threat event or the hazardous condition would cause major crippling injury or death.

Impact on Reputation

1. The postulated threat event or the hazardous condition would not harm my reputation or status.
2. The threat event or the hazardous condition would temporarily harm my reputation or status, but I could easily recover.
3. The threat event or the hazardous condition would cause some degradation of my reputation or status over time, requiring an investment of time and resources to recover.
4. The threat event or the hazardous condition would cause significant degradation/damage to my reputation or status in a short time, from which I could only partially recover.
5. The threat event or the hazardous condition would permanently damage or destroy my reputation or status.

Impact on Recoverability

1. I could fully recover all functions from the postulated threat event or hazardous condition within 24 hours.
2. I could fully recover all functions from the postulated threat event or hazardous condition within 24–48 hours.
3. I could fully recover or restore most functions from the postulated threat event or hazardous condition within 48 hours to one week.
4. I could fully recover or restore most functions from the postulated threat event or hazardous condition within one to six months.
5. I will be unable to fully recover or restore most functions from the postulated threat event or hazardous condition within six months.

STEP 2: IDENTIFY AND CHARACTERIZE
THE THREAT TO SPECIFIC ASSETS

There are a lot of threat actors, or agents, in the world today. For the purposes of your own personal risk situation relative to where you are located or where you are traveling, it does not make sense to identify all threat actors, along with their capabilities. Think of this stage of the analysis as a threat filter. The goal of the threat analysis is to identify and prioritize those threats that are relevant to you or your team and then estimate the degree of threat posed by the adversary to you, your health, communications, information, etc. A team of kidnappers operating in Colombia, for instance, has no relevance to you when your travel is to corporate offices in London. On the other hand, the presence of world-class pickpocket artists on Regent Street might be a threat on which you need to focus your attention and analysis. One of the reasons that I prefer the identification and the classification of assets and undesired events criticality before turning to threat is to ensure that I have a context to guide relevancy. Threat, at least in my view, should not be identified and estimated in the absence of the context that makes it relevant to your analysis. Otherwise, you will waste time and resources scenario spinning—looking for worst-case situations that are implausible, at best. The following are the stages of threat filtering.

Identify Threat Categories and Potential Adversaries

Threat categories are essentially buckets used to classify and subcategorize threats and adversaries that might put identified assets at risk, for example, categorization by motive such as "intentional, unintentional, and accidental." Subcategories under the category of *intentional* would represent types or classes of threat actors. Subcategories under *unintentional* or *accidental* would represent types of hazards or threat agents, either natural or human-made events. Note the distinction between threat actor and threat agent or hazard. The former assumes intent, motive, and opportunity—something premediated and planned. The latter assumes that there will be a history or a favorable environment for the event to occur, but since these are hazards, they are not targeting you—they just occur. You get caught in the path of a tsunami or not. A fire consumes your hotel, and if you are inside, you are directly affected. But it is not something that seeks you out. Categorize and subcategorize all the threats and the threat agents (hazards) that are relevant to you. This is the first threat filter (Table 9.3).

TABLE 9.3   Example of Threat Categories Used to Identify and Classify Various Types of Threat Events and Threat Actors

Intentional (Threat Actors)	Unintentional (Natural Hazard or Agent)	Accidental (Artificial Event)
Terrorist organization	Hurricane	Oil spill
Hackers	Tsunami	Road accidents
Kidnap gang	Famine	Fire
Pickpockets	Earthquake	Inaccessibility to drugs
Insurgents		

Assess Degree of Threat

Once relevant threats have been classified, the degree of threat to you must be estimated. This is done by examining various characteristics of the adversary or the hazard (Table 9.4). Each degree filter measures the levels of intensity, capability, past history (validation), and environmental suitability. When considering intent or motivation, look for evidence or indicators of the threat actor's resolve or desire to target you, your team, or someone who fits your profile. This is done through a set of questions regarding the adversary, such as whether the adversary has knowledge of the asset, a need for the asset, or a declared or a demonstrated interest in the asset. Working from broad to specific, estimate the following:

Intent and Motivation

1. There is no indication or evidence of intent or motivation by the threat actor to target you, your team, or area of operations (AORs).
2. General statement by the threat actor(s) of intent to target assets, which may or may not be associated with you or your team, in your AOR.
3. General statement by the threat actor(s) of intent to target assets directly associated with you or your team, in your AOR.
4. Credible indicators or evidence of intent or motivation by the threat actor(s) to target individuals or teams like yours (if not you or your team, personally), in your AOR.
5. Credible indicators or evident of intent or motivation by the threat actor(s) to *specifically* target you and your team, in your AOR.

TABLE 9.4 Example of a Threat Assessment Matrix

		Threat Assessment						Rating	
Threat Event	Asset	Intent and Motive	Capability (Competent)	Capability (Logistics)	History	Ops Environment	Total	No.	Linguistic
Kidnap	You	5	3	2	5	4	19	0.70	High
Suicide attack	Your team	3	3	2	2	2	12	0.35	Medium
Hacker	Your information	4	5	4	5	5	23	0.90	Critical
Lack of drug supply	Your equipment/ material	N/A	N/A	N/A	5	5	10	0.25	Medium

Scaling Criteria for Threat

Total	Vulnerability Rating	Rating
		Critical
25	1.0	
24	0.95	
23	0.90	
22	0.85	
21	0.80	
20	0.75	

(Continued)

TABLE 9.4 (CONTINUED)   Example of a Threat Assessment Matrix

Total	Scaling Criteria for Threat	
	Vulnerability Rating	Rating
19	0.70	High
18	0.65	
17	0.60	
16	0.55	
15	0.50	
14	0.45	Medium
13	0.40	
12	0.35	
11	0.30	
10	0.25	
9	0.20	Low
8	0.15	
7	0.10	
6	0.05	
5	0.01	

Skill and Workforce Capability of the Adversary

The degree of capability further delineates and adds (or subtracts) weight to the threat actor, providing a picture of your adversary's facility and aptitude to carry out an attack on you. Working from broad to specific, estimate the following:

1. The adversary does not have resource potential (workforce) or competency to carry out an attack on you or your team.
2. The adversary has little workforce potential and amateur-level familiarity with the skill set required to carry out an attack on you or your team.
3. The adversary has some workforce potential and some basic training or competency on skills needed to carry out an attack on you or your team.
4. The adversary has adequate workforce potential and intermediate-level training or skill needed to carry out an attack on you or your team.
5. The adversary has abundant workforce potential. Training and proven competency with skills to carry out an attack on you or your team are advanced (professional level).

Determine the Logistic Capability of the Adversary

The degree of logistic capability further delineates and adds (or subtracts) weight to the threat actor, providing a picture of your adversary's ability to acquire explosives, tools, safe house, or weapons to carry out an attack on you. Working from broad to specific, estimate the following:

1. The adversary does not have a logistic capacity or an acquisition network to carry out an attack on you or your team.
2. The adversary has very basic logistic capacity but no acquisition network required to carry out an attack on you or your team.
3. The adversary has minimal logistic and acquisition network capacity needed to carry out an attack on you or your team.
4. The adversary has adequate logistic and acquisition network capacity to carry out an attack on you or your team.
5. The adversary has sophisticated logistics and acquisition networks.

Determine Frequency of Threat-Related Incidents Based on Historical Data

This is an important category in assessing threat, because the presence, the absence, or the degree of *incidents* directly attributable to an identified *threat actor* informs you as to the malignancy or the benignity of the threat. For example, in the late 1990s, I was working in a Middle

Eastern capital. While there, I walked past the headquarters of a known terrorist group being given safe haven in the country on a daily basis. The guards outside of the main entrance knew that we were Americans but left us alone. Now, this group was and remains a capable, motivated terrorist threat actor. However, we knew that there was no history of direct attacks on US personnel inside this particular location at that time. Yes, the group was a threat. However, for the location and the time, our exposure was considered an acceptable risk because the group's history against us was benign. They merited careful watching, of course, but complete avoidance of the risk was not necessary or practical. Also, it is in the category of event history and frequency that relevancy of natural or human-made hazards becomes apparent.

Working from broad to specific, estimate the following:

1. No history of attacks or hazard events, successful or otherwise, on targets such as you or your team in the area to which you are traveling or are currently working
2. History of infrequent, unsuccessful attacks or unintentional disruptions on targets such as you or your team in the general region to which you are traveling or are currently working
3. History of infrequent successful attacks, hazard events, or unintentional disruptions on targets such as you or your team in the specific area to which you are traveling or are currently working
4. Recent history of frequent unsuccessful attacks, some unintentional disruptions, or minor hazardous events on targets such as you or your team in the general region to which you are traveling or are currently working
5. Recent history of frequent successful attacks, major hazard events, or chronic disruption on targets such as you or your team in the specific area to which you are traveling or are currently working

Determine the Favorability of the Operational Environment

What is *operational environment* in terms of suitability to me or to my adversary? When considering this category, I am reminded of a situation in which I found myself hunting Cape buffalo in Africa (outlined earlier in the book when illustrating an aspect of the principal of detection). Our party came up on a small group of Cape buffalo resting beneath some thorn trees, about 350 m from our Land Rover. I made the decision to move in closer to the buffalo, in order to get a clean shot. As I began to carefully move closer through the Savannah grass—which was waist high when I entered it—I quickly learned that the terrain beneath the grass was uneven. I found myself in thick grass that was over my head—and the realization dawned on me that I could no longer see or anticipate the movements of a quarry that weighed between 1100 and 2000 lb and had an excellent sense of smell and a reputation for being extremely aggressive. I had gone from being the hunter to potentially being the hunted. The operational environment literally shifted beneath my feet from one favorable to me to one favorable to the adversary. The operational environment is a composite of physical, cultural, political, and cyber conditions, circumstances, and influence that favor either you or your adversary's operational capabilities (US Army Combined Arms Center, 2009).

On a physical level, factors within one's operational environment include observation (the ability to observe or be observed), avenues of approach by you or by your adversary (this would include chokepoints, for instance), terrain obstacles or assets, and cover or concealment. To this last feature, I would add contrast, which is a concept used in the surveillance world to *force* contrast between you and your adversary in order to detect the threat. On a cultural level, factors within the operational environment include language, mannerisms, and traditions. Political factors can be organizations, tribes, political groups or parties, or other government agencies; cyber conditions in many ways can mirror the physical world in the sense that observation (for assessment purposes), pathways of access into your systems or devices, existing firewalls or physical obstacles to access, and concealment all apply to the virtual environment.

Working from broad to specific, estimate the following:

1. The operational environment greatly favors me or my team and represents a distinct disadvantage to the adversary. There are geophysical, climatic, or locational conditions that disfavor natural or accidental hazards.
2. The operational environment slightly favors me or my team and represents somewhat of a disadvantage to the adversary. There are geophysical, climatic, or locational conditions that usually disfavor natural or accidental hazards.
3. The operational environment is neutral. Neither I nor my team or the adversary is at an advantage or disadvantage. Geophysical, climatic, or locational conditions are benign.
4. The operational environment slightly favors the adversary and represents somewhat of a disadvantage to me or my team. There are geophysical, climatic, or locational conditions that might favor natural or accidental hazards.
5. The operational environment greatly favors the adversary and represents a distinct disadvantage to me or my team. There are geophysical, climatic, or locational conditions that greatly favor natural or accidental hazards.

STEP 3: IDENTIFY AND CHARACTERIZE VULNERABILITIES

Vulnerabilities are either inherent weaknesses with you or your team or shortcomings with existing countermeasures that you are using to protect yourself that can in either case be used to gain access to you or your team members (Table 9.5). For example, if you are out of shape and suddenly find yourself in a situation where you need to run to escape an assailant, your inherent lack of physical conditioning leaves you vulnerable to assault and potential abduction by the adversary. It is a physical weakness within you. Similarly, if you habitually overindulge in alcohol while on a trip, your habit can be an inherent susceptibility easily exploited by an adversary who is interested in what you know, who you are, or where you are going. Alternatively, if your team is taking counterkidnap measures by alternating the routes to and from their residence or hotel to work but remain consistent with the time of departure, they exhibit a shortcoming in your antikidnap countermeasure that can be identified and exploited by an adversary intent on abducting them.

Vulnerabilities can result from several conditions that include the following:

- Your own physical and mental conditioning, habits, and presence or lack of self-discipline
- Vulnerabilities in your own personal technical gear, such as lack of or weak passwords on laptops or other media
- Personal behavior, such as predictable habits in arrival and departure from your hotel, overindulging in alcohol, or other vices
- Your location. An example would be checking into a ground floor room of a hotel.
- Operational and personnel practices. An example of this would be using outdated procedures for situations that have evolved and are very different from when the procedure was first developed. In the late 1990s, I was involved in testing new procedures at US embassies for reacting to bomb threats. At one major US mission, we executed an unannounced bomb drill to see what the reaction would be. When the threat was announced over the intercom, I watched officers methodically gathering up their classified documents and folders and locking them securely in the safe. They then filed down the hallways, like so many sheep, and gathered dutifully out in front of the mission grounds on a main thoroughfare, all clustered tightly together—one big fat target. All were according to the existing procedure and practice. Those practices that were being followed were in compliance

TABLE 9.5 Example of a Vulnerability Assessment Chart

		Vulnerability Assessment						Rating	
Threat Event	Asset	Public Knowledge	Predictability	Physical Protection	Accessibility	Proximity	Total	No.	Linguistic
Kidnap	You	2	2	4	1	3	12	0.35	Medium
Suicide attack	Your team	3	4	5	5	3	20	0.75	Critical
Hacker	Your information	3	1	5	3	3	15	0.50	High
Lack of drug supply	Your equipment/ materials	5	5	4	2	4	20	0.75	Critical

Scaling Criteria for Vulnerability

Vulnerability Rating	Rating
	Critical
Total	
25	1.0
24	0.95
23	0.90
22	0.85
21	0.80
20	0.75

(Continued)

TABLE 9.5 (CONTINUED)   Example of a Vulnerability Assessment Chart

Total	Scaling Criteria for Vulnerability	
	Vulnerability Rating	Rating
19	0.70	High
18	0.65	
17	0.60	
16	0.55	
15	0.50	
14	0.45	Medium
13	0.40	
12	0.35	
11	0.30	
10	0.25	
9	0.20	Low
8	0.15	
7	0.10	
6	0.05	
5	0.01	

(i.e., they had a procedure—check!) but were outdated and represented a severe vulnerability—they matched a threat profile from the 1960s when bombs were hidden in packages or devices with a timer affixed to them (the Baader-Meinhof Gang or Red Brigade but not al Qaeda).

Identify Vulnerability Vectors with Public Knowledge (Recurring, Nonrecurring, and Time)

1. Event, meeting, or conference that you are attending is as follows:
   a. Nonrecurring (one off)
   b. Location/your affiliation not public knowledge, corporate confidential, or classified
   c. Your itinerary not public knowledge, corporate confidential, or classified
   d. Your movement and attendance not public knowledge, corporate confidential, or classified
2. Event, meeting, or conference that you are attending is as follows:
   a. Recurring
   b. Location of the event not public knowledge
   c. Your location at the event not public knowledge
   d. Your itinerary to the event not public knowledge
   e. Your movement and attendance not public knowledge
3. Event, meeting, or conference that you are attending is informally locally known and is as follows:
   a. Recurring
   b. Location, itinerary, movement, and attendance released to the public at such short notice that only the most skilled adversary would have time to exploit the knowledge.
4. Event, meeting, or conference you are attending is high profile (symbolic), known informally by the public and is as follows:
   a. Nonrecurring (one off)
   b. Location, itinerary, movement, and attendance released to the public with sufficient time that most adversaries would have time to exploit the knowledge.
5. Event, meeting, or conference that you are attending is high profile (symbolic), officially known by the public and is as follows:
   a. Recurring
   b. Location, itinerary, movement, and attendance released to the public with sufficient time that most adversaries would have time to exploit the knowledge.

Predictability (Itinerary, Movement, and Accommodation)

1. First time you or your team has traveled to the location or the event; first iteration of itinerary, movement, and activity in country
2. Recurring travel to a location or an event where all (major and minor) details of itinerary, movement, and accommodation have been changed
3. Recurring travel to a location or an event where major details of itinerary, movement, and accommodation have been changed and randomization of time, route, and mode of transportation security procedure on a routine basis
4. Recurring travel to a location or an event where only minor details of itinerary, movement, and accommodation have been changed and implementation of security procedures and randomization of selective elements of travel only when threat levels escalate
5. Recurring travel to a location or an event; no details of itinerary, movement, and accommodation have been changed. No changes in security procedures used within the past 12 months. Randomization not used

Physical Protection

1. Facility in which you or your team is residing is specifically designed to defeat external ground threat. There is a protected and monitored physical perimeter, standoff from public road, armed guard force, high-security gate (barriers and blast protection), security lighting, and facility access control.
2. Facility in which you or your team is residing has been retrofitted to mitigate, to some degree, external ground threat. There is a protected and monitored physical perimeter, standoff from public road, contract guard force with proprietary supervision, 24-hour gate security for access control, security lighting, and facility access control.
3. Facility in which you or your team is residing has been retrofitted to mitigate, to some degree, external ground threat. There is a physical perimeter, some standoff from public roads, contract guard force with contract supervision, security lighting in high-traffic areas only, and access control in residence areas only.
4. Facility in which you or your team is residing has not been retrofitted to mitigate external ground threat. There is a physical perimeter; however, there is little to no standoff from public

roads. There is contract guard force with rotating supervision, ambient lighting only, and access control in residence areas only.

5. Facility in which you or your team is residing has not been retrofitted to mitigate external ground threat. There is no physical perimeter and no standoff from public roads. There is only concierge control in lobby area and no security guard force. There is little to no protection at all from adversarial attack on premises.

Accessibility

1. Multiple layers of personal security countermeasures addressing detection, deterrence, delay, defense, and recovery elements are in use by you and your team to effectively control access to you by an adversary.
2. Multiple layers of personal security countermeasures addressing detection, deterrence, delay, defense, and recovery elements are in use by you and your team, but at least one weakness exists in the layers that an adversary could exploit to gain access to you or your team.
3. Despite some layers of personal security countermeasures in use by you and your team, several weaknesses exist across the layers that several different adversaries could exploit to gain access to you or your team. Very limited or ineffective detection capability (surveillance/threat awareness detection).
4. No effective countermeasures in use by you and your team. Most known adversaries could gain access to you or your team. There is no detection capability (surveillance/threat awareness detection).
5. You or your team is completely open to public access. No security countermeasures exist.

Proximity (Collateral Damage Potential)

1. You or your team is not located in close proximity to another potential/alternative target. You or your team will not be moving through a high-crime/high-threat area or region. There is no exposure.
2. You or your team is located in close proximity to another potential/ alternative target that, if attacked, would result in minor injury (to you or your team) because of collateral damage. You or your team will be moving through a high-crime/high-threat area or region between 1% and 25% of the time. There is minimal exposure.
3. You or your team is located in close proximity to another potential/ alternative target that, if attacked, would result in significant

injury (to you or your team) because of collateral damage. You or your team will be moving through a high-crime/high-threat area or region between 26% and 50% of the time. There is medium exposure.

4. You or your team is located in close proximity to another potential/alternative target that, if attacked, would result in mass casualties, potential fatalities, and significant injury or possible loss of life (to you or your team) because of collateral damage. You or your team will be moving through a high-crime/high-threat area or region between 50% and 75% of the time. There is high exposure.

5. You or your team is located in close proximity to another potential/alternative target that, if attacked, would result in loss of life or mass casualties for that target and also yourself or your team. You or your team will be moving through a high-crime/high-threat area or region between 75% and 100% of the time. There is very high exposure.

STEP 4: ASSESS RISKS AND DETERMINE PRIORITIES FOR YOU AND YOUR TEAM'S PROTECTION

This stage of the analysis is where you pull everything together and estimate the likelihood (probability) that a specific undesirable event, which you have previously identified, will occur given certain conditions or what-if scenarios (Table 9.6). Your scenarios should be anchored in fact-based estimates that are integrated with data collected on assets, threat, and vulnerabilities. As an exercise in informed judgment, avoid the temptation to leap exclusively to worst-case scenario spinning.

Estimate the Degree of Impact Relative to Yourself or Your Team Members

Review your impact ratings from step 1, where you determined what were the most critical asset(s) and supportive assets and identified undesirable events and impacts of loss and prioritization of assets.

Estimate the Likelihood of Attack by a Potential Adversary

Review your threat ratings from step 2, where you identified threat categories, potential adversaries, potential hazards or hazard agents, types of adversaries, intent, motivation, capability, history, and degree of

TABLE 9.6 Exemplar of a Risk Assessment Matrix, Pulling All of the Elements of the Risk Analysis Together

Threat Event	Asset	Risk Assessment						Risk Rating	
		Impact		Threat		Vulnerability			
		No.	Linguistic	No.	Linguistic	No.	Linguistic	No.	Linguistic
Kidnap	You	75	Critical	0.70	High	0.35	Medium	12.75	Medium/medium
Suicide attack	Your team	95	Critical	0.35	Medium	0.75	Critical	24.9	Low/high
Hacker	Your information	50	High	0.90	Critical	0.50	High	22.5	Low/high
Lack of drug supply	Your equipment/materials	80	Critical	0.25	Medium	0.75	Critical	15	High/medium

Scaling Criteria for Risk

Total	Risk Rating	Linguistic
20	100	High critical
19	95	
18	90	
17	85	
16	80	Medium critical
15	75	
14	70	

(Continued)

TABLE 9.6 (CONTINUED) Exemplar of a Risk Assessment Matrix, Pulling All of the Elements of the Risk Analysis Together

	Scaling Criteria for Risk	
Total	**Risk Rating**	**Linguistic**
13	65	Low critical
12	60	
11	55	
10	50	High–high
9	45	
8	40	Medium–high
7	35	
6	30	
5	25	Low–high
4	20	
3	15	High–medium
		Medium–medium
2	10	Low–medium
1	5	Low

threat. Take into consideration your impact ratings and identified vulnerabilities (step 3).

Estimate the Likelihood That a Specific Vulnerability Will Be Exploited

Review your impact rating from the vulnerability assessment in step 3, taking into consideration information obtained in the initial impact assessment in step 1 and the threat assessment in step 2. Include other judgments and make the necessary revisions to your analysis.

Determine the Relative Degree of Risk

Your individual judgments should be identified and tracked, which will provide you an overall risk level. When the threat (T) and the vulnerability (V) levels are calculated together, you can estimate the probability or the likelihood of occurrence of the undesirable event. The probability of occurrence $(T \times V)$ and the expected impact (I) are considered in the estimate of the risk level. The overall risk (R) can be computed using the formula $R = I \times (T \times V)$. Why multiply? Using multiplication in the formula is based on the premise that all three elements (I and T and V) must be present to have risk (R). If there is no threat (T), there is no risk. Likewise, if there is no vulnerability (V) for the threat to exploit, there is no risk. Furthermore, even if there is a threat and a vulnerability to exploit but there is no consequence or impact (I) of that exploitation, there is no risk.

STEP 5: IDENTIFY UNACCEPTABLE RISKS AND DETERMINE RISK MITIGATION PRIORITIES

Once you have identified risks, determine your security protection priorities. All the previous steps have been done to make a rational and realistic assessment of risks; determine which are the most serious and rank them in order, relative to each other. The acceptable level of risk for you cannot just be determined by a formula. It helps, but it may vary with time, circumstances, and your own attitude toward risk in the environment. Ultimately, you must decide what is an acceptable level of risk for you, your supporting assets, or your team. However, the ratings that you derive will help you make rational, fact-based decisions about what is or is not acceptable.

Based on the information in your analysis, you can identify focused countermeasures that address the discrete elements of risk. For example, in the previous tables, I concluded (hypothetically) that my risk of being kidnapped was medium. However, I may not be satisfied with that level of risk, so to reduce it further, I might examine my program of detection, deterrence, delay, deny, or defense to see if there are elements lacking or additional layers that can be designed in reducing the risk. Also, I could shift my location or operation to a location where there is a much lower assessed threat level of kidnapping.

A countermeasure or several in combination can lower the risk. By using a principled approach to personal security, you will be able to identify countermeasures that detect, deter, delay, deny, or defend threats to varying degrees.

Identify the Benefits and Costs of the Countermeasures

Countermeasure benefits can be defined in terms of the level of risk reduction that they provide. A countermeasure option package can be defined as "grouping of security countermeasures that work together as a security system to guard against the significant risks identified during the risk assessment phase." To determine the most effective sets of countermeasures for each of the undesirable events that you have listed, you must determine the effect that each countermeasure option will have on the existing risk level. This can be accomplished by answering the questions about vulnerability again (step 3) and also by considering if the countermeasure options will have an effect on the threat (intent and/or capability) or on the asset (a lessening of impact). The analysis of countermeasure functions supports your risk reduction analysis. Following this procedure, a determination can be made of the new level of risk. Certain countermeasures may appear several times in your matrix. If one of these countermeasures is selected, it could mitigate the risk of several undesirable events.

Identify the Cost of the Countermeasures

You must consider the cost of materials, training, or other ongoing operational costs associated with countermeasure implementation. Bear in mind that using specified procedures is typically the least expensive countermeasure. With regard to personal security, this is good news because much of personal security risk reduction is through learning and using good procedures and protocols. Hardware is more expensive, and workforce (bodyguards or personal executive protection specialists) is the most expensive form of countermeasure. Every countermeasure has a cost associated with it that is measured in dollars and cents, inconvenience, time, or personnel. In order to select the most appropriate countermeasure option, the cost associated with each countermeasure must be determined.

- When determining the dollar cost of a countermeasure, include the purchase price as well as the life cycle maintenance costs. The life expectancy of the countermeasure should be considered when determining cost.
- When determining the cost of a countermeasure in terms of inconvenience, consider whether the inconvenience caused is offset by the measure of risk reduction gained. If a countermeasure is inconvenient, you or your team will be tired of it and ultimately find a way to bypass it. It is possible that through procedure redesign, the same or greater level of risk reduction can be achieved with far less inconvenience.
- When determining the cost of a countermeasure in terms of time, include the time to implement the countermeasure and the time to prepare for implementation, as well as any time required for follow-up and evaluation.
- When determining the cost of a countermeasure in terms of the personnel required to use it, consider the number of staff needed to use the countermeasure as well as the skills, the knowledge, and the abilities of the personnel involved. Additionally, staff training needs/costs should be considered.

The general principle to follow when analyzing countermeasures is to select the least expensive countermeasure that will resolve your security needs and reduce risk to an acceptable level. Since a countermeasure can potentially protect against more than one vulnerability and since compensating countermeasures are used in a complementary manner to form a security system, it is important to determine the cost of the various optional countermeasure groupings. A particular grouping may be less expensive than the sum of the costs for the least expensive countermeasure for each significant unwanted event identified and provide adequate protection at an overall lower cost. After the cost of each optional countermeasure grouping is determined, the cost differences and the marginal benefits of each option can be compared.

REFERENCE

US Army Combined Arms Center, "Understanding the operational environment in COIN" [PowerPoint presentation, no. 13], presented at the 1st Army West COIN Workshop, Ft. Leavenworth, Kansas (February 13, 2009).

ENDNOTE

1. The ARM method was first developed by the Training and Professional Development Working Group of the US Security Policy Board in 1993–1994. Much of its methodology and training materials were developed in the Analysis and Policy Center of the Central Intelligence Agency's Office of Security. The author was one of the first officers at Central Intelligence Agency (CIA) trained and certified in the use of ARM. Subsequent to the methodology and the course development, the CIA's ARM Training Program was launched. This training expanded well beyond CIA into the Department of Defense and numerous other agencies and departments of the federal government.

CHAPTER 10

Personal Security and Transportation
Securing Your Movement

INTRODUCTION

Your personal movements when traveling, whether locally by taxi or by foot or between cities or countries by train or by airplane, are when you are most vulnerable to security incidents targeting you specifically or from simply being in the wrong place at the wrong time. Ground transportation, in particular, can be fraught with risk in the third world. For example, in the Mexican city of Poza Rica, home to the national oil company Pemex, the Zeta-organized criminal cartel recently took over some of the bus and taxi transportation companies. Taxis that are affiliated with the Zeta cartel have red triangles on them, and if someone is unlucky enough to have an accident with a cartel taxi, criminal gang members are on the scene in short order. The local police steer clear and let the cartel work out the details. If you happen to be in one of those taxis, you are exposed to risk of KFR, collateral injury, or death from an attack on the taxi by a rival cartel or a disgruntled gang member or a shakedown by the driver or a member of the cartel. At the very least, they learn about who you are, where you are staying, what you may want, and who you are working with.

BY FOOT

As a general statement, traveling by foot in an urban area is when you are most exposed to attack by an adversary. You are limited by speed, your own stamina, and the urban topography and dynamics of traffic and crowds. Depending on your location, your physical condition compared to that of a potential adversary, and your own personal knowledge of the urban space through which you are moving, foot travel can be turned to your advantage.

- Location: If you are moving along Fifth Avenue, New York City, at lunchtime, it is typically very crowded. Your speed of travel is necessarily limited to the flow of foot traffic around you. (Change your location relative to direction of travel.)
- Stamina: The better your physical conditioning, the more options you have on foot in terms of speed and distance. If your physical conditioning is not good, this is a limitation you need to consider when moving from one location to another.
- Urban topography: As noted in Chapter 2, mentally knowing where you are going and your urban environment will pay real dividends when you are on foot moving through the city. Knowing in advance your options for change in direction of travel, shortcuts, chokepoints, and ever-shifting kinds of districts or neighborhoods that vary according to ethnicity, market, exterior or interior design, or level can all play a part in how you use the urban environment to your benefit or find yourself utterly challenged and helpless at its complexity. It is all up to you and whether you do your homework in advance.
- Shelter or cover: There are two considerations when selecting a route that provides shelter or cover for your journey by foot. The first is simply weather considerations. I once was required to work in a Northern Baltic city in the middle of December. Temperatures hover around 28°F (–2°C) during the daytime and much lower at night. I ensured that my route by foot included at least three small cafes where I could duck in, get a hot drink, and warm up before resuming my walk through the city. I had a similar experience in the Middle Eastern city where I was caught out in a sudden, severe sandstorm. I fortunately knew where I was in relation to my hotel and what options were available for shelter so I was able to ride out the worst of the storm indoors. Cover is a different consideration. Lowering your profile when moving from point A to B in a city could entail planning your route through a crowded marketplace, a building interior that has large public space front and back entrances, or back streets. This can break up your visible exposure to potential threat actors.
- Sustenance: We all assume that there will be a place where we can get a bottle of water or food when in the developed world. In third-world countries, sampling what there is to eat and drink on the street is not such a good idea. Keep a small bottle of water with you and a granola bar or something to eat, when

going out on the street. It lowers your dependency on what is in your immediate environment should you get hungry or thirsty, so that you can move quickly and effectively through it and get to your destination.

- Clothing: Northern Sweden, near the Arctic Circle, can be unforgivingly cold. Residents of this region have a saying "There is no such thing as cold weather, only poor clothing." There is truth to this. When in cold regions, layer your clothing. Next to the skin, the main job of this layer is to wick sweat away from your skin. Wool, synthetics, and a wool–synthetic blend are good for this because they are efficient—warm when it is cold and cool when it is hot. This base layer should be snug, because, if it cannot touch your skin, it cannot wick sweat. Sweat that stays on your skin will leave you shivering. The next layer is for insulation, which traps your body heat. It can range from lightweight fleeces and wool sweaters to full-on puffy down jackets; it just depends on the season. Finally, the third (outer) layer is your shell, which cuts wind and keeps you dry. The guiding principle of layering is that you are regularly adding and removing layers to keep your body temperature even (Hostetter, 2016). Alternatively, in desert climates, be prepared for sandstorms or dust storms. Having experienced several, if I am in a place where these can be expected, I carry small clear plastic swim goggles in my backpack and a scarf (besides the antihistamines outlined in Chapter 2). The goggles will protect your eyes and allow you to navigate to safety, since visibility can be severely reduced. The scarf, wrapped around your nose and mouth, keeps particulates from getting in and clogging your airways. The antihistamines are for later, once I am sheltered, to help open passageways in my nose, throat, and lungs.

GROUND TRANSPORTATION: VEHICLE AND RAIL

Bicycle

Utilizing a bicycle, a motor scooter, and a motorcycle in a city are all excellent ways to mitigate exposure to risk because of limitations on speed of travel and stamina. The principle threat to a cyclist or a motorcyclist is traffic. In the third world, this can be a substantial risk, so I would recommend strongly against the use of bicycles or motorcycles to get around a city until you have a good sense of traffic flow and direction, as well as the urban topography itself. I cannot emphasize enough how crucial situational awareness is to operating a bicycle or a motorbike in the developing world. Traffic rules tend toward the *law of the jungle*, meaning the survival of the fittest and the largest.

Once you get acclimatized to using this kind of transportation, the benefits to your security can be significant. I worked in Uganda during their civil war. During that tense period and afterward, I purchased and used a motorbike to get around the city. The bike gave me the ability to blend into traffic (most of the traffic on the road was via bicycle or motorbikes), which lowered my profile. There are many places in the world that we live in today where traveling in an armored limousine can draw out your adversary, whereas moving along with the masses on a bicycle or a motorbike will not draw even a second glance from potential threat actors. If you have the option and are adequately prepared to use it, bicycle or motorbike travel can be quite useful. As outlined in Chapter 3, various military factions or the police could throw up roadblocks with no notice, reducing traffic to a standstill. With a cycle, you retain the option to change course and take a rutted track or road that is not passable by car, to circumvent the roadblock. You have flexibility, which travel by foot also provides, with the benefit of speed. Knowing by heart the urban terrain around you is a must.

If you choose to employ a bicycle or a motorbike, your safety as well as the security of your bike is a key consideration. Here are some important principles to securing your bike (Dahr, 2012):

General Bike-Locking Principles

1. Your bike should be more secure than the bike parked next to it. There is old adage, if you are camping in the woods with a friend and see a bear, you do not have to outrun the bear, you just need to outrun your friend. Similarly, you will never be able to 100% secure your bicycle, but you can make your bike the least accessible target on the block for a thief.
2. Never rely solely on a cable lock to secure your bike, ever. These cables can be snipped so easily that it will blow your mind. You would not tie your bike down using twizzlers—so do not tie your bike down using cables.
3. The smaller the u-lock, the better. Not only is it lighter to carry around, the smaller size gives the thief less room to mount a leverage-based attack on the lock (i.e., pry it open with a crowbar).
4. Use multiple locking mechanisms. With one u-lock, there is no possible way to secure all the components on your bike that a thief might steal. You need a u-lock plus something else (another u-lock, a cable lock, locking skewers, etc.).
5. Make your bike ugly. Wrap electrical tape around the seat. That small change can give the appearance that the bike is older and less valuable.

How to Lock the Bike

The primary component to securely locking your bike is a mini u-lock. This u-lock goes through the back wheel (inside the rear triangle of the frame), securing the bike to something solid. The beauty of this approach is that it locks the rear wheel and the frame, even though you are technically not even locking the frame! It turns out that it is impossible to pull the frame away from the wheel when the lock is positioned inside the triangle of the bike frame. Is there a weakness in this method? Well, you could cut the rear wheel to pull out the bicycle. In practice, this usually does not happen because cutting the wheel is very hard to do and you would be destroying a very valuable part of the bike. If you are worried about this issue, you could use a slightly larger u-lock that can go through the rear wheel and part of the frame. The second component of this strategy is to secure the front wheel via cable lock or even a second u-lock. This is to make sure that your front wheel is secure. Front wheels are not that expensive so it is unlikely that a thief will break out tools to only steal a front wheel (they will steal it if the front wheel is not secured at all though).

Motorbike Security

The most serious risk to your use of a motorbike, aside from traffic, is thieves. In the third world, this can be an especially acute problem. The following are some key principles to follow when securing your motorbike (Bonnier Corporation, 2009; Steube, 2009):

1. Park your motorbike out in the open in a well-lit place, preferably where people can see it and walk past it. If you are within view of a CCTV camera, that is even better. Do not give thieves cover to work—most are lazy; even professionals prefer not to be seen or watched when stealing a bike. Good criminal prevention through environmental design techniques employ light, and natural public surveillance is an excellent deterrent principle. Use them.
2. If you do not have a garage, cover your bike. Not only will this protect it from the weather, it also makes it harder for potential thieves to quickly assess whether the machine is worth stealing and how difficult or easy it is to steal. Given options, they will move on to one that is easier. It is another deterrent layer of security.
3. Lock the ignition and take the keys with you. Lock your forks in place and keep the bike in first gear rather than neutral when it is stopped and shut off.

4. Two locks are better than one: A case-hardened u-lock should be locked (ideally) through the frame or at least the forks or the wheel. Do not rest on the ground, as it gives thieves leverage to defeat the lock. Use a secondary cable lock system (asymmetrical chains 5/8 in. or greater), anchored to something solid. Most thieves are prepared to defeat one lock, but not two different kinds. Alarmed disk locks are good. If disk locks are used, turn them inward rather than facing outward so that the locks on them cannot be easily *punched* by a thief.
5. Consider wiring in a kill switch or simply removing and pocketing the main fuse when you park the bike.

Rickshaws

One of the quickest, cheapest, and more efficient ways to move through crowded urban environments in many third-world countries is via the *tuk tuk* or auto rickshaw. In many countries, however, mechanical quality standards and driver licensing are minimal to nonexistent. Furthermore, since this kind of transportation is often unlicensed and the preferred mode of transport in slum areas of the cities, it is also a vector for crime and theft. In fact, there are some countries where the tuk tuk is specifically targeted by thieves. More than any other mode of transport, knowing your urban topography in advance will pay strong dividends. Tuk tuk drivers are notorious for taking the roundabout way to your hotel or destination and charging a lot of money for the ride.

The following are important considerations regarding your security, when opting to use motor rickshaws:

1. Do not get into a tuk tuk with no meter. If you do not have a choice, then make sure to negotiate your fare in advance. Keep a close eye on the meter. Drivers have been known to alter them, so that the meters run fast. If it appears that the meter is not working or has been altered to run fast, tell the driver to fix it or you will tell the police.
2. Be wary of the common scam about "discounts" if you visit certain jewelry stores, hotels, etc. Your driver gets a commission from these businesses, and the multiple stops will expose you to aggressive salespersons and slow down your journey. When you check into your hotel or residence, to the extent possible, ask about reasonable rates to common destinations around the city. With this general rate structure in mind, always get a price quote and agree to the price up front.

3. As outlined in Chapter 2, it is important that you know your geography and way around the city in advance. A common ploy by drivers is to claim ignorance, saying that they do not know where a certain hotel is or that it is closed for a special ceremony and that you should go to another one. Do not fall for it. The best antidote to this kind of scam is to be firm and crisp—show them you know your way around and cannot be fooled.

4. Be deliberate and certain about the denomination of bills, in local currency, that you give the driver for payment. To the extent possible, as pointed out in Chapter 2, break up large bills that you have and keep smaller ones readily available. Know what you have and what you have given the driver. They will sometimes claim you gave them a 10 or a 100 Rupee bill, for instance, when, in fact, it was not. At night, in a darkened tuk tuk, it can be hard to tell, and they do not usually have an over-head dome light.

5. Beware of fake road fees. A man in civilian clothes or a local police officer working with the driver will stop the tuk tuk and demand additional fees. The driver will usually argue and say no, so the police officer or the alleged authority will then turn to you. They might ask for your passport (reason to carry only a copy) to see your visa. Do not fall for it.

Taxis

Taxis and taxi drivers in the third world have always held a special place in my own personal security program. While it is important to be wary of taxi drivers, in a new and strange place, a good driver who is reputable can become an excellent source of information about the city and the places to avoid, as well as a trusted transportation contact. Both characteristics are invaluable, so more often than not when I end up in a new city, my interaction with the driver is part job interview and part solicitation for local intel. I want the inside scoop on where I am. As aforementioned, be prepared to have a good cover story for the driver. Drivers are collectors of information and, in many countries, are regular sources for the local intelligence service, the police, or the organized crime cartel that owns them (in parts of Mexico, the Zeta cartel taxis have small red triangles on the back windshield or bumper). I prefer a story that is innocuous and boring and keeps the focus off me. A "Canadian businessman soliciting tractor parts or selling refrigeration units" with a local distributor is as exciting as watching paint dry and much better than "an American security consultant" helping the government, a national oil company, or a private client.

As aforementioned, there are—just as with other modes of public transportation—distinct things that you should watch out for and do for yourself to ensure your own security (Hodson, 2011). These include the following:

1. Never get in without agreeing on a fare. Just as with tuk tuks, your fare is based on two options: a metered fare or a negotiated rate. In the third world, the meter itself can be an antiquated analog device that was last operational in the 1960s. Alternatively, it can be a digital meter that is mysteriously not working or meters the ride suspiciously fast. Or there just is no meter at all (Figure 10.1). Make sure that you agree before you get in the cab—before you put your briefcase, shopping bag, or anything in the cab—on exactly how much the fare is going to be.
2. Keep your bags close to you, not in the trunk. Whether it is a large suitcase or a small one and your laptop bag or just a backpack and a larger case, keep them in the backseat next to you. *Insist on it.* When you arrive at your destination, if you are able, get out first *with your cases* and then pay the driver. Otherwise, pay him/her and then have him help you get your larger case out followed directly by you (it ensures that he or she is out of the

FIGURE 10.1 The meter in this ancient taxi that the author took, in Cairo, in 2011 had seen its best days—perhaps two decades ago. It belonged in a museum. In this instance, I halted the taxi and negotiated my price to the airport before proceeding any further.

cab when you alight). Typically, a good cabbie will go out of his/
her way to do just that. In the event of a dispute, either way, you
will have all your stuff with you.

3. Know where you are going. Have the address of your destination written out in the local language and carry it with you. Get
a map and learn the route to your destination (see Chapter 2);
note if a taxi driver takes you to a different or longer way and
if he or she does, *do not hesitate to quickly question him/her or
redirect him/her—be polite but firm about it.* Your hotel should
have a business card with the address and a basic map printed
in the local language. Always grab one or two when you check
in. Additionally, if you are going anywhere by cab (or any transportation really), always have someone at the front desk of the
hotel write out where you are going in the local language on a
scrap of paper. Also, do not forget to ask the front desk or the
concierge what sort of fare is expected for the cab ride so that
you can properly negotiate.

4. Stick to licensed cabs. To be on the safe side, make sure to use
a licensed cab. In some places, you can tell by the license plate
whether the cab is legitimate or not. Alternatively, you can
observe whether the license is printed on the cab itself. If the
driver's photo and his or her license and name are not on the
front visor of his cab, get out and find another. Or, check to
ensure that the driver's photo and the driver are one and the
same person. Usually, taxis have the number of the service plas-
tered on it or on the interior. Ask the information desk or the
concierge at your hotel what to look for. As a rule of thumb,
if you are out on the town, look or ask for the location of taxi
stands. Typically, only licensed taxis can use that stand.

5. Make the rules and the relationship from the outset clear: No
sharing or stopping for a buddy. I have had this happen and end
up taking a completely different route than originally intended.
Part of the relationship, particularly in the third world, that I
establish from the outset is (a) negotiating the fare or ensuring
the meter works and (b) making it clear that I want to go from
point A to point B and not stop for friends, family, or otherwise. This can be a common occurrence in Africa and parts
of the Middle East so it is good to establish the rules from the
beginning.

6. Have the proper change. Carry lots of small bills, so you can
give the exact amount to the taxi driver and be on your way.
Otherwise, you will be exposed to the "I do not have change"
scam, which can delay your travel.

Buses

Roads and highways in the developing world are often narrow, curvy, in bad condition, and poorly maintained. Speed limits and rules of the road are nonexistent, and on dark stretches at night in some countries, there is the threat of hijack by criminal gangs. Combine this with buses or minibuses that are mechanically challenged, badly driven, and packed to the gills, and you have a recipe for serious risk to life and limb.

One of the worst accidents that I have ever witnessed was two over-loaded *Tata* buses, one passing the other at high speed on a rural two-lane road in Ecuador. A third bus, coming from the opposite direction, slammed into the oncoming bus. The carnage from that accident was terrible. Anyone who has ever lived for a long period in the developing world has seen these kinds of accidents. They happen all too frequently. Transportation by bus or minibus in the third world is exceedingly dangerous.

If you do survive an accident, chances are that emergency medical care and evacuation will be severely delayed since it is usually very limited or nonexistent.

Besides accidents, the crowded bus terminals in capital cities or provincial towns attract pickpockets and thieves. In some countries in the Middle East, the danger is terrorism. Bus terminals or crowded buses are targeted by terrorist bombers because, as with marketplaces, they are crowded and vulnerable to the carnage and the chaos that a suicide bomb attack produces.

If you must use local buses, the following precautions are recommended:

1. Schedule your travel so that you depart and arrive at your destination during daylight hours. There are several reasons for this: First are the drivers themselves and the traffic that they deal with. It is a fact: Third-world bus drivers can be drunk or high, extremely tired, underage (I once rode a bus in South America where my driver was 14, and his seat was a lawn chair wired tied to the floor), poorly skilled, or poorly compensated. They are negotiating roads where the drivers of trucks or other buses are the same. They pass on hills and blind curves or play chicken with massive diesel lorries. If you must risk your life on a local bus transportation, making sure you travel during the daytime lowers your risk to some degree. After dark, all the aforementioned bad behaviors and habits occur on really bad, narrow, eroding unlit roads at speed. Second, you want to avoid arriving in a strange city or town after dark.
2. Keep your most important items close to you; money and travel documents such as passport and ID should be kept on your

person. If something happens to the bus and you are able to get out, you will not have the time or the ability to go searching for your backpack with all your valuables inside. I usually layer items on my person by priority—passport, mobile phone, and money/credit card on my person; a small first aid kit, shaving kit, toiletries, and some critical medicines in a backpack along with my laptop; change of underwear and socks; and a guidebook. That backpack goes between my legs on the floor or under the seat in front of me, not overhead. Whenever the bus stops to unload or load passengers, check for your luggage each time to make sure that it does not "walk away" when bags are offloaded underneath or on top of the bus.

3. Bus stations are magnets for petty thieves. Be especially careful of pickpockets when arriving at your destination, retrieving your luggage, and departing the area. The principal technique used by pickpockets is distraction. They can be quite creative at distracting your attention while picking your pocket and snatching your bag or luggage. Stay frosty and focused; get through the crowd and on to your next destination.

Trains

Personal security is very important for train travel, because there is very little in the way of physical and procedural security measures on the train itself or at train terminals. You are your own first and last line of defense. A good example of this is the August 21, 2015, terrorist attack by a lone gunman on a Paris-bound high-speed train in France. The well-armed gunman had just initiated his attack when he was tackled and subdued by several passengers that included two off-duty US service members. They were alert and quickly grasped the situation, which prepared them to take timely action when it was most needed.

As aforementioned, the following measures should be considered when using trains:

1. As with bus travel, keep your most important items close to you: money and travel documents such as passport and ID, credit cards, and camera memory cards on your person. If something happens to the train and you are able to get out, you will not have the time or the ability to go searching through your luggage for important items. I usually layer items on my person by priority—passport, mobile phone, and money on my person; a small first aid kit, shaving kit, toiletries, and some critical medicines in a backpack along with laptop; change of underwear

and socks; and a guidebook. That backpack goes between my legs on the floor or under the seat in front of me, not overhead. Whenever the train stops to unload or load passengers, check for your luggage each time to make sure that it does not walk away when bags are offloaded from luggage bins at the front or the back of the train car.

2. If taking a cheap, third-class train, make sure that you request or receive the top bunk. Do not expect a restful sleep. Relax and try to get some rest, but with your belongings in the spoon position. If you have an extra strap, tie the strap around your torso and one end of the bag so you will awaken if being robbed.

3. While traveling on a train, do not fall asleep with your laptop out and exposed as a thief can easily take it and get off at the next stop. Do not place it on the seat next to you unless the laptop is in its bag and you wrap the bag's strap around your arm. Do not place your laptop on the overhead rack. Not only might it be stolen, but it might also get damaged if bounced around. Possibly, the best place to store a laptop is on your lap with your arms over it. Another option is to place it on the floor between your legs and wrap the strap around one of your legs.

4. Train stations, like bus stations or other mass transit-type terminals, are magnets for petty thieves. Be especially careful of pickpockets when arriving at your destination, retrieving your luggage, and departing the area. The principal technique used by pickpockets is distraction. They can be quite creative at distracting your attention while picking your pocket and snatching your bag or luggage. Stay frosty and focused; get through the crowd and on to your next destination. Be particularly careful around large schedule boards that provide train number, time of arrival and departure, and destination of trains. People become absorbed with the schedules and temporarily lose their awareness of what is going on around them. Pickpockets will target individuals in areas such as this. Also, if you are on a long layover between trains and want to take a nap, do not tune out with your earbuds in and your favorite music. You completely nullify an important security sensor, your hearing, and the distraction can be enough for an accomplished thief to make off with some of your possessions.

Rental Car and Driving

Driving in the third world poses challenging safety and security problems. It requires acquired skills that are part instinct, part abdication of all the normal Marquess of Queensberry rules of the road that you learned in the developed world, and part planning ahead. When these conditions are overlaid with a hostile situation featuring armed militia or army roadblocks, criminal gangs, corrupt police, and intermittent conflict, you take you and your passengers' lives in your hands if you decide to make this a learning adventure and drive anyway. Having more than once witnessed the result of poor judgment in this regard in several developing countries, I strongly recommend against it. Even if you are an experienced driver in hostile or developing countries, these are the points that you should consider if you must drive:

Safety and Security Risk Considerations

Navigating roads and cities in the third world is challenging and dangerous. Road surface conditions are poor, lighting is usually nonexistent, and driver competency and behavior are sporadic and unpredictable. In East Africa, for instance, asphalt-paved roads can be notoriously bad with massive parts of the road washed out or with deep potholes. Navigating around these axle-breaking obstructions often forces traffic to come at each other head on or forces you into unpaved, muddy detours thick enough to get stuck in during rainy season. With roads such as these, it is important to remain hyperalert if you hit a patch that is smooth and obstruction free; the bad portions of these roads tend to come up quickly, with no warning. In below-freezing conditions, driving in the third world can be lethal. Black ice on roads that have not been sanded or salted is a huge hazard in the cold climates of the world; coupled with long-haul diesel trucks driven at prohibitive speeds by untrained drivers, the result can be massive kilometer-long pileups.

Drivers in the third world follow their own rules. They can be high, drunk, underage, or exhausted because they are working under unreasonable, unregulated conditions. They will pass at the crest of hills or on blind corners of two-lane mountain roads with a thousand foot drop-off. Their lights may not work, and in some countries, drivers turn them off at night due to the mistaken belief that the lights drain their batteries. Drivers will not look but pull into oncoming traffic, turn unexpectedly directly into traffic, proceed at speed the wrong way down a one-way street, or just stop in the middle of the road—without rhyme or reason.

Livestock in the road is a common hazard, and if you hit a chicken, a goat, or a cow and kill it, you are liable for it. In cities, should you be involved in an accident where someone is injured or killed, you can find yourself in a flash mob in an instant and quickly become a victim yourself.

- Insurance: Check with your insurance company to confirm what they cover, or do not cover, and where you are going. The important coverage that you want includes collision damage waiver (CDW), in the country where you are going. Read the fine print—there are circumstances where the insurance company does not pay for damage or loss to the vehicle, leaving you completely exposed to the loss financially. This can be an unacceptable risk, because, in some countries, if you cannot settle the bill, you will be jailed.

These are just in normal, peaceful times. In hostile countries or regions that have endemic lawlessness or war, security conditions only compound these challenges. With the mentioned reminders in mind, the following are considerations to remember for planning purposes the next time that you intend to drive in third world or hostile areas of the world:

1. Absolutely do not leave home without first finding out what your major credit card or your auto insurance policy provides in terms of coverage where you are traveling. In general, your US auto insurance does not cover you while you are abroad, except in some countries neighboring the United States, such as Canada. Forget Mexico. Renting a car in Mexico can be infuriating (Delsol, 2012). The country's infamous mandatory insurance has left more than one unwitting tourist absolutely fuming at the rental car counter in Mexico City's airport. Mexican car rental rates look wonderfully cheap on comparison websites, but they do not include insurance, which can easily double, and in some cases triple, the cost. Declining to buy the insurance (some of which is mandatory, anyway) is foolhardy to the extreme, but buying the full package without knowing what you are buying is also foolish. Mexican car rental companies offer various levels of insurance, and only one is mandatory. Here are the basics (costs listed are typical but variable):
   a. Basic personal liability: Sometimes called *third-party liability insurance*, this is the one, incontrovertibly mandatory insurance in Mexico. It covers claims for injury or damage that you cause to another driver, car, or other property damaged in an accident, but it does not cover injury to you or damage to the rented vehicle. Mexico does not accept liability coverage from US auto policies or credit card insurance.[1] You simply cannot rent a car without buying Mexican liability insurance. But here is what most renters do not know: By law, the mandatory liability insurance is already included in the rental price.
   b. Supplemental liability insurance: Sometimes called the *additional liability insurance*, this is not mandatory, although many rental companies will tell you (or let you assume) it is.

Still, it is worth considering. The basic liability coverage is usually Mex$50,000, or about US$3800, which would not go far in anything beyond a fender bender.

c. Loss damage waiver (LDW): Also called CDW or LDW/CDW. You are responsible to the rental company for any loss or damage to the vehicle *no matter what the cause is or who is at fault*. Typically, your credit card insurance benefits cover collision damage. However, it is crucial that you verify what your credit card covers, and does not, before you go. American Express Gold Card, for example, does not cover damage or loss of the vehicle due to war or military activity, off-road operation (some companies have denied reimbursement for vehicles damaged in a dirt parking lot, for instance), and some four-wheel drive vehicles. If you need this flexibility, then you should consider other options to ensure that you have this coverage. This one requires some research and some careful thought.

To collect on your credit card insurance, you must use that card when you rent the car and when you pay the final bill. Carry proof of coverage with you, although rental companies do not always require it. You must also explicitly decline the offered insurance, which is not possible with companies such as Avis and National, which include LDW/CDW in their rates or bundle it with the required liability.

d. Personal accident insurance: Neither the included nor the supplemental liability insurance covers injury to you or your passengers. This optional insurance does, including ambulance, doctors, and hospital. This might be covered by your health insurance—again, verify—and it is not required.

If you rent a car in Europe, be sure to check the country's auto insurance requirements. You may be required to buy specific types of coverage. To rent a car in Italy, for example, you must purchase a CDW and theft protection, according to Auto Europe, a provider of car rental services in 130 countries. You also must be at least 21 years old with a driver's license that has been valid for at least one year and have an international driving permit as well.

2. Route planning (McGill, 2016): The principle of preparation should be implemented before you travel anywhere by car. There are basically three types of journeys: daily, special events, and unscheduled. Daily trips are dangerous because they imply a routine, which is a known quantity and can be exploited by threat actors who are casing you as a potential target. Special events are less dangerous if they are not necessarily public knowledge.

If they are, then they can attract the attention of threat actors. Finally, there are unscheduled journeys. These are unplanned, spontaneous, and the safest because they do not give a threat actor the ability or the time to plan and execute an attack.

The most likely places for any attacks to occur will be those that are known and predicted. That is why the areas in and around the residence and the office are considered danger areas. Identify over time vehicles that are parked in the area of your residence or your work. By doing so, you can implement the "absence of the normal and the presence of the abnormal" rule and pick out vehicles that should not be there, are new, different, and a potential threat. Know where the closest hospitals, police stations, etc., are so that, at any stage when required, you can move quickly to them.

3. Emergency kit: Ensure that your vehicle is equipped with good communications, a first aid kit, a fire extinguisher, a spare wheel and tire (check it before leaving the rental lot), a wheel changing kit, spare keys, a flashlight, and maps. Maps are important because there is a good chance that your smartphone or GPS will not work where you are going. It is also a good idea to have a small multitool with you and a folding knife.

4. Special events and pickup: Ensure that you have communications with all parties concerned, whether it is via mobile phone or radio. In advance, know where your arrival point will be, routes to and from the event, security at the venue (or not), and timing and alternate routes to and from the event. Use the "one-minute pickup" rule wherever possible. Advise your party of your approach by mobile phone, and once alongside, stay in the vehicle with the engine running. Keep doors locked on approach and lock doors as soon as your party is in the car, at which point you move away from the pickup zone as quickly as possible. Similarly, do the same for drop-off.

5. Hide in plain sight. Rent a vehicle that blends in with the rest of the cars on the road. This lowers your profile by making you inconspicuous, so that you virtually disappear. While in Yemen, I used an older beige Toyota sedan that was a bit dented and mud spattered with local plates. In Mexico, I always prefer a light-colored, very boring small SUV such as a Ford EcoSport or a VW CrossFox. They are local models that are common, inconspicuous, and easy to fix. You can find spare parts for those brands in most Mexican towns. In places such as Iraq, a Hyundai, a Kia, or a Toyota is the best. I look for the nearest mud puddle and make sure that my vehicle is well spattered with it. Leave it dirty. In all cases, stay away from luxury brands such

as Mercedes, Lexus, or BMW. Also, do not rent large pickup trucks or SUVs. At best, they draw unwanted attention to you, and at worst, you become a target for carjacking by thieves.

6. Park your car in well-lit, secure areas. Throughout Mexico and Central and South America, there are car parks in and around tourist areas and in downtown areas that are good choices. Avoid parking your car on quiet, dark side streets—you just give thieves or potential abductors the cover that they need. When parking in lots, never park nose in. You should park back in, so that you can move quickly out of the parking lot when you are in the car.

7. If you have a briefcase or bags, lock them in the trunk of the car or put them out of sight. Be aware of drawing attention to yourself when putting valuables in the trunk.

8. Try to avoid parking your car next to vans on the driver's side. If you return and there is a van parked next to your car, get someone to approach the car with you. If you are alone, enter from the passenger's side and lock the doors immediately upon getting into your vehicle.

Driving

9. When driving, keep your doors locked at all times and your windows up or at least not more than two inches down. This will provide a deterrence to bag snatchers at traffic stops, who often pose as windshield washers or roam up and down stopped traffic to sell roses, candy, or cigarettes (squeegee merchants). When you get into your car, make it a habit to lock the car first, before putting the key in the ignition.

10. When driving in the city, leave room between yourself and the car in front of you in the event that you need to maneuver out of a situation. Do not allow yourself to be hemmed in. This means staying alert and aware at all times while driving. Give any road hazards or obstacles a wide berth, since they can provide cover for attackers. Maintain a watchful, critical eye on the traffic ahead of you—brake lights, sudden lane changes, or other indicators of what could be happening ahead of you give you the opportunity to position your vehicle in the most optimum way, in advance.

11. Plan your travel during daylight hours. Leave at sunup, to skirt traffic in large cities. In Mexico and other countries, using the toll roads (called *cuotas* in Mexico) is more secure than free roads.

Tactical Driving If you regularly travel into hostile regions, particularly where there are criminal gangs who use roadblocks to extort money or terrorist groups who regularly kidnap individuals for ransom,

I strongly suggest that you invest in a tactical driving course. Tactical driving gives you the practical skills to aggressively and competently maneuver your vehicle around or away from threats, under all conditions. I was fortunate enough to be given this training early in my career and put much of what I learned into practice in a hostile war zone environment in Africa in the 1980s. The following are two practical recommendations for this kind of driving, among the many things that are taught, that you should know:

1. Roadblock withdrawal: In Chapter 3, we discussed the various kinds of roadblocks encountered in the third world, or in conflict zones, including illegal criminal blockades. Quick review: An illegitimate roadblock is typically thrown up after dark, on blind curves or over the crest of a hill, and is manned by criminals who, more often than not, are not uniformed and are not carrying standard military issue or police issue weaponry. If you approach one of these roadblocks, you need to be very alert in terms of how the individuals at the blockade are behaving, how they are armed, or how they are treating individuals in front of you. If individuals are being pulled from their cars, or otherwise being mistreated, you can reasonably assume that this is not a standard blockade. Under the circumstances, there are two relatively simple tactical driving maneuvers available to you.

   a. One hundred eighty reverse: In the 180 reverse maneuver, you check your mirror to see if anyone is behind you or you are able to back around someone, at speed, behind you. You then throw the vehicle into reverse gear, floor it, and back away from the roadblock at speed—counting four seconds off aloud. At the count of "four one-thousand" (or four Mississippi), you crank the wheel hard to the fat of the road. That means that the direction where you have the most road. The centrifugal force and weight of the engine will slew your front end around 180 degrees, at which time, you slam the vehicle (ideally as its coming around) into a forward gear and floor it, moving quickly away from the threat.

   b. Ramming: The second maneuver is ramming the blockade. As you come up on the roadblock, you want to give the appearance that you are stopping for the adversaries who are stationed at the blockade. You never want to hit a blockade at high speed, because you lose the forward kinetic force and the weight of your engine block as it hits the barrier, and if your vehicle is unstable, it can flip or become high centered on the barrier, stopping you. As you slow down to less than 20 mph and get within about 15–20 ft of the blockade, floor the accelerator. If vehicles are being used to blockade the road, aim for the rear of the vehicles and not the front where the engine block is located. When you hit the vehicle, maintain your foot on the accelerator and push through the barrier. If someone is foolish enough to be in your way, hit them and drive over them—it is not the time to be squeamish about injuring or killing someone.

AIR TRANSPORTATION

Unlike other modes of transportation, an entire regime of physical security has evolved around the commercial aviation industry. This is particularly true since the terrorist attacks of September 11, 2001, in New York. The focus of airport security in the United States is principally about keeping bad things off airplanes as opposed to bad people away from the aircraft. Given recent incidents overseas, the Transport Security Administration may be forced to review that policy. The terrorist threat has substantially evolved and is increasingly targeting airport workers themselves who have physical access to the aircraft. The downing of Metrojet 9268 over the Sinai Peninsula on October 31, 2015, after it took off from Sharm el Sheikh with 224 passengers and crew aboard turned out to be the result of a bomb smuggled onto the aircraft by an EgyptAir mechanic whose cousin was affiliated with ISIS. A bomb that blew a hole in the fuselage of Daallo Airlines on February 2, 2016, shortly after takeoff from Mogadishu International Airport turned out to be a laptop computer with a bomb in it carried aboard by a suicide bomber affiliated with Al Shabaab. Two airport workers smuggled the bomb through security screening and then handed the device over to the bomber in the departure lounge. In both instances, terrorist planners have found that the weakest link in the chain of airport security is insiders—workers who can be bribed, extorted, or otherwise persuaded to cooperate in getting a bomb aboard an aircraft.

Terrorist threat actors are not the only adversaries that you should be concerned about when flying. Criminal theft and—more recently—hackers exploiting onboard WiFi connections are of concern. Business travelers are particularly vulnerable on long-haul overseas flights, because criminals have the time to work patiently in the cabin, while passengers are sleeping.

Prepacking for Security and Safety

The Zen to good security and safety in and around international airport terminals is two things: (a) a good, well-thought-out prepack routine and (b) early arrival at the airport. It is really that simple. Both measures keep you centered, calm, and able to be aware and alert for anything out of the ordinary, since you are not in a rush and not so disorganized that you lose focus. The following is the way to prepare your pack load for travel:

1. Keep your most important valuable items on your person. The most crucial things to have with you on the plane are your ID (passport), credit card, mobile phone, and—if required—prescription medications. With these items, should you have to suddenly bail out of an emergency exit into a life raft, or onto the tarmac with the fuselage blazing behind you, you can survive.
2. Your carry-on will have the next most important items, including toiletries, change of underwear, socks, an empty (preferably fold-up) backpack in the event that you must check your carry-on and transfer important items to another bag, and other items as necessary. Once you have extracted the credit card that you will carry in your front pocket on the plane, take your wallet with any other cards and cash and bury it deep in the carry-on.

At Security Screening

1. When you are going through security, if you need to remove your wallet, watch, iPhone, or Mont Blanc pen, make sure to say it out loud to the security attendant—"Here is my wallet, watch, iPhone, etc." as you hand it over. It puts security attendants on notice that you are security aware—many items often go missing while passengers are processing through security screening.
2. When you are in line to be x-rayed, wait until you are ready to walk through before releasing your purse, laptop, or wallet for separate screening. Beware if someone ahead of you keeps getting sent back for repeat screening. A common scam at airports is for thieves, working in pairs, to collect other passengers' valuables as they come through the x-ray machine while the other holds up the line.

In the Terminal

1. I use my time inside the terminal to rearrange valuables and documents before proceeding to the boarding gate. If you are not traveling business class and cannot avail yourself of the

semiprivacy of the lounge area, just choose a small café' or a deserted seating area away from the gate itself and prying eyes. The reason for this is that thieves arrive early at boarding gate areas and position themselves so that they can case potential targets for exploitation later on the aircraft. Use this time to put only essentials on your person (credit card, ID, medicine, phone) and stuff the rest deep inside your carry-on bag. I typically travel with a small backpack and a small roller board that is carry-on compliant. Your wallet and valuables should be stuffed deep in the backpack.[2] I lock my roller board at this time, since it will be overhead and out of view.

2. While in the terminal area, beware of free WiFi hot spots (see Chapter 7). These areas are commonly targeted by cybercriminals.

On the Plane

1. If you are wearing a jacket and the flight attendant offers to hang it up for you, make sure that the pockets are completely empty before turning it over to him/her.

2. Keep a distinctive ribbon or a cord with you that you can tie on your carry-on to distinguish it from other bags or backpacks. This is especially important if you have to check your carry-on at planeside due to lack of space in the overhead compartments. Also, to the extent possible, place your carry-on in the overhead compartment across from you and not above you. That way, you can observe when someone is potentially tampering with your bag.

3. Make sure that you place your carry-on upside down in the compartment. The bag should be resting on the outer compartment, which is often where people stash electronics, books, or cash that they want to use later. This is the first area targeted by thieves onboard.

4. Your ID, credit card, and phone should be either in a zippered pocket on your person or in your front pocket to deter pick-pockets onboard. Women should keep their purses secured in front of them, not hanging over the shoulder. The purse should be firmly secured with a zippered flap or similar—it should not be an open model satchel.

5. Never leave valuables in your seat when you have to get up to go to the lavatory or to stretch. Also, if you do see someone delving into your overhead bin and handling your bag, do not be afraid to politely but firmly *speak up*. If they are innocent, they will explain why they are handling your bag; if they are not, you put them on notice that you are watching your bag. It is a deterrent measure.

Emergency Situations

In my 40+ years of flying throughout the world, I have only had to deal with genuine in-flight emergencies on two occasions. Both of these incidents were very instructive. In 1982, I was on a Boeing 747 that lost its forward cargo hatch while taking off from Kai Tak International Airport in Hong Kong. The sudden loss of the door affected the plane's aerodynamic stability, and it was immediately apparent that there was a problem. Had the door separated at altitude, it might have been a much more serious situation. The pilot handled the emergency very professionally, turning the jumbo jet around and landing it without further issue. In 1998, while at cruising altitude of 33,000 ft on an overnight flight between New York City and Paris, there was an electrical fire on board the 747 aircraft. We descended quickly to less than 10,000 ft and diverted to St. John's, Newfoundland, in Canada. In both instances, I was struck by the almost immediate sense of restlessness and fear that sets in with passengers when they know that they are on a stricken airliner. It can be infectious, and it is easy to let it get to you. Fortunately, crewmembers were very professional, and the pilot—in both instances—immediately let us know precisely what was going on and our status. Having those expectations met quickly helped substantially. In the event of an emergency in flight, the following are additional considerations for your own emergency response planning:

1. Take charge of your own sense of unease by helping to ease the nerves of passengers around you. It worked very well for me in both situations, because I was able to focus on someone else and not me. There is nothing you can do, in terms of whatever the situation is with the aircraft. It is an opportunity to get to know passengers around you, in the event that you need their help later on in the emergency.

2. Let the flight attendants do their job. They are well trained and, in both instances, were able to rapidly assess the situation and manage the passengers.

3. Pay strict attention to the safety briefing that proceeds every routine flight. I still, despite all my years of flying, put down my book or music and listen to the briefing. I check the safety card in the pocket, to determine what type of aircraft that I am in and where the safety exits are located. Finally, I always count the number of seats between myself and the emergency exit. In the event of an emergency, it could be pitch dark, over the Atlantic. Knowing where to go, and counting the seats on the way, could be the difference between surviving and perishing in an accident.

4. Do not, under any circumstances, stop to retrieve belongings—let them go. When you can evacuate—move! There is a reason why it is good to keep your most important possessions on your person. You will not have to think about these things, if you find yourself in a strange terminal and country, after having survived an evacuation from an aircraft. With a credit card, you can buy food, lodging, transportation, and clothing. With your documentation, you can travel to another location and authenticate who you are. Your phone gives you communication to key individuals, and medicine ensures you remain healthy. Keep these four things on your person while on board.

5. Save the high heels for the boardroom or the terra firma. Your footwear should be comfortable, durable, and flat. You need footwear in which you can run. Wear natural fabrics such as cotton, wool, denim, or leather. Avoid synthetics, as these melt in a fire.

6. If you survive the initial impact, evacuation becomes the imperative. It also becomes the imperative of a host of other people. The quicker you can think, keep your wits about you, and be able to move, the better your chances of survival. Smoke may begin to fill up the cabin. In this event, get as low as you can. Smoke rises to the top, and breathable oxygen will be down at the floor level. This is when you need to remember how many seats are between you and the exit.

REFERENCES

Bonnier Corporation, "12 Ways to prevent motorcycle theft/motorcycle," *Cruiser*, accessed March 13, 2006, http://www.motorcyclecruiser.com/12-ways-to-prevent-motorcycle-theft (February 24, 2009).

Dahr, R., "The proper way to lock your bicycle," *Lifehacker*, accessed March 12, 2016, http://lifehacker.com/5942301/the-proper-way-to-lock-your-bicycle (November 9, 2012).

Delsol, C., "Renting a car in Mexico: What you need to know," *SF Gate*, accessed March 12, 2016, http://www.sfgate.com/mexico/mexicomix/article/Renting-a-car-in-Mexico-What-you-need-to-know-3787891.php (August 14, 2012).

Hodson, M., "The taxi cab guide: What you need to know," *Go-See-Write blog*, accessed March 12, 2016, http://www.goseewrite.com/?s=taxi+cab+guide&submit.x=0&submit.y=0&submit=Go (March 30, 2011).

Hostetter, K., "How do I layer for cold weather," *Backpacker*, accessed February 26, 2016, http://www.backpacker.com/gear/experts/ask-kristin/how-do-i-layer-for-cold-weather, (February 2016).

McGill, T., "Evasive driving and the awareness of threats," *The Tips Bank*, accessed April 17, 2016, http://www.thetipsbank.com/evasive -driving.htm (2016).

Steube, W.B., "How to prevent motorcycle, scooter & moped theft," Bradenton, FL: Manatee County Sheriff's Department, accessed March 10, 2016, http://www.manateesheriff.com.

ENDNOTES

1. If you have Allstate auto insurance, you are covered throughout all Canadian provinces and territories and between all ports, the company says. This insurance also is valid in US territories, such as Puerto Rico, Guam, and the US Virgin Islands. If you are driving south into Mexico, your policy will protect you if you will be traveling within 75 mi of the border for a maximum of 10 days on each separate entry or trip.
2. A slash-proof portable safe, or travel safe, is highly recommended.

CHAPTER **11**

Managing Your Team's Personal Security

INTRODUCTION

Managing the logistics of a group of employees, whether they are engineers or senior vice presidents of the company, can be like herding cats. They all have their own travel habits, expectations, experience, and assumptions about how much they know about where they are going, how to behave, and what to do whether in transit or in the city. Personally, I have seen it all. Managing human beings through these situations requires skill, patience, and firmness. The first step in being able to manage your team is having the confidence that you can handle yourself. The next step is having a plan to handle the team and the authority to implement it.

When shepherding a team of individuals into and out of international locations that are potentially hostile, you need to be confident first of your own personal security program and your ability to adhere to it and execute it. Having the confidence and the self-discipline inherent in your own plan will extend to the self-confidence and the authority that you need to have in order to manage and execute your team's personal security while on assignment. Make no mistake about it: Whether these individuals are long-time colleagues or a group of strangers from different companies thrown together for a project, while they are with you, *think of them as your team.* You need to take firm ownership of their security. Making this your first priority, when you first meet, sets the right tone and direction moving forward. You will need that to exercise the authority required to manage their movements and behavior on the ground.

AUTHORITY

Establishment of authority is a key element to group cohesion and execution when it comes to personal security planning. Ideally, you should have or seek designation as the principal in terms of the security plan. This should come from management, and typically, you will be designated formally as the team leader. You must couple this formal authority with informal authority. These are the actions that you take to set up prebriefings, awareness and threat briefings, protocols, and procedures prior to travel. Taking care of these details cements your natural authority within the group. I have found it indispensable to have clear guidance from management or company authorities dispatching team members, on what to do in the event that there is an issue with an employee while deployed. Being able to spell this out, in a predeployment briefing, attaches consequences to disciplinary issues. When you are managing down, this is helpful. It is not something that is of use when managing up. That requires a different set of skills.

COMMUNICATIONS

Both operational and technical communications between team members are crucial while en route on travel status and on the ground. Every team member should have a call list, with names and mobile numbers of everyone as well as key contacts in the company office and personal contacts of each individual. This list should be established at the very first prebrief meeting. If not, then it should be accomplished before the team goes wheels up to an overseas location. Even if it means a 5- or a 10-minute huddle in the airport prior to departure, it is important to have this contact mechanism in place.

There should also be a backup means of communications. Mobile phones do not always work in certain countries. If possible, issue prepaid telephone cards for use with hard-line phones. Also, determine a rendezvous point at intermediate airports and the final destination. Who to call, what to do if the team gets separated, or arrival times are going to be different. Murphy's law dictates that your phone will not work when you get to where you are going. You want to be able to make some contact. Know the name, the physical description, and some response-and-challenge questions with the local expeditor that is meeting you and the team on the ground. Two a.m. in Beirut's International Airport, going with your gut, is not fun.

Technically, before you depart, make sure that you have called your mobile phone carrier and confirmed that your phone will work in the regions/countries to which you are traveling. You can sometimes purchase a temporary international plan that covers phone calls made from these locations. Make sure that your data roaming is turned off; WiFi is okay, but if data roaming charges kick in, you could be in for a very hefty bill. Once you have confirmed your own gear works, then at the team briefing, make sure to give instructions to the team members to make sure that their own phones work as well, and on what to do once they arrive. On the ground, it is a good idea to purchase a temporary burner phone with a local SIM card, for use in the country. This saves charges on long-distance calls on your primary mobile phone, which reverts to emergency use only in country while you use a locally pro-cured phone. Once your team has local phones, make sure that they lock their primary phone away in the hotel safe. As with the wheels-up briefing, once local mobile phones are procured, distributed, and tested, a call list should be provided to the group with the local phones. Send a follow-up e-mail to the appropriate contact at the corporate office with these local numbers so that the security operations center has them in case of emergency. This keeps communications both within the group and with management seamlessly stitched up.

THE TEAM BRIEFING

It is important for the team to formally meet before wheels up. Make time for it. This session establishes several key objectives: First is your authority and expectations for the team—good and bad (remember—note explicitly that there are consequences to behavior that puts the team and/or the individual at risk). The second is a threat and risk briefing on the location(s) to which you are going and what the team can expect. This is an abbreviated security awareness brief, and it can be tailored so that you lay out basic detection, deterrence, delay, defense, and response protocols for the team that they can follow. The third is communication protocols, procedures (contact lists), and technology checks; and fourth, make sure that everyone has the right kit moving forward, to include meds, documentation, money, and clothing. This, as noted earlier, is the ideal situation. It rarely happens.

More common is the situation where team members are pulled together at the last minute and end up meeting for the first time at the gate before departure. With time at a premium and no formal authori-tative structure established, key objectives can still be met. First, take the initiative in introducing everyone, their titles and roles, and ask everyone to exchange contact information. Second, without going into detail about where you are going or what the risks are, establish a meet-up procedure for the destination airport. If there is a layover, use that time to further establish your relationship to the team and provide the necessary briefings on the location to which you are headed. Provide the security awareness briefing and security protocols for team members. Test communications if time permits and check with everyone regarding documents, money, clothing, and the like. Even if discussed informally, which is typically the way that it will be in a team of peers, it is best to acknowledge and be proactive about the requirement to have good team security.

ON THE GROUND

Your team is most vulnerable during movements between locations. This begins at the airport, on arrival. If you are fortunate enough to have traveled with your group, whether it is a small group of two or three or a larger group, it is crucial that you establish structure from the outset before moving into the public area of the terminal (out of customs). Ensure that you circle up with team members between baggage and customs and the public terminal. The best place is usually just inside the airport terminal in the debarkation area. This meeting gives team members a chance to ask any question or advise of any issues that they might have (forgot cash, mobile phone not working or charged, need medicine, etc.), and it gives you a chance to take stock of any of their needs and also provide instructions on what to do after entering the public area of the terminal. Getting this out of the way, out-of-public view lowers your team's profile and keeps your movements as a group deliberate and confident. Circling up in the public terminal and exhibiting any confusion, indecisiveness, or issue for anyone to see or hear is a bad idea. Keep group coordination and instructions on movements low profile and as discreet as possible.

Once inside the terminal and before obtaining transportation, it is important to ensure that communications work for everyone. This is most important should you have a team that is larger than three individuals because you may have to divide the team into two groups when it comes to transportation from the airport to the hotel or the residence. Test your mobile phones, to make sure that they work. If they do not roam or sync with the local network, this is the time to find a local phone and SIM card (most international airports have them) and activate it. It is important to have communications between the two parties during this time, in the event that there are any disruptions or incidents that could separate you en route to the hotel or the residence. If you are a small team (three persons or less), this is less of an issue, because you can remain together. In any case, it is still a good idea to make sure that your communications work locally before shoving off from the airport.

You should also make certain that you and your team all have at least US$100 in cash before departing the airport. Try to get your cash in small denominations. This gives you the currency needed to tip for information or pay "roadblock fees" should this become an issue en route to the hotel.

Third, if you are in a country where the language is foreign to you or anyone in your group, make certain that you have directions written on a paper to the hotel or the residence to which you are going. This is less of an issue in developed countries; however, in third-world countries and particularly as one gets further into the interior of these countries, language becomes a formidable barrier. Thinking ahead with this challenge in mind will save you time and trouble, particularly if you get separated.

If you divide into two groups, maintain control over the transportation discussion—do not cut loose the second group with instructions to find transport or take a taxi. The best option is to arrange the transport within the terminal, rather than outside the terminal at the taxi stand. You may not have a choice. If you do not, stick with both groups and make sure that your drivers both understand, from you, where the ultimate destination is. Back this up with written instructions that are kept by one of the second group's team members. Verbal instructions get forgotten or confused. Make sure that the group has them in writing.

ROADBLOCK PROTOCOL

En route from the airport to the hotel, in many countries, roadblocks are common. Usually, they can be pretty casual affairs, where the police or the militia will either take a cursory glance and wave you on or briefly chat with the driver and then send you on ahead. Brief your team, in advance, to have their documents ready and to let the driver do the talking. Keep answers to a minimum, and if a fee is requested, pay it and smile. The objective is to get past the roadblock, not get engage in a back and forth that, I guarantee you, will not end well.

If your vehicle clears the roadblock but the other is delayed, have your driver pull over and wait for the second vehicle. If you cannot pull over, the fallback option is either to make sure that someone in the second vehicle calls ahead to you to confirm that they are clear. The third option is the written directions that they have to the hotel or the residence.

AT THE HOTEL

Once everyone has arrived and checked in the hotel, it is best to schedule a follow-up briefing before settling into the project schedule. This follow-up briefing is to tie up any loose ends such as communications issues. It is also to set expectations for coordination while in the country. Finally, at these briefings, it is important to reemphasize existing threats in the area, in spite of what may appear to be a calm business-as-usual atmosphere. Being lulled into a false sense of security can be a fatal mistake. Keep your team's understanding of threat and risks finely honed, so that they do not become complacent and make mistakes.

The follow-up briefing is also your opportunity to reiterate the rules and the principles of personal security that you expect from team members. This is usually not necessary if your group consists of veteran travelers. However, I have had the experience of leading a team of inexperienced, green contractors or employees into hostile regions. My advice is to come across strong, firm, and no nonsense from the beginning, and as the days and the weeks progress, you can ease off as team members internalize good security into their daily routine.

Key points to hit at this briefing are the following:

- Reemphasis of the threat
- Principles of preparation (locally)
- Detection, deterrence, and delay
- Synching up communications
- Development of contingency scenarios (what-if)
- End-of-week briefs (under routine circumstances)

MANAGING CRISIS SITUATIONS

There is nothing like a full-blown crisis to put to test your own personal security and the plans that you have developed to manage the security and the safety of others. From my own experience, I learned very quickly that the human factor and other unforeseen events have a way of quickly overtaking and sidelining the best-made plans. As noted wryly by Prussian field marshal Helmuth von Moltke, "no plan survives first contact with the enemy." Not as well known, but equally true, was what Moltke said after his observation about planning. "Strategy," he added, "is a system of expedients."

Third-world countries or hostile regions where you may be living and working require a clear-eyed, hands-on approach to security for you and your team. In addition, it is important that you have the capability to be flexible in the plans and the procedures put into place. They will change, based on circumstances, and you need to be able to adapt accordingly. If not, the cruelty of events out of your control will crush your spirit and initiative. I have witnessed this firsthand, so I cannot emphasize enough the importance of being capable of adjusting as you and your team move through the event together.

Principle of Planning

In the mid-1980s, I had the fortunate experience of taking over as an officer in charge in an African country. I inherited a situation where emergency planning was nascent, at best. The planning stages, therefore, were mine alone to develop. My brief was in communications; I was running, at the time, the longest high-frequency communication path in Africa—a 2000-plus path into a large relay in West Africa. The philosophy that drove operations in those days focused on making sure that all paths and modes of communication were backed up. The rule was tough: no more than two hours off the air or there was hell to pay!

So, needless to say, multiple backups went into every aspect of planning. It was a principle that was sound then, and I believe that it is sound up to this day. Planning when you have the luxury of time prepares you for the dynamics of a crisis when the time has run out. The time to think, to prepare, and to adapt becomes the first thing that you lose.

Loss of Mobility

The conflict area in which I was operating deteriorated gradually at first. As rebel forces encroached on the capital, roadblocks increased along with the time that it took to get around the city. Roadblocks were manned by militias that were increasingly tense, inexperienced, and uncertain about their role or protocols for dealing with individuals. More often than not, they defaulted to aggressiveness—most were on a hair trigger. Moving equipment, supplies, or personnel around the city provoked suspicion and invited additional scrutiny. My planning, which was done before mobility became an issue, included prepositioned alternative communication sites in the city. In addition, these sites were each provisioned with extra supplies of diesel fuel, generator power, food, and water. I began a regime of testing each site once every other week. This ensured that senior management, at a moment's notice, could elect to evacuate and disperse personnel into the relative safety of residences scattered throughout the city.

At some stage of the crisis, a tipping point will be reached and the security situation will deteriorate very, very rapidly. Ironically, the prelude to this is usually an eerie calm and an absence of the roadblocks normally seen. Do not be fooled. This usually comes as opposing forces dig into respective positions and prepare for an assault. You and your team should be buttoned down and prepared to ride out the crisis when it begins to unfold into its more violent stage. Regrettably, even at this stage, there will be individuals around you who want to maintain status quo up until the last minute and then hurry into emergency procedures that they have not reviewed or only given a cursory glance. These individuals unfortunately add to, rather than help manage through, the chaos. It is your job beforehand to recognize these individuals and be prepared for their reaction.

Loss of Command and Control: Criticality of Communications

When an evacuation occurs, one of the critical elements at risk is command and control over your organization. During a crisis, corporate expectations as to what is happening on the ground with company assets and employees are crucial. Every violent crisis, whether it is conflict originated or disaster originated, has in common the trait of casting an opaque curtain of uncertainty over the city or the region where it is occurring. Building in resilience and operability to both long-haul company-to-corporate communications and local tactical communications is the key to surviving an extended crisis event. This communication capability must be tested and ready when the balloon goes up. There will not be time to adjust in to the situation.

Ideally, your backup communication facility should be off site in a location that will be shared with local management. Having a key decision maker at hand, on site will streamline the myriad of executive decisions that need to be made with regard to events on the ground and simultaneous decisions at the corporate level. If there is physical separation between you and the management when the crisis inexorably shuts down mobility and critical infrastructure on the ground, unless there is a robust tactical backup communication capability, local command and control will be lost. This is not a situation that you want for your team or the company as a whole. In the absence of a command structure, individuals make decisions on their own that may or may not be the best. These decisions are usually impulsive and taken based on fear and emotion. Some normally intelligent, confident individuals can devolve into severe impediments—untrained or inexperienced type A personalities in an active crisis are, regrettably, the worst. Control is their first and last imperative; this—coupled with an inherent rigidity and temper when things inevitably do not go their way—can be utterly disastrous. The consequences can be fatal, and in the aftermath of the crisis, there will be liability issues that are tough to deal with if the proper planning steps to handle the crisis were not made in the first place.

As alluded to, the second capability that should already be in place, tested, and ready is a tactical communication network. You should not rely on mobile phones for this capability, because cellular communication is usually the first thing to go when a crisis hits. It is well worth the time and the investment of the company to put into place a very high-frequency/ultrahigh-frequency radio communications network that has extended range and coverage through a series of repeaters. This is particularly important if the company footprint is countrywide or region-wide. The radio communication network should utilize light-voice privacy-level encryption, since more robust encryption tends to affect transmission and reception performance and easily breaks apart in hilly areas or dense urban terrain.

Loss of Security and Safety

The loss of your personal security and safety, and that of your team, deteriorates in a crisis situation to the point where it is nonexistent. If you are dealing with an urban conflict situation, unless you have found adequate shelter, you will be exposed to the vicissitudes and the cruelty of combat. Your preparations should also take this into consideration. Observe locations of military emplacements, defenses, government ministries, and main thoroughfares between sectors of the city. In battle, all these will be in play and hotly contested. If your location is alongside or in the middle of any of these kinds of military objectives, you will come under heavy artillery, mortar, and small-arm fire. There is the chance that your vantage point could be exploited by an opposing force, seeking to place fire on an enemy combatant.

You need to consider these aspects of your physical security and defense measures in the event that a crisis unfolds and you and your team must seek cover.

Postcrisis Considerations

The day after a coup d'etat or insurgent victory, the city in which you are located may be in a state of shock as people slowly come out to survey damage and check on friends, relatives, and neighbors. It is important to maintain your vigilance during this time. In the days and the weeks after, the security situation can actually be more uncertain than before. The following are issues to be aware of and plan for under the circumstances:

- Curfew and curfew conditions—Typically, there will be a dusk-to-dawn or a 7 a.m. to 7 p.m. curfew. If insurgents have taken over from former government troops or if government troops were victorious, enforcement of the curfew will likely be by military forces, and they can be under shoot-on-sight orders. It is not a time to test the curfew; if you have to be out and about, try to be back inside, buttoned up at least an hour before the curfew goes into effect. A sign that things are getting under control is when uniformed police take over roadblock and curfew duties.

- If you are traveling out of the country following a conflict, make certain that you have hard copies of your itinerary and associated travel documents. You should have your ID (passport) with you at all times.
- Avoid areas where there were extended battles or contact between forces. Years ago, I was part of a team in Africa that went in to assess the scene of a hard-fought battle. It was a fresh scene, with corpses of government troops who manned artillery pieces and communications to the bitter end, to cover a general retreat. We learned that the retreating soldiers left weapons and other battlefield items in plain sight but were booby-trapped. There were live grenades, mortar rounds, and explosives left out in the open, not to mention the dead. These areas can be dangerous because they are mined or booby-trapped and also because unexploded ordinance can explode. Avoid large gatherings or protests such as food riots. These can be exceedingly dangerous.
- Expect electricity to be interrupted or nonexistent and water to be contaminated.
- There will be looting and violent crimes such as rape, assault, and murder. Reprisal killings will take place, and the police will deal harshly with thieves or criminals when they are caught. Summary execution is quite common.
- Discipline with the winners is not the best. It is typically restored after a few days, but in the interim, the occupying force is usually allowed to "let off steam." This is a dangerous time, because armed soldiers can be drunk and violent. Keep a low profile.
- In the weeks and the months after a crisis, there will be an increase in armed robbery and banditry, typically committed by soldiers from the losing side that need to secure resources. They still have weaponry and could mount a counterinsurgency.

Conclusion

Personal security training and awareness are, in my opinion, the red-headed stepchild of the overall discipline of security. From my perspective, I have repeatedly seen its implementation fragmented across several different components of an organization. This is unfortunate because it dilutes and essentially neutralizes the benefits of an integrated, well-thought-out program. Travel or human resources will provide a list of dos and don'ts to travelers going to a higher-risk location, downloaded from a travel website or the US State Department. Security awareness training might consist of a quick 45 minutes with corporate security, where they brief you on threats in a location and give you a few tips on what to do if something goes bad. Executive protection gets contracted.

Of course, there are distinct exceptions with large corporations or government organizations (although I am surprised that some large corporations still have paltry personal security programs). Unfortunately, the majority of business or nongovernmental organization (NGO) travelers around our increasingly insecure globe do not have the benefit of a team of elite ex-special forces commandos as 24/7 executive protection specialists, constantly scouting ahead and behind you and discreetly well armed. What is consistently missed in this approach is the one true asset requiring protection: you. A good personal security program that takes a thoughtful, systematic approach to your needs and capabilities as opposed to a procedural standard operating procedure checklist on a PowerPoint presentation that is more for the corporate compliance team than the individual is what is lacking. All too often business travelers, NGO representatives, or journalists find themselves, quite unexpectedly, at the tip of the spear of the company's latest business development gambit into third-world markets or that story that is breaking in some small, obscure, undeveloped part of the world. Increasingly, there is evidence that it is these employees that are the most vulnerable to threat events and threat actors. In Mexico, for instance, KFR—once focused on senior executives of companies and multimillion dollar ransoms—has shifted to midlevel employees. The reason is hostage negotiators have priced themselves out of the market (they typically ask for fees in excess of US$100,000), so to avoid further delay, the companies pay up. Perversely, this provides a strong incentive for kidnappers to continue targeting midlevel employees—folks like you and I. Unfortunately, companies have not caught up to this fact and still fork out big bucks for high-priced executive protection courses and measures for only the most senior employees. In Africa and the Middle East, countries are under siege from a growing Islamic extremist insurgency that is targeting hotels, resorts, shopping malls, and markets, along with all the usual targets such as air travel. This heavily impacts business travelers or others who may not be traveling into the most hostile environment but find themselves trapped in a relatively benign environment that has become host to hostile threat actors.

Surviving in a high-risk environment requires preparation, planning, and some luck. It is said that one makes their own luck, and in terms of personal security, that is very true. Luck is the confluence of timing and opportunity; without doing your homework, memorizing the terrain, practicing observation skills, and rehearsing self-defense techniques, it becomes harder and less apparent to recognize the right time to act and the right opportunity on the mean streets of many places in this world today.

The program outlined in this book takes into account our personal foibles and weaknesses and provides a systematic framework for mitigating these vulnerabilities. Your corporation's world-class physical or cybersecurity designs and systems on its premises are not worth a plugged nickel to you once you step across the street, step into a third-world airport at 2 a.m., or check into a strange hotel in some downtown provincial capital. Ironically, in today's world, all those things that your company studiously strives to physically protect on it premises stay in your head or on your electronic media. It is when these things occur, away from the protective cocoon of the corporate campus or cozy ivy-covered halls of academia, that things get messy and risky.

Welcome to my world. I have lived it most of my life, on the streets and not in a comfortable office chair behind company or residential iron gates. I sincerely hope that my experiences and wisdom passed along in the pages of this book serve to secure you, your team, or family from the growing insecurities that we all face in today's world.

Best of luck!

Index

Page numbers followed by f, t, and n indicate figures, tables, and notes, respectively.

Motorcycle, use for transportation, 213

Motor rickshaws, security considerations, 216–217

Motor scooter, use for transportation, 213

Movement, preparation for, 11–12

Mucinex D, 15

The Mungiki gang, 116

Museveni, Yoweri, 112

Muslim Brotherhood in Egypt, 77

Muslim Umma, 180

N

Narcobloqueos, 57

Nardia, Major Avi, 172

National Resistance Army (NRA), 112

Natural disasters, 2, 191t
  crime rates and, 129–132
  emergency phase, 130
  impact phase, 130
  reconstruction phase, 131
  recovery phase, 130–131
  warning phase, 129–130

Neck grab, 42

Negotiation, in KFR, 83–84

Nexium, 15

Nieto, Enrique Peña, 72, 73

Nigeria
  kidnapping threats in, 71–72, 75

Nighttime, 56

Nihilists, 179

9/11 attacks, 137, 139, 229

No money, no politics, kidnapping for, 66–67

Nusra Front, 71

O

Oberoi Trident hotels (India), attack on, 140

Observation, 29, 30

Occupy Movement (2012), 132

One hundred eighty (180) reverse, 228

Operational environment
  defined, 195–196
  favorability of, 195–196

Operations center and response requirements, executive protection program, 101

Organization of Petroleum Exporting Countries (OPEC), 39

P

Packing, for mobility and portability, 26–27

Pain/fever medicine, in travel medical kit, 14–15

Pakistan
  kidnapping threats in, 72

Paramilitary checkpoints, 55–56
  in conflict zones, 54–55

Paris (France) terrorist attacks (2015), 169, 174

Parking, car, 227

Peace of mind, 12; *see also* Mental health
  engineering, 21–25

Peer-to-peer networks poisoning, 156

Pemex, 211

Pepper spray, 34, 36

PeptoBismol, 15

Perimeter, residential security and, 149

Perimeter security, in hotels, 143

Personal accident insurance, 225

Personal cybersecurity program, for business traveler, 160–164
  defense, 163
  delay, 162–163
  detection, 162
  established secure baseline of information security, 160–161
  preparation, 161–162
  response, 163–164

Personal identification number (PIN), 23

Personally identifiable information (PII), 164, 165; *see also* Identity theft

Personal security, 1
  broken windows theory, 113–115
  effectiveness of, 2